John Zinkin, Chris Bennett

The Challenge of Leading an Ethical and Successful Organization

John Zinkin, Chris Bennett

The Challenge of Leading an Ethical and Successful Organization

—

DE GRUYTER

ISBN 978-3-11-078081-9
e-ISBN (PDF) 978-3-11-078087-1
e-ISBN (EPUB) 978-3-11-078095-6

Library of Congress Control Number: 2022946186

Bibliographic information published by the Deutsche Nationalbibliothek
The Deutsche Nationalbibliothek lists this publication in the Deutsche Nationalbibliografie;
detailed bibliographic data are available on the internet at http://dnb.dnb.de.

Typesetting: Integra Software Services Pvt. Ltd.
Printing and binding: CPI books GmbH, Leck

www.degruyter.com

Acknowledgments

We were helped by many people in developing our thoughts, refining our arguments, and making the case.

We would like to thank the following for the time they invested in reading our drafts to ensure that the case we make is correct, clear, and, relevant; based on their respective experiences as academics, company director of long standing; senior management consulting partner; entrepreneur; central banker and capital markets regulator; and lawyer: Professor Sander van der Leeuw, Professor John Rudd, John Colvin, Dato Dr R. Thillainathan, Edward Clayton, Tony Heneberry, Tan Sri Andrew Sheng, and Sujata Shekar Naik. If we have misunderstood or misrepresented their views, the fault is entirely ours. We would like to thank Stefan Giesen, our excellent editor, for challenging our assumptions robustly and constructively, including simplifying the structure of the book. We would like to thank Jaya Dalal for her excellent coordination of production, as usual; and Mervin Ebenezer for final production.

John Zinkin
Chris Bennett
Kuala Lumpur

https://doi.org/10.1515/9783110780871-202

Advance Praise for *The Challenge of Leading an Ethical and Successful Organization*

"The Challenge of Leading an Ethical and Successful Organization demonstrates that there are serious external obstacles to being both ethical and successful. Obeying the law provides minimum guidelines, and the law does not treat corporations as moral agents. The resulting focus by judges, investors, and analysts on shareholder value maximization often leads to breaking the law and behaving unethically, as long as the so-called 'cost of doing business' is less expensive than the extra profits achieved through malpractice.

The end does not always justify the means. The outcome does not always justify the process. The process must be morally upright and ethically sound. It must stand the scrutiny of good decency. Ethical decisions are more complicated when *the world as it is*, differs from *the world as it ought to be*; and reconciling duty-based and consequential ethics may prove impossible because of different cultural assumptions and individuals' 'multiple ethical personas.' Choices are often between complicated 'shades of gray' rather than between simple 'black and white' answers.

John Zinkin and Chris Bennett show in detail how leaders can overcome the barriers to ethical and effective decision-making by building an ethical and successful organization – where ethics defines its mission, vision, and values, combining the 'Five P' performance checklist (covering 'Purpose,' 'Principles,' 'Power,' 'People,' and 'Processes') with a simple six-step ethical process that allows leaders to confront their ethical dilemmas successfully.

I highly recommend this book to anyone in a leadership position who has to make difficult ethical choices in *the world as it is* as opposed to the ideal *world as it ought to be* that does not exist."

–*Devaneson Evanson, CEO, Minority Shareholders Watch Group (MSWG)*

"What ought I do? This is increasingly becoming a challenge – society today demands that we take into account a vast number of factors when deciding whether or not a course of action is ethically acceptable or not. This can lead to many unfortunate outcomes – virtue signalling, where we act in a way, we believe others will find acceptable, kneejerk reactions, where we do what feels right at the time, often based on a simple set of 'rules' we have constructed. Or else to complete and utter confusion as we seek to navigate our way intelligently and ethically through the challenges we face at work and in wider society.

The Challenge of Leading an Ethical and Successful Organization is an enormous help to the confused – as well as to kneejerkers and virtue signallers – because it takes the reader back to first principles of ethics, and shows, with numerous contemporary and historical examples, the underlying issues and how they can be handled.

https://doi.org/10.1515/9783110780871-203

It equips readers with a toolkit which cuts through the confusion of modern continuously changing ethical priorities.

Reading this book provided many 'aha' moments and clear insights which I found extremely helpful as I advise clients and mentor staff."

–Edward Clayton, Partner, Advisory, PwC Malaysia/Vietnam

"*The Challenge of Leading an Ethical and Successful Organization* is filled with examples of our ultimately self-destructive nature. Given the current state of the world, perhaps it is not dark enough, nor imbued with a sufficient sense of urgency.

John Zinkin and Chris Bennett have again written a book which is profoundly informative and challenging, leaving me hoping it provides conclusive solutions to the problems business leaders face. It describes a world where the tramlines (rules and regulations) are designed to control the majority, for the benefit of the political and financial minorities (read elites), for whom the tramlines appear not to apply.

The final chapter brings light to the darkness with practical suggestions for change. I wonder, however, whether a global system of taxation, variable according to an organization's positive impact on society and on the environment, should be added to this recipe for redemption."

–Tony Heneberry, Founder and CEO of CEO Solutions

"With *The Challenge of Leading an Ethical and Successful Organization*, John Zinkin and Chris Bennett have come out with a three-volume masterpiece. After dealing ably and comprehensively with *The Principles and Practice of Effective Leadership* in their first volume, in their second volume, *Criminality and Business Strategies: Similarities and Differences*, they make it overwhelmingly clear that the similarities between organized crime and legitimate businesses are a lot greater than their apparent differences. Instead of leaving their readers with this depressing conclusion, in this, their third volume, they demonstrate masterfully, using their trans-disciplinary toolkit, how business leaders can confront the ethical issues and challenges they face in decision making as well as building and guiding enterprises that are both ethical and successful.

Their trilogy on effective leadership is a must read for all executives."

–Dato Dr R. Thillainathan, Director of Genting Berhad,
Public Investment Bank Berhad, IDEAS Policy Research Berhad

Contents

Acknowledgments —— V

Introduction —— XIII

Chapter 1
Ethics and the Law —— 1
    Ethics —— 1
        Professional Ethics —— 2
        Business Ethics —— 3
        Personal Ethics —— 4
    The Law —— 5
        Reality is Different —— 5
        Rule of Law —— 7
        The Workings of the Law —— 10
    Summary —— 15
    Appendix 1.1: Introduction to Business-related Professional
    Codes of Conduct —— 17
        Accountancy —— 17
        Engineering —— 17
        Finance —— 18
        Journalism —— 18
        Law —— 19
        Medical —— 20

Chapter 2
The Ethics Continuum —— 23
    "Ought" Versus "Is" —— 23
    Duty-based Versus Consequential Ethics —— 26
    Different Axioms, Different Choices —— 28
        Virtue —— 28
        Effectiveness —— 33
        Mutuality —— 34
        Predictability —— 35
        Utility —— 36
        Self-image —— 36
    Multiple Ethical Personas —— 37
    Reward and Punishment —— 39
        Ford Pinto Case —— 41
        Boeing 737 MAX Case —— 42
    Summary —— 43

Chapter 3
Barriers to Ethical Behavior — 48
  Evolution — 48
    System 1 and System 2 — 48
    Rhetoric — 50
    Volatility, Uncertainty, Complexity, and Ambiguity (VUCA) — 51
  Maslow's Five Needs — 51
    Survival — 51
    Safety — 51
    Belonging — 52
    Esteem — 53
    Self-actualization — 53
  Inappropriate Role Models — 53
  Increasing Impunity, Declining Accountability — 54
  Media and Reality TV — 56
  Vested Interests — 58
  Inappropriate Regulation? — 60
  Deception — 62
  "Bad Apples" — 63
  Rules-based and Principles-based Regulation — 66
    Cultural Complications — 67
    Weak Enforcement — 68
    Inappropriate KPIs — 69
  Summary — 71

Chapter 4
Handling Ethical Dilemmas — 76
  Establishing an Ethical Baseline — 76
  Establishing Personal "Moral Capital" — 77
  Ethics are Situational — 78
  Determining "Kaleidoscopic Ethical Personas" — 82
    Dealing with the State — 82
    Dealing with Employees — 83
    Dealing with Peers — 84
    Kaleidoscopic Ethical Personas — 84
  Confronting Ethical Dilemmas — 85
    Determining Areas of Conflict — 86
    Making Decisions — 88
  Applying the Six-Step Ethical Framework — 89
    Purpose — 89
    Principles — 90
    Power — 92

People —— 92
Processes —— 93
Assessing Resulting "Moral Injury" —— 94
Reassessing "Moral Capital" —— 94
Summary —— 95

Chapter 5
Building an Ethical Organization —— 99
"Mission and Vision" —— 99
Purpose —— 101
Principles —— 104
Power —— 110
People —— 112
Processes —— 113
Stakeholder Expectations —— 116
Summary —— 118
Appendix 5.1: Two Approaches to Stakeholder Engagement —— 119

Chapter 6
Leading Ethical and Successful Organizations —— 124
Ethical Obstacles —— 124
The Law —— 125
Maximizing Profits —— 125
Social Media —— 126
Decision-making —— 126
Vested Interests —— 127
Cognitive Dissonance —— 127
Inappropriate Regulation —— 128
Deception —— 128
Inappropriate KPIs and Investor Demands —— 129
Handling Ethical Dilemmas —— 129
Establishing Ethical Baselines —— 129
Confronting Ethical Dilemmas Successfully —— 131
Ethical *and* Successful Strategies —— 132
Purpose —— 133
Principles —— 135
Power —— 137
People —— 138
Processes —— 139
Personal "Moral Capital" —— 139
Summary —— 140

List of Figures —— 143

List of Tables —— 145

About the Authors —— 147

Index —— 149

Introduction

When we were commissioned to write *The Principles and Practice of Effective Leadership*, published in 2021, we agreed to write a sequel about the lessons legitimate businesses could learn from organized crime (OC). Our research led us to some surprising conclusions, in particular, that the similarities between OC and legitimate businesses were significantly greater than the differences.

Instead of leaving our readers with this depressing conclusion, we decided we should write two books instead of one. This is the second book; it focuses on how to confront the ethical challenges decision-makers face in leading sustainable organizations. The first book, *Criminality and Business Strategy: Similarities and Differences*, focuses on the lessons to be learned from OC. Some of the ideas in *The Principles and Practice of Effective Leadership* were developed further in both follow-up books. We wrote them as standalone books, but they work even better as companion volumes to give readers an integrated perspective of ethical issues faced by business leaders when making decisions. Since they were written as standalone volumes, there is inevitably some textual overlap between the two books but the arguments are developed differently. Should this textual overlap be onerous for you, we have flagged sections that have overlapping text in the footnotes.

The first three chapters of this book explain why making ethical business decisions is harder than is generally understood.

Expecting the law to give more than minimum guidance is unrealistic. Legal systems focus on achieving predictability of outcomes and due process rather than on natural justice and "fairness." Commercial law is complicated, technical, and time consuming. To be effective it requires more than a statement of *what* needs to be done, and needs to define precisely *how* it is to be done.

Ethical decision-making is difficult because real-world issues are more complex than those of ideal worlds; because reconciling duty-based and consequential ethics is often impossible; because underlying values and beliefs derived from different religious or cultural assumptions clash; because people respond in unexpected ways as a result of their multiple ethical personas, and their often unpredictable reactions to reward and punishment.

Real issues in ethical decision-making result from the evolution of the human brain, which seeks simple "black and white" ethical answers whenever volatility, uncertainty, complexity, and ambiguity (VUCA) creates moral issues that are varying "shades of gray." Inappropriate role models and regulations, irresponsible media reporting, and vested interests further complicate ethical decision-making.

The last three chapters of the book show how leaders of organizations can build and guide organizations that are both ethical and successful, taking account of all the problems discussed earlier.

Ethical decision-making is complex. Individuals need to establish ethical baselines that they will not cross when making decisions. To do this, they must establish

https://doi.org/10.1515/9783110780871-205

their personal "Moral Capital" and recognize they have "kaleidoscopic ethical personas" that affect their ethical choices based on contexts and conditions that are unique to every decision they make. Their "Moral Capital" is an amalgam of the "Universal Core" values of all of humanity, the "Cultural Mantle" values of each individual's cultural and religious background, and the "Regulated Atmosphere" created by the laws and regulations of the jurisdictions in which they live. To further complicate matters, how people make ethical choices depends on whether they adopt duty-based or consequential ethics to make decisions and how they seek to reconcile these two approaches.

The legal basis on which corporations are established makes it clear that they are not moral agents. Nevertheless, leaders of modern corporations are expected by society to consider ethical issues. An organization's "Five Ps" ("Purpose," "Principles," "Power," "People," and "Processes") determine its ethical stance; they depend on the mission and vision, established by its founder, senior management, owners, and/or board.

Ethics are at the heart of successful, sustainable enterprises, even if they are not moral agents. The key to developing a sustainable mission and vision is to remember that it is the customer who determines what value the enterprise offers, and then to ensure that the organization's "Five Ps" are properly aligned with its mission and vision.

"Purpose" defines an organization's beneficiaries, how it will make a positive difference in their lives, and the rates of return required to satisfy different types of shareholders (family, dispersed investors, or the state). Ranking and prioritizing the needs of stakeholders reflects the personal ethical values, principles, and rewards of the people working in the organization. "Principles" are reflected in policies regarding *Caveat Emptor*, competition, ethical "fading," equal opportunity, information, marketing, pricing, and technology, incorporated into codes of conduct. "Power" in the organization is a function of organizational structures ("Incubators," "Family Firms," "Eiffel Towers," or "Guided Missiles"). "People" make all the difference in terms of choosing, retaining, and promoting the right number of personnel, with relevant skills and suitability of character to ensure that the organization achieves its mission and vision. "Processes" set appropriate key performance indicators (KPIs) and include the feedback mechanisms needed to achieve ethical success, while striking the right balance between extrinsic, and intrinsic, motivators, after allowing for personal autonomy, self-development, and the desire to make a difference.

When the mission and vision are based on firm ethical foundations and the "Five Ps" are correctly aligned to deliver the agreed mission and vision, the result is an ethical and successful organization.

Book Outline

Chapter 1 explains the role of ethics in general, of professional and business ethics, and of personal ethics in particular. It discusses how, sometimes, professional or business ethics and personal ethics clash to create moral conflict. The same is true of ethics and the law. It explains that there are two ways of applying laws: liberal societies' "Rule *of* Law" where nobody is above the law; and totalitarian governmental "Rule *by* Law." It shows why the law can only provide minimum guidance for running an ethical and successful organization.

Chapter 2 discusses the ethical difficulties leaders face as a result of differences in context and circumstances. It explores the five causes of such difficulties: that the world as it *ought to be* is not the world *as it is*; reconciling duty-based and consequential ethics can be impossible; different cultural assumptions and religious axioms lead to different ethical resolutions; organizations and individuals have multiple ethical personas, the salience of which depends on the circumstances of the choices they face; and the impact of rewards and punishments affects ethical decision-making. It explains how the interaction of these factors can lead to inconsistent decisions, resulting in individual "moral damage" and a loss of self-respect.

Chapter 3 explores the barriers to ethical behavior. It describes how the brain works to minimize the cognitive load of complex decision-making. It explains how misleading rhetoric and a desire to minimize the dissonant effect of VUCA by choosing overly simple solutions in a complicated world affects ethical decisions. It discusses the ethical damage caused by inappropriate role models, regulation, and media reporting that reflect vested interests and increase impunity and diminish accountability. It shows how deception caused by inappropriate KPIs undermines ethical behavior.

Chapter 4 recognizes the complexity of ethical decision-making. It shows how individuals need to establish ethical baselines that they will not cross when making decisions. It explains the concepts of "moral injury," personal "Moral Capital," and "kaleidoscopic ethical personas" that affect individuals' ethical choices based on contexts and conditions that are unique to every decision they make. It explains the concepts of "Universal Core," "Cultural Mantle," and "Regulated Atmosphere" values and beliefs and how they can interact to create ethical conflicts.

Chapter 5 shows how business ethics are the heart of enterprises' mission and vision, explaining how the customer determines what value the organization is offering and not the shareholder or the organization's management. It discusses "Purpose" and the appropriate rates of return for different ownership structures, and how "Principles" are incorporated into policy guidelines and codes of conduct. It discusses "Power" and how it is a function of one of four appropriate organizational structures. It explains the importance of "People," and analyzes the role of "Processes" in setting appropriate KPIs and feedback mechanisms to achieve ethical success.

Chapter 6 shows how long-term success is based on firm ethical foundations with a mission and vision that satisfies stakeholders and regulators. It brings together the arguments of the preceding chapters and revisits ethical obstacles and the challenges they create in leading an ethical and successful organization. It then discusses ways of handling ethical dilemmas successfully. It explores the need to determine in advance the potential areas of ethical conflict, and the potential costs of such conflicts so that leaders can make appropriate decisions by applying a six-step ethical framework to ensure they are both ethical and effective, thereby creating ethical and effective strategies, using the "Five Ps" as a decision-making checklist.

Chapter 1
Ethics and the Law

People who lead ethical and successful organizations should appreciate the different constraints posed upon their freedom of action by ethics, and the law.

Ethics

Ethics, as the thought of Man about his action, is as ancient as Man itself . . . ethical systems changed through time, gaining more and new concepts to think about new human realities in the world and to communicate them. An example would be the constellation of four concepts needed in ancient Greek philosophy to explain moral life – good, end, happiness, and virtue – to which medievalism added the concept of God, modernity the concept of liberty, and contemporaneity the concept of responsibility. . . . *Ethics originally heteronomous, being given to Man (from a higher entity: Nature or God), becomes autonomous, being made by Man to Man.* Finally, ethics turned out to be applied to many different concrete fields of human activity – engineering, media, economics, politics, etc. – but none more developed than in biomedical (and environment) field through bioethics.

. . . ethics has always been and still is a rationalization of human action (the logic underneath human actions) concerning the principles it is grounded on, the ends it aims toward, and the processes it entails.[1]   [Emphases ours]

Many ethicists consider ethics and morals to be related concepts. The difference is that morals reflect intentions and whether we perceive our behavior as "good" or "bad," whereas ethics defines what practical behaviors are "right or wrong." Ethics can be classified into three types:
1. General, covering issues that affect humanity as a whole
2. Institutional ethics, dealing with issues that affect given organizations, with professional and business ethics as distinct subsets and/or
3. Personal ethics affecting the choices of individuals in their relations with society and the organizations that they work for.

Problems arise when the three classes of ethics come into conflict with one another, the law, and varying societal expectations. The conflicts create ethical dilemmas that are difficult to resolve:

Ethics refers to well-founded standards of right and wrong that prescribe what humans ought to do, usually in terms of rights, obligations, benefits to society, fairness, or specific virtues. Ethics, for example, refers to those standards that impose the reasonable obligations to refrain from rape, stealing, murder, assault, slander, and fraud. Ethical standards also include those that enjoin virtues of honesty, compassion, and loyalty. And, ethical standards include standards relating to rights, such as the right to life, the right to freedom from injury, and the

https://doi.org/10.1515/9783110780871-001

right to privacy. Such standards are adequate standards of ethics because they are supported by consistent and well-founded reasons.[2]   [Emphases ours]

Ethics is a branch of philosophy that *aims to answer the basic question, "What should I do?" It's a process of reflection in which people's decisions are shaped by their values, principles, and purpose rather than unthinking habits, social conventions, or self-interest.*

Our values, principles, and purpose are what give us a sense of what's good, right, and meaningful in our lives. They serve as a reference point for all the possible courses of action we could choose. On this definition, an ethical decision is one made based on reflection about the things we think are important and that is consistent with those beliefs.

While each person is able to reflect and discover their own sense of what's good, right, and meaningful, the course of human history has seen different groups unify around different sets of values, purposes and principles. *Christians, consequentialists, Buddhists, Stoics and the rest all provide different answers to that question, "What should I do?" Each of these answers is a "morality".*[3]   [Emphases ours]

Professional Ethics

Professional ethics are a form of applied ethics governing the behavior of members of a professional body. Shared ethical principles form the basis of professional codes of conduct, though they may differ according to profession. They provide agreed rules on how members, when acting as representatives of their profession, should act toward other people, and institutions in their work, sharing a common morality, seeking efficient and effective solutions:

Applied ethics is a branch of ethics specific to a concrete social domain of activity, grounded on common morality and addressed to all people possibly involved in that activity.

All applied ethics are of a theoretical–practical nature, having a double requirement: *on the one hand, a sound theory to guarantee the objectivity of its justifications and the coherence of its orientations and, on the other hand, efficient and efficacious interventions in concrete situations to assure the real and satisfactory resolution of problems.*[4]   [Emphasis ours]

Professional codes of conduct reflect the unique circumstances and conditions of a given profession, and share ethical principles: honesty, trustworthiness, loyalty, respect for others, adherence to the law, doing good and avoiding harming others, and accountability. They confirm the expectations that the profession has of members, providing guidelines to set minimum standards of appropriate behavior.[5]

Professional codes of conduct provide benefits to the:
1. Public in general and clients in particular by building confidence in the trustworthiness of the profession
2. Clients by providing greater transparency and certainty about how their needs are met

3. Members by providing support to resist pressure to behave inappropriately and for advice on how to handle "gray areas"
4. Profession as a whole through the common understanding of acceptable practice, creating collegiality and fairer, transparent disciplinary procedures and
5. Outsiders dealing with the profession because the profession is regarded as more reliable and reputable to deal with.[6]

For professional codes of conduct to be effective:

> Codes should be regulative; should promote the public interest and the interests of those served; should not be self-serving; should be specific and honest, and should be both policeable and policed.[7]

The major business-related professions are accountancy, engineering, finance, journalism, law and medicine.[i] Appendix 1.1 (Introduction to Business-related Professional Codes of Conduct) provides a snapshot of their professional codes of conduct.

Business Ethics

Business ethics are not an oxymoron. Ethical behavior creates sustainable businesses. Achieving sustainable ethical organizational success presents individuals with ethical challenges that can be anticipated. The skill of organizations in resolving their ethical challenges provides the foundations for sustainable success.

Ethical business practices add to the boundaries of the law as it applies to customers, employees, and the communities impacted by their operations. Potentially, they build trust between customers and the organizations that serve them. They can act as a "quality signal" in achieving repeat business and enhancing brand equity. With the increased interest in environmental, social, and governance (ESG) matters, ethically run organizations have become more attractive to investors and prospective employees, making it easier to attract and retain scarce talent.

Organizations with good business ethics are trustworthy: keeping promises, transparent and honest in communications, and diligent in following up. They respect customers and their needs, treat employees with empathy and understanding while at the same time setting them challenging objectives that allow them to see how they can contribute to achieving the organization's mission and vision. They treat customers and employees fairly, according to clearly communicated standards in their codes of conduct, that apply to all.

---

i There are many other respected professions, for example in architecture; entertainment; first responders (firefighters, military, and police); dentistry and nursing; sports; and teaching, but their direct relevance to commercial organizations is rather limited, so we have excluded them.

Organizations that behave in this way put their customers first, recognizing that the purpose of business is to create and maintain loyal, satisfied customers while optimizing shareholder value.[ii]

Personal Ethics

Personal ethics are the ethics people adopt in dealing with everyday dilemmas. Professional and business ethics are adopted in interactions and business dealings in professional lives. Sometimes, professional or business ethics and personal ethics clash:

> [Professional] ethics are basically an institution's attempt to regulate behavior with rules based on a shared moral code. Violating ethics has the same consequence as breaking a rule, while violating one's morals results in personal guilt and shame instead of a societal consequence. *Ethical dilemmas occur when an institutional set of ethics conflicts with one's personal moral code.*[8]   [Emphasis ours]

In our book *Criminality and Business Strategy: Similarities and Differences* we show that many people struggle to accept that changes in circumstances, conditions, and scientific knowledge justify amending laws based in history or religion. Consequently, reconciling ethical (morality-based) and effective (law-based) decision-making is complex, and contextually dependent. Unsurprisingly, individuals often experience stress, confusion, anger, shame, guilt, and a sense of powerlessness when making choices that violate their values, even if they are legal or commonly accepted practice.

Choosing the best way for individuals to deal with so many factors is complicated. We suggest an approach that depends on circumstances and which of people's multiple ethical personas are in play. It recognizes the "moral injury"[iii] they may suffer as a result. In order to appreciate the extent to which they are susceptible to "moral injury," people need to establish a baseline that represents their beliefs and values. To establish this ethical baseline, they need to assess their personal "Moral Capital" and define their "kaleidoscopic ethical personas." (This approach is the subject of Chapter 5: Building an Ethical Organization.)

---

ii If we were to use Operations Research's mathematical approach, the "objective function" would read "successful ethical organizations maximize customer satisfaction, subject to constraints created by other stakeholders and the need to create positive net present value, given appropriate hurdle rates of return."

iii "Moral injury is understood to be the strong cognitive and emotional response that can occur following events that violate a person's moral or ethical code. Potentially morally injurious events include a person's own or other people's acts of omission or commission, or betrayal by a trusted person in a high-stakes situation . . . morally injurious events threaten one's deeply held beliefs and trust."

Williamson, V. et al. (2021), "Moral injury: The effects on mental health and implications for treatment," *The Lancet*, Volume 8, Issue 6, June 1, pp. 453–455, https://www.thelancet.com/journals/lanpsy/article/PIIS2215-0366(21)00113-9/fulltext, accessed July 11, 2021.

The Law

Law is distinct from morality and ethics. The *Oxford English Dictionary* defines the law as:

> The body of rules, whether proceeding from formal enactment or from custom, which a particular state or community recognizes as binding on its members or subjects.

In the ancient world, philosophers, jurists, and theologians assumed there was no difference between morality, ethics, and the law. The law was morality made manifest either by divine revelation ("natural law") or by the commands of the sovereign interpreting those manifestations for enforcement by the state.[iv] This explains the popular misconception that

> [t]he law exists in some way to promote morality, to preserve those conditions which make the moral life possible, and then to enable men to lead sober and industrious lives. The average man regards law as justice systematized, and justice itself as a somewhat chaotic mass of moral principles. *On this view, the positive law is conceived of as a code of rules, corresponding to the code of moral laws, deriving its authority from the obligatory character of those moral laws, and being just or unjust according as it agrees with, or differs from them.*[9]   [Emphasis ours]

There are a number of reasons why this idealized view of the relationship between morality/ethics and the law does not reflect the practice of law. The idealized view assumes that the ruling elites that control the state have a strong sense of morality and are motivated by what is best for its subjects. This idea dates back to Plato's *Republic*[10] in the West, and Confucius's *Analects*[11] in the East that extolled the virtues of idealized benevolent rulers.

Reality is Different

The reality – *how the world is,* as opposed to *how it ought to be* – is different. Plato failed miserably by his own admission when he tried to apply his ideas in Syracuse;[12] and Confucius's disciple Xunzi disagreed with both Confucius and his other famous follower, Mencius, arguing that people were selfish and envious.[v] History is full of leaders who used the power of the state and its control over the writing of

---

iv For example, the Bible and the Quran for the Abrahamic faiths; and the Code of Hammurabi for Mesopotamians and the *Book of Lord Shang* for the Qin emperor in China.
v "Confucius did not explain why the superior man chooses righteousness rather than personal profit. This question was taken up more than 100 years after his death by his follower Mencius (Mengzi; c. 372–c. 289 BCE), who asserted that humans are naturally inclined to do what is humane and right. Evil is not part of human nature but is the result of poor upbringing or lack of education. But Confucius also had another distinguished follower, Xunzi (c. 300–c. 230 BCE), who said that humans naturally seek profit for themselves and envy others."

laws to treat subjects cruelly, amorally, and unjustly, showing that subjects cannot rely on laws to protect them.

Acemoglu and Robinson point out in their book *Why Nations Fail* that the most important single factor in explaining why some nations flourish and others fail is the philosophy of ruling political and economic elites, enabled by the social and bureaucratic elites. Ruling elites that adopt an inclusive approach create conditions for economic growth and a fair distribution of wealth. Ruling elites that adopt an extractive approach to governing create institutions, that are designed to benefit themselves at the expense of the rest of society, using the law to enforce their governance malpractices:

> *Secure property rights, the law, public services, and the freedom to contract and exchange all rely on the state [and its laws], the institution with the coercive capacity to impose order, prevent theft and fraud, and enforce contracts between private parties.* To function well, society also needs other public services: roads and a transport network so that goods can be transported; a public infrastructure so that economic activity can flourish; and *some type of basic regulation to prevent fraud and malfeasance.* Though many of these public services can be provided by markets and private citizens, the degree of coordination necessary to do so on a large scale often eludes all but a central authority. *The state is thus inexorably intertwined with economic institutions, as the enforcer of law and order, private property contracts,* and often as a key provider of public services. Inclusive economic institutions need and use the state.
>
> . . . Private property is non-existent in North Korea. In colonial Latin America there was private property for Spaniards, but the property of indigenous peoples was highly insecure. In neither type of society was the vast mass of people able to make the economic decisions they wanted to; they were subject to mass coercion. In neither type of society was the power of the state used to provide public services that promoted prosperity . . . *In neither type of society was there a level playing field or an unbiased legal system. In North Korea, the legal system is an arm of the ruling Communist Party, and in Latin America it was a tool of discrimination against the mass of the people. We call such institutions, which have opposite properties to those we call inclusive, extractive because such institutions are designed to extract incomes and wealth from one subset of society to benefit a different subset.*[13]   [Emphases ours]

This is not to deny that when the law is working at its best, it does reflect the ideas of right behavior expressed in a society's morality/ethics. For example, a basic principle of common law is that people are obliged to take care of their neighbors, and to avoid harming them, reflecting the moral injunction of reciprocity that exists in all moral codes. How this is expressed in the law might be worded differently, but the principle is the same, illustrated by Lord Atkin's statement in *Donoghue v. Stevenson* giving restricted specificity to a vague, diffuse rule, providing the ground for deciding future cases of tort:

Singer, P. (2021), "Ethics," *Encyclopedia Britannica*, December 15, 2021, https://www.britannica.com/topic/ethics-philosophy, accessed 22 December 2021.

The rule that you are to love your neighbour becomes in law, you must not injure your neighbour; and the lawyer's question, Who is my neighbour? receives a restricted reply. *You must take reasonable care to avoid acts or omissions which you can reasonably foresee would be likely to injure your neighbour.* Who, then, in law is my neighbour? The answer seems to be – *persons who are so closely and directly affected by my act that I ought reasonably to have them in contemplation as being so affected when I am directing my mind to the acts or omissions which are called in question.*[14]   [Emphases ours]

The key point here is that the application of law requires more than just a statement of *what* needs to be done, but must define *how* it is to be done, for it to be effective – hence the restricted specificity of Lord Atkin's judgment. This lies at the heart of the arguments between those who believe that there is such a thing as "natural law" that all of humanity must follow, versus the positivists who argue that law is man-made and therefore reflects the socio-political contexts applicable of each jurisdiction.[vi] We would argue that *it is precisely in deciding how the law is applied that we see the difference between law and morality/ethics*:

Experience does indeed show that no human society is viable unless certain practices are outlawed in order to protect life, personal integrity, and goods. This statement concerning a "minimal" or "empirical" natural law (as H. L. A. Hart calls it), however, simply says that life, limbs and goods **must** be protected, if a society is to be viable. It does not say anything, though, about **how** life, limbs and goods **ought** to be protected; nor does it say anything about **whose** life, limbs and goods ought to be protected. *The whom and the how of such a "minimal natural law" constraints are precisely where group- and personal- interests and preference step in; where a variety of ultimate, incompatible, principles of justice has been adopted over times and places*; where the most different social arrangement, all taking into account those "natural constraints", have been established, each one claiming for itself the blessing of absolute justice.[15] [Emphases ours]

Additionally, there are two quite distinct approaches to the application of laws, namely liberal societies' "Rule *of* Law" where nobody is above the law; and totalitarian governmental "Rule *by* Law" advocated by Hobbes in *Leviathan,* where he argued that the sovereign was necessary to make and enforce laws to keep the peace, but that the sovereign was above the law, because being bound by laws created for subjects to obey was incompatible with being the sovereign.[16]

Rule of Law

The "rule of law" is one of the fundamental concepts of liberal society, along with democracy, human rights, social justice, and economic freedom. Some argue that

---

vi For an excellent exposition of the legal positivist refutation of the Natural Law Theory, see Chiassoni, P. (2014), "Kelsen on Natural Law Theory," *Revus*, Volume 23, November 18, 2014, https://doi.org/10.4000/revus.2976.

the "rule of law" is separate and distinct from these other concepts and applies only to the formal and procedural aspects of government institutional decision-making as it affects policy.[17] Others believe there is overlap that leads to integration of the different elements. The key requirement of the "rule of law" is:

> People in positions of authority should exercise their power within a constraining framework of well-established public norms rather than in an arbitrary, *ad hoc*, or purely discretionary manner on the basis of their own preferences or ideology. *It insists that the government should operate within a framework of law in everything it does, and that it should be accountable through law when there is a suggestion of unauthorized action by those in power.*

> But the Rule of Law is not just about government. It requires also that citizens should respect and comply with legal norms, even when they disagree with them. When their interests conflict with others' they should accept legal determinations of what their rights and duties are. Also, *the law should be the same for everyone, so that no one is above the law, and everyone has access to the law's protection.* The requirement of access is particularly important, in two senses. First, law should be epistemically accessible: it should be a body of norms promulgated as public knowledge so that people can study it, internalize it, figure out what it requires of them, and use it as a framework for their plans and expectations and for settling their disputes with others. Secondly, *legal institutions and their procedures should be available to ordinary people to uphold their rights, settle their disputes, and protect them against abuses of public and private power. All of this in turn requires the independence of the judiciary, the accountability of government officials, the transparency of public business, and the integrity of legal procedures.*[18]   [Emphases ours]

When non-specialists ("the Man on the Clapham omnibus") refer to "rule of law" they mean the absence of corruption; the independence of the judiciary; speedy sentencing (since "justice delayed is justice denied"[19]); and a presumption in favor of liberty. However, when jurists refer to the "rule of law" they tend to mean the rule by general norms rather than by decree; that the norms are publicly available; and that they are clear and determinate and not so vague that their interpretation is subject to the whims of officials.[20]

For some jurists, all that matters is that the courts are the final arbiters; others who worry about the political leanings of judges recognize that in such circumstances where the politics of judges have a role to play, as for example in the US Supreme Court's alleged attitude toward *Roe v. Wade*,[21] "rule *of* law" comes dangerously close to "rule *by* man."

"Rule of law" meets the common expectations most clearly in the case of common law, with its evolutionary development that is less subject to state control than statute law. Statute law is created by political elites, who frame statutes to reflect their interests. As a result, statute law can become "rule *by* law" as opposed to "rule *of* law" in the hands of illiberal or dictatorial regimes.

The World Justice Project defined the four universal principles for a society to have "rule of law":

As used by the World Justice Project, the rule of law refers to a rules-based system in which the following four universal principles are upheld:

- – The government and its officials and agents are accountable under the law.
- – The laws are clear, publicized, stable, and fair, and protect fundamental rights, including the security of persons and property.
- – The process by which the laws are enacted, administered, and enforced is accessible, fair, and efficient.
- – Access to justice is provided by competent, independent, and ethical adjudicators, attorneys or representatives, and judicial officers who are of sufficient number, have adequate resources, and reflect the makeup of the communities they serve.[22]

Despite this definition, morality as a principle of the "rule of law" failed the important test of fairness in the South African apartheid government's judicial regime:

> [T]he apartheid government, its officers and agents were accountable in accordance with the laws; the laws were clear; publicized, and stable, and were upheld by law enforcement officials and judges. What was missing was the substantive component of the rule of law. The process by which the laws were made was not fair (only whites, a minority of the population, had the vote). And the laws themselves were not fair. They institutionalized discrimination, vested broad discretionary powers in the executive, and failed to protect fundamental rights. *Without a substantive content there would be no answer to the criticism, sometimes voiced, that the rule of law is "an empty vessel into which any law could be poured."*[23]   [Emphasis ours]

South Africa's failure to meet the "fairness" test is an example of a society where ruling elites adopted extractive political and economic practices supported by extractive institutions, in particular by a form of the law that (when answering the "how" and "whose" questions raised earlier) provided an opportunity for unjust, unfair, and immoral judgments as a result. As another example, the law protecting property is a fundamental pillar of successful commercial societies, yet it has no interest in ensuring that wealth is distributed equitably. From at least 1619 in Jamestown[vii] until 1833 it

---

vii "To ignore what had been happening with relative frequency in the broader Atlantic world over the preceding 100 years or so understates the real brutality of the ongoing slave trade, of which the 1619 group were undoubtedly a part, and minimizes the significant African presence in the Atlantic world to that point," Guasco explains. "People of African descent have been 'here' longer than the English colonies. . . . Prior to 1619, hundreds of thousands of Africans, both free and enslaved, aided the establishment and survival of colonies in the Americas and the New World. They also fought against European oppression, and, in some instances, hindered the systematic spread of colonization."

Christopher Columbus likely transported the first Africans to the Americas in the late 1490s on his expeditions to the island of Hispaniola, now Haiti and the Dominican Republic. Their exact status, whether free or enslaved, remains disputed. But the timeline fits with what we know of the origins of the slave trade.

European trade of enslaved Africans began in the 1400s. "The first example we have of Africans being taken against their will and put on board European ships would take the story back to 1441," says Guasco, when the Portuguese captured 12 Africans in Cabo Branco – modern-day Mauritania in north Africa – and brought them to Portugal as enslaved peoples."

"America's history of slavery began long before Jamestown," *History*, August 26, 2019, https://www.history.com/news/american-slavery-before-jamestown-1619, accessed May 14, 2022.

was legal in the British Empire to own slaves,[24] as it was in the Southern United States until after the end of the American Civil War in 1865 or Cuba until 1878 and Brazil until 1888.[25] This was a violation of human rights, but justified by the individual's right to own property in a legal system where enslaved people were regarded as chattels to be bought and sold like livestock.

The law has additional roles to acting as an enforcement channel of morality/ethical behavior: it is the guarantor of commercial activity; it can be used to oppress people, assisting in the transfer "of incomes and wealth from one subset of society to the benefit of a different subset," or as the French philosopher/writer Voltaire put it:

> In general, the art of government consists of taking as much as possible from one class of citizens to give to another.[26]

The Workings of the Law

The way the law works in practice is another reason why the idealized view of the law and morality/ethics being one and the same is mistaken:

> Legal work and ethical behaviors are often entangled in a way that can be difficult to decipher. However, it's important to understand the difference between a legal judgment and an ethical decision, as the two may seem at odds with one another.
>
> First: what is ethics? In general understanding, ethical behavior falls under a system of morality concerned with what's good for both individuals and society. It concerns how people should and shouldn't behave, and different societies and cultures have different ideas of ethical behavior.
>
> In contrast, *the law is a system of rules and guidelines that are meant to be separated from ethics and morality and are enforced through social institutions like courts and law enforcement. In general terms, the law affords punishment through fines, community service, jail time, etc. when one breaks the rules. However, when one breaks an ethical rule, enforcement is more often public shame or the loss of personal relationships rather than money or time.*[27]   [Emphasis ours]

Table 1.1 compares and contrasts the workings of the law with those of morality:

Given that regulations are needed, the question arises, "How best to regulate?" There are two approaches to regulation: rules-based and principles-based. Table 1.2 compares and contrasts the two:

The "rule of law" requires everybody to respond in the same way to rules and regulations to be effective. Problems can arise from a mismatch of axiomatic assumptions between the Universalist and Particularist worldviews of ethical behavior, illustrated in Table 1.3, which shows the differences in axioms between the two systems.

Table 1.4 presents a hypothetical car accident in which you might find yourself as a witness.

How people respond to the hypothetical example above indicates their position on the Universalist–Particularist continuum. Universalists would argue that being

Table 1.1: Law and morality compared.

Law (in "rule *of* law" societies)	Morality
1. The law regulates and controls the observable human behavior. It is not concerned with inner motives. The law is not interested in intentions unless they translate into actions that harm another person.	1. Morality regulates and controls both the inner motives and the external actions. It is concerned with the whole life of a person.
2. The law applies universally in a particular society. All individuals are equally subjected to it. It does not change from person to person.	2. Morality condemns a person if he or she has evil intentions, whereas laws only apply once these intentions are manifested externally and harm another person.
3. Application of the law is determined by precise and specific judgments that take the particular context into account and any mitigating circumstances.	3. Morality is variable. It changes from person to person and from age to age. Every person has their own moral principles.
4. The law is man-made, backed by the powers of the state.	4. Moral laws lack precision and specificity as there is no human authority to make and enforce them.
5. Law-breaking is punished proportionately to the harms it causes, through fines or custodial sentencing.	5. Morality is not defined or enforced by secular authority. It is a private matter of conscience in a secular state. Breach of moral principles does not lead to punishment in a secular state.
6. The fear of punishment acts as an imperfect deterrent to law-breaking.	6. The only check against the breach of morality is social condemnation or individual conscience.

Based on: Singh, M. *Theory of Relationship between Law and Morality*, http://www.legalservicesin dia.com/article/1931/Theory-of-Relationship-between-Law-and-Morality.html, accessed December 22, 2021.

Table 1.2: Rules-based and principles-based regulations compared.

Rules-based regulations	Principles-based regulations
1. Address the "What" and "How" question	1. Addresses the "Why" question
2. Clear what is permitted and what is not	2. Often unclear what is permitted
3. Risk of form over substance	3. Substance above form
4. Box-ticking rather than exercising judgment	4. Requires exercise of judgment above all
High risk of "breaking the law legally" to get around the spirit of the law by focusing on the wording.	*High risk of poor execution because of insufficient detailed direction on "How to implement".*

Source: Zinkin, J. (2019) *Better Governance across the Board: Creating Value through Reputation, People and Processes* (Boston and Berlin: Walter de Gruyter Inc), p. 34.

Table 1.3: Rules-based versus relationship-based morality.

Universalist rules-based	Particularist relationship-based
Underlying beliefs:	**Underlying beliefs:**
1. What is good and right can be defined and always applies regardless of circumstances	1. Obligations to in-group relationships considering special circumstances come first
2. No exceptions to applying rules; relationships do not matter	2. Waivers are necessary because special circumstances always exist
3. Only one reality – that which has been agreed in a code of conduct or applicable laws	3. Several realities exist based on changing circumstances and relationships
4. Trustworthy person honors their word or contract, regardless of impact on relationship	4. Trustworthy person honors changing mutual ties, despite what the law may say

Based on: Zinkin, J. and Bennett, C. (2021) *The Principles and Practice of Effective Leadership* (Berlin and Boston: Walter de Gruyter GmbH), p. 268.

Table 1.4: Witnessing a car accident.

Situation:

You are in a car with a close friend driving when he hits a pedestrian at more than 70 kph in an area where the speed limit is 50. There are no witnesses and no forensic evidence to prove the speed at which he was driving. His lawyer says if you testify that he was going at less than 50, it will help your friend.

Question: Does your friend, as a good friend, have the right to expect you to lie for him?

Differing beliefs give different answers
Answer 1: He has the right to expect me to testify to the lower speed.
Answer 2: He has some right to expect me to testify to the lower speed.
Answer 3: He has no right to expect me to testify to the lower speed.

What would you do?
1. Testify he was going at less than 50 kph?
2. Not testify he was going at less than 50 kph?

How much difference would it make to your answer if the pedestrian was badly hurt?

Differing beliefs
Universalist Approach
1. The truth must be told.
2. The law was broken and the serious condition of the pedestrian underlines the importance of upholding the law.
3. It is more important to tell the truth the more serious the injuries.

Table 1.4 (continued)

Situation:

Particularist Approach

1. The need to support my friend comes first.
2. My friend needs my help even more now he is in trouble with the law.
3. It is more important to lie for my friend the more serious the injuries.

Based on: Trompenaars, F. and Hampden-Turner, C. (1998) *Riding the Waves of Culture* (London: Nicholas Brealey Publishing), pp. 33–49.

loyal may be important, but greater harm would be created by letting friends get away with breaking the law and allowing them to do it again. It is the differences in the underlying beliefs and values that determine what we do. Particularists will find reasons why "in these particular circumstances" the law should not apply – in this example, the need to be loyal to a close friend.

Commercial law in different jurisdictions has different approaches to regulation with the US relying on rules-based "black letter law" and Commonwealth countries increasingly relying on principles-based regulation that focuses on intended outcomes rather than the prohibition of specific behaviors. "Black letter law" focuses on predictability of legal outcomes rather than the ethical consequences of actions and, as a result, is criticized for fostering a "tick in the box" mentality, devoid of moral intent. It is designed to protect those in positions of responsibility when challenged in a court of law by demonstrating that they followed due process (ticked all the relevant boxes), and therefore cannot be held responsible for any unethical outcomes. Even in principles-based regulatory regimes, if defendants can prove under challenge in court that they did what they were required to do (that is, follow the letter of the law) regardless of the outcome, and whether they violated the "spirit" of the law, they may not be penalized for what they have done. The law may then be changed after the event to rectify the injustice. For example, during the Congressional hearings into Goldman Sachs's Abacus and Timberwolf deals in 2010, when Senator Carl Levin, Chair of the Committee investigating the deals, was told that what Goldman had done was legal, his reaction was that the law needed changing. The success of Goldman's lawyers in defending the three Goldman employees from being found guilty offended the Committee's sense of ethics and led to the development and passage of Dodd–Frank legislation changing banking regulation.[28]

There are two reasons why businesspeople are willing to treat ethics and the law as separate issues and are willing to ignore the ethical dimensions of decisions they make. The first is the legal opinion of Lord Thurlow that "corporations, have neither bodies to be punished nor souls to be condemned, they therefore do as they like"[29] and that though subject to law, they were beyond ethical claims. "Did you ever expect a corporation to have conscience, when it has no soul to be damned and no body to be kicked?"[30] The second is the Friedman doctrine that the purpose of business is to maximize shareholder value. Combining the two means that decisions cease to be moral decisions and become ones of risk management[31] and the "cost of doing business." As long as the costs of unethical or illegal behavior including fines and the damage to reputation and market capitalization are less than the profits to be derived from that behavior, then there is no reason not to behave unethically or break the law, particularly if fines are paid by the corporation at the expense of innocent shareholders.

If executives – those who make the decisions – do not pay the fines personally and are not jailed, we should not be surprised at companies behaving unethically and being willing to break the law with executives regarding the issue as one of risk management. For that to change, judges would have to punish directors and senior managers and shareholders in their personal capacities, lifting the veil of incorporation and going after the decision-makers who have bodies to punish and souls to condemn, which in turn would negate most of the economic advantages of the limited liability company.

This raises a further question regarding how the "rule of law" works in practice, namely that the legal process is technical, expensive, and time-consuming. As a result, equitable or just verdicts can sometimes be denied because the resources, skills, and willingness to "run down the clock" of powerful defendants fighting a case against less well-resourced plaintiffs overwhelm the merits of the plaintiffs' case, or the case is heard before a technically incompetent or politically motivated judge who favors the arguments of one side in a biased way.

Commercial law is technically complex, expensive, and time-consuming. The main objective of common law judges when making decisions is to provide certainty to future litigants, and limit the costs of litigation by maximizing the chances that disputes can be settled out of court. As Lord Neuberger, then President of the UK Supreme Court, said in a speech in 2016 at the Singapore Management University (SMU) Law School:

> *Certainty is a quality to be prized in the law. It is an essential ingredient of the rule of law that the law has to be as certain, as clear and as accessible as possible. The more uncertain, the more unclear, the more inaccessible, the law, the less people feel free to act, in their private and public activities and in their private and public disputes, and therefore the more constrained and more unfree is society and the greater the risk of commerce withering.* That is as true of interpretation of legal documents as of any other branch of legal activity. And, in order to have certainty (or at least as much certainty as possible), *there have to be principles which are of general application, and which are reliably applied by judges when it comes to resolving disputes.*[32]   [Emphases ours]

The law can only provide minimum guidance for running an ethical and successful organization. There are many instances where there are conflicts between what is morally right, what is ethically appropriate, and what is legal. The issue then becomes what has priority – the demands of ethical behavior or the requirements of the law? Moreover, many ethical considerations do not fall under the purview of the law, but reflect conventions designed to make doing business easier. That is why companies make it clear in their codes of conduct that they will obey the laws of the jurisdictions where they operate, and why *successful and ethical companies make it clear that their values require them to go beyond what the law demands.*

Summary

Ethics can be classified as: being general, covering issues that affect humanity as a whole; as institutional ethics, dealing with issues that affect given organizations, with professional and business ethics as distinct subsets; and/or as personal ethics affecting the choices of individuals in their relations with society and the organizations that they work for. Problems arise when these three classes of ethics conflict with one another, the law, and varying societal expectations, creating ethical dilemmas that are difficult to resolve.

Professional ethics govern the behavior of members of a professional body. They provide agreed rules on how members, acting as representatives of their profession, should act towards other people, and institutions in their work, sharing a common morality, seeking efficient and effective solutions.

Business ethics help organizations to be trustworthy: keeping promises, being transparent and honest in communications, and being diligent in following up. Organizations with business ethics respect customers and their needs, treat employees and suppliers with empathy and fairness, according to clearly communicated standards in their codes of conduct, and put their customers first, recognizing that the purpose of business is to create and maintain loyal, satisfied customers in order to optimize shareholder value.

Personal ethics are those adopted by people dealing with everyday dilemmas. Professional and business ethics are adopted in interactions and business dealings in professional lives. Sometimes, professional or business ethics and personal ethics clash in a moral conflict.

Law is distinct from morality and ethics. There are a number of reasons why the idealized view of the relationship between morality/ethics and the law does not reflect the practice of law. Reality – *how the world is,* as opposed to *how it ought to be* – is different: elites often use the power of the state and its control over the writing of history to adopt an extractive approach to governing through institutions that are designed to benefit themselves at the expense of the rest of society, and use the law to enforce their governance malpractices.

At its best, the law reflects the ideas of right behavior expressed in a society's morality/ethics. However, the application of law requires more than just a statement of *what* needs to be done, but must define *how* it is to be done, for it to be effective. This lies at the heart of the arguments between those who believe that there is such a thing as "natural law" that all of humanity must follow, versus the positivists who argue that law is man-made and therefore reflects the socio-political contexts applicable in each jurisdiction. It is precisely in deciding *how* the law is applied that the difference between law and morality/ethics arises.

There are two distinct ways of applying laws: liberal societies' "Rule *of* Law" where nobody is above the law; and totalitarian governmental "Rule *by* Law" advocated by Hobbes in *Leviathan.* "Rule *of* law" meets common expectations most clearly in the case of common law, with its evolutionary development that is less subject to state control than statute law. Statute law is created by political elites, who frame statutes to reflect their interests. As a result, statute law can become "rule *by* law" as opposed to "rule *of* law" in the hands of illiberal or dictatorial regimes.

Four universal principles support the "rule *of* law": government officials and agents are accountable under the law; laws are clear, publicized, stable, and fair, protecting fundamental rights including security of the person and property; legal processes are accessible, fair, and efficient; and access to justice is provided by competent, independent, and ethical adjudicators. In addition, the law should be seen to be fair, a test that the Apartheid South African judicial regime failed.

The "rule *of* law" requires everybody to respond in the same way to rules and regulations to be effective. Problems can arise from a mismatch of axiomatic assumptions between the Universalist and Particularist worldviews of ethical behavior.

Commercial law in different jurisdictions has different approaches to regulation with the United States relying on rules-based "black letter law" and Commonwealth countries increasingly relying on principles-based regulation that focuses on intended outcomes rather than the prohibition of specific behaviors. "Black letter law" focuses on predictability of legal outcomes rather than the ethical consequences of actions and as a result is criticized for fostering a "tick in the box" mentality, devoid of moral intent.

Businesspeople treat ethics and the law as two separate issues because "corporations, have neither bodies to be punished nor souls to be condemned, they therefore do as they like" in the words of Lord Thurlow; and the Friedmanite doctrine that the purpose of business is to maximize shareholder value. Combined, they justify breaking the law as long as the costs of breaking the law are less than the profits to be gained by so doing.

Commercial law is technically complex, expensive, and time-consuming. The main objective of common law judges when making decisions is that they provide certainty to future litigants, and limit the costs of litigation by maximizing the chances that disputes can be settled out of court.

The law can only provide minimum guidance for running an ethical and successful organization. There are many instances where there are conflicts between what is morally right, what is ethically appropriate, and what is legal. That is why companies make it clear in their codes of conduct that they will obey the laws of the jurisdictions where they operate, and why successful *and* ethical companies make it clear that their values require them to go beyond what the law demands.

Appendix 1.1: Introduction to Business-related Professional Codes of Conduct

Accountancy

The Chartered Institute of Management Accountants (CIMA) states in its preamble to its code of ethics:

> A distinguishing mark of the accountancy profession is its acceptance of the responsibility to act in the public interest. A professional accountant's responsibility is not exclusively to satisfy the needs of an individual client or employing organisation. Therefore, the Code contains requirements and application material to enable professional accountants to meet their responsibility to act in the public interest.[33]

According to the International Federation of Accountants (IFAC), five principles of ethics for professional accountants ensure that accountants act in the public interest. They are integrity; objectivity; professional competence and due care; confidentiality; and professional behavior.[34]

Engineering

The National Society of Professional Engineers (NSPE) states in its preamble to its code of ethics:

> Engineering is an important and learned profession. As members of this profession, engineers are expected to exhibit the highest standards of honesty and integrity. Engineering has a direct and vital impact on the quality of life for all people. Accordingly, the services provided by engineers require honesty, impartiality, fairness, and equity, and must be dedicated to the protection of the public health, safety, and welfare. Engineers must perform under a standard of professional behavior that requires adherence to the highest principles of ethical conduct.[35]

According to the NSPE six duties for engineers ensure that they act in the public interest. They are that they hold paramount the safety, health, and welfare of the public; perform service only in areas of their competence; issue public statements only in an objective and truthful manner; act for each employer or client as faithful agents or trustees; avoid deceptive acts; and conduct themselves honorably, responsibly, ethically, and lawfully so as to enhance the honor, reputation, and usefulness of the profession.[36]

Finance

The Chartered Banker Professional Standards Board's Code of Professional Conduct sets out the ethical and professional values, attitudes, and behaviour expected of all professional bankers, and all member banks are expected to sign up and adhere to the Code.

The Code sets out "how individuals should follow best practice and demonstrate their personal commitment to professionalism in banking, by: treating all customers, colleagues and counterparties with respect and acting with integrity; developing and maintaining their professional knowledge and acting with due skill, care and diligence; considering the risks and implications of their actions and advice, and holding themselves accountable for them and their impact; being open and cooperative with the regulators; complying with all current regulatory and legal requirements; paying due regard to the interests of customers and treating them fairly; observing and demonstrating proper standards of market conduct at all times; acting in an honest and trustworthy manner, being alert to and managing potential conflicts of interest; and treating information with appropriate confidentiality and sensitivity."[37]

Journalism

The Society of Professional Journalists (SPJ) states in its preamble to its code of ethics:

> Members of the Society of Professional Journalists believe that public enlightenment is the forerunner of justice and the foundation of democracy. Ethical journalism strives to ensure the free exchange of information that is accurate, fair and thorough. An ethical journalist acts with integrity.[38]

According to the SPJ four principles ensure that journalists act in the public interest. *First, seek truth and report it*, ensuring that they are accurate, using original sources wherever possible; providing context and avoiding oversimplification; allowing subjects of the news to respond to criticism and allegations of wrongdoing; holding those in power accountable and giving voice to the voiceless; supporting open and civil exchange of views even when they find them repugnant; never distorting the facts or stereotyping and attributing the sources. *Second, minimize harm*, treating sources, colleagues, and members of the public as deserving of respect by balancing the public's need for information against potential harm or discomfort; show compassion for those affected by the coverage and consider cultural differences when reporting; recognizing that legal access to information is not an ethical justification to publish; respecting the right to privacy; balancing a suspect's right to a fair trial with the public's right to know; and considering the implications of the extended reach and permanence of publication (particularly in social media). *Third, act independently*, remembering that "the highest and primary obligation of ethical journalism is to serve the public, by avoiding conflicts of interest; refusing gifts, favors, fees or any other activities that may compromise integrity or impartiality; distinguishing news from advertising, and labelling sponsored content prominently. *Fourth, be accountable and transparent* by responding quickly to questions about accuracy, clarity, and fairness; acknowledging mistakes and correcting them quickly and prominently, explain the corrections; exposing unethical conduct in their organizations, and abiding by the same high standards expected of others.[39]

Law

The American Bar Association (ABA) states:

[1] A lawyer, as a member of the legal profession, is a representative of clients, an officer of the legal system and a public citizen having special responsibility for the quality of justice. As a representative of clients, a lawyer performs various functions.

[2] As advisor, a lawyer provides a client with an informed understanding of the client's legal rights and obligations and explains their practical implications. As advocate, a lawyer zealously asserts the client's position under the rules of the adversary system. As negotiator, a lawyer seeks a result advantageous to the client but consistent with requirements of honest dealings with others. As an evaluator, a lawyer acts by examining a client's legal affairs and reporting about them to the client or to others.

[3] In addition to these representational functions, a lawyer may serve as a third-party neutral, a nonrepresentational role helping the parties to resolve a dispute or other matter.[40]

According to the ABA, lawyers should act in the public interest and help the bar regulate itself accordingly. They should be competent, prompt, and diligent; their conduct should conform to the requirements of the law (in both business and personal matters); they should use the procedures of the law for legitimate purposes only and not to intimidate or harass others. Given the important place the law has in the smooth workings of government, society, and business, lawyers as public citizens should seek to improve the law, access, administration of justice, and the quality of service provided. Lawyers are also expected to "cultivate knowledge of the law beyond its use for clients, employ that knowledge in reform of the law and work to strengthen legal education" and further the public's understanding of and confidence in the "rule of law" and the justice system. Lawyers, recognizing that the poor cannot afford adequate legal counsel, should devote time and resources to ensure equal access to the justice system and to adequate legal counsel.[41]

Medical

The American Medical Association (AMA) states:

As a member of this profession, a physician must recognize responsibility to patients first and foremost, as well as to society, to other health professionals, and to self. The following Principles adopted by the American Medical Association are not laws, but standards of conduct which define the essentials of honorable behavior for the physician.

I.   A physician shall be dedicated to providing competent medical care, with compassion and respect for human dignity and rights.

II. A physician shall uphold standards of professionalism, be honest in all professional interactions, and strive to report physicians deficient in character or competence, or engaging in fraud or deception, to appropriate entities.

III. A physician shall respect the law and also recognize a responsibility to seek changes in those requirements which are contrary to the best interests of the patient.

IV. A physician shall respect the rights of patients, colleagues, and other health professionals, and shall safeguard patient confidences and privacy within the constraints of the law.

V.   A physician shall continue to study, apply, and advance scientific knowledge, maintain a commitment to medical education, make relevant information available to patients, colleagues, and the public, obtain consultation, and use the talents of other health professionals when indicated.

VI. A physician shall, in the provision of appropriate patient care, except in emergencies, be free to choose whom to serve, with whom to associate, and the environment in which to provide medical care.

VII. A physician shall recognize a responsibility to participate in activities contributing to the improvement of the community and the betterment of public health.

VIII. A physician shall, while caring for a patient, regard responsibility to the patient as paramount.

IX. A physician shall support access to medical care for all people.[42]

References

1 Neves, M. P. (2016), "Ethics, as a philosophical discipline," Bioethics Research Centre, Bioethics Institute, Catholic University of Portugal, Porto, Portugal, published in *Encyclopedia of Global Bioethics*, January, 2016, pp. 2–3.

2 Velasquez, M. et al. (2010) "What is ethics?", Markkula Center for Applied Ethics, January 1, 2010, https://www.scu.edu/ethics/ethics-resources/ethical-decision-making/what-is-ethics/, accessed December 22, 2021.

3 "Ethics explainer: Ethics, morality and law," Ethics Centre, September 27, 2016, https://ethics.org.au/ethics-explainer-ethics-morality-law/, accessed December 21, 2021.

4 "Ethics explainer: Ethics, morality and law," p. 16.

5 "Professional ethics and codes of conduct," Ministry of Business Innovation and Employment, 2021, https://www.iaa.govt.nz/for-advisers/adviser-tools/ethics-toolkit/professional-ethics-and-codes-of-conduct/, accessed December 28, 2021.

6 Ibid.

7 De George, R. T. (1982), *Business Ethics* (New York: Macmillan) quoted in Werhane, P. and Freeman, R. (eds), *Encyclopedic Dictionary of Business Ethics* (Oxford: Blackwell Business, 1998), p. 114.

8 Gunner, J. (2021), "What's the difference between ethics, morals and values?", *YourDictionary*, 2021, https://examples.yourdictionary.com/difference-between-ethics-morals-and-values.html, accessed December 23, 2021.

9 Singh, M., *Theory of Relationship between Law and Morality*, http://www.legalservicesindia.com/article/1931/Theory-of-Relationship-between-Law-and-Morality.html, accessed December 22, 2021.

10 Bauman, D. C. (2018), "Plato on virtuous leadership: An ancient model for modern business," *Business Ethics Quarterly*, Volume 28, Issue 3, 2018, pp. 251–274.

11 Confucius (1997 [479 BCE]), *Analects of Confucius* (New York: Norton).

12 Plato, "Epistles," LCL 234, pp. 388–389, *Loeb Classical Library* (Harvard University Press, 2022), https://www.loebclassics.com/view/plato-philosopher_epistles/1929/pb_LCL234.389.xml, accessed December 23, 2021.

13 Acemoglu, D. and Robinson, J. A. (2012), *Why Nations Fail: The Origins of Power, Prosperity, and Poverty* (New York: Currency), pp. 75–76.

14 Atkin, J. (1932), "Donoghue v Stevenson [1932] Doctrine of negligence," *Donoghue v. Stevenson* [1932] A.C. 562, [1932] UKHL 100, 1932 S.C. (H.L.) 31, 1932 S.L.T. 317, [1932] W.N. 139, *LawTeacher*, October 22, 2021, https://www.lawteacher.net/cases/donoghue-v-stevenson.php, accessed December 23, 2021.

15 Chiassoni, P. (2014), "Kelsen on Natural Law Theory," *Revus*, Volume 23, November 18, 2014, DOI: https://doi.org/10.4000/revus.2976, accessed December 23, 2021.

16 Hobbes, T. and Tuck, R., eds (1991 [1651]), *Leviathan* (Cambridge: Cambridge University Press), p. 184, cited in Waldron, J. (2020), "The Rule of Law," in *The Stanford Encyclopedia of Philosophy* (Summer 2020 Edition), Edward N. Zalta, ed., https://plato.stanford.edu/entries/rule-of-law/, accessed December 26, 2021.

17 Waldron (2020).

18 Waldron (2020).

19 Gladstone, W. E., *Forbes Quotes*, https://www.forbes.com/quotes/9805/, accessed December 26, 2021.

20 Waldron (2020).

21 Roberts, W. (2021), "Abortion: Will the Supreme Court overturn Roe v. Wade in 2022?" *Aljazeera*, December 27, 2021, https://www.aljazeera.com/news/2021/12/27/abortion-will-us-supreme-court-overturn-roe-v-wade-2022, accessed December 29, 2021.

22 Agrast, M., Botero, J., and Ponce, A. (2011), "WJP Rule of Law Index 2011" (Washington, D.C.: The World Justice Project), p. 1, https://worldjusticeproject.org/sites/default/files/documents/WJP_Rule_of_Law_Index_2011_Report.pdf, accessed December 27, 2021.

23 Chaskalson, A. (2011), World Justice Project, 2011, *Rule of Law Index* (2011 edition), p. 9, https://worldjusticeproject.org/sites/default/files/documents/WJP_Rule_of_Law_Index_2011_Report.pdf, accessed December 27, 2021.

24 Oldfield, J. (2021), "Abolition of the slave trade and slavery in Britain," *British Library*, February 4, 2021, https://www.bl.uk/restoration-18th-century-literature/articles/abolition-of-the-slave-trade-and-slavery-in-britain, accessed January 9, 2021.

25 Bergad, L. W. (2012), "Abolition," Chapter 8 in *The Comparative Histories of Slavery in Brazil, Cuba, and the United States* (Cambridge: Cambridge University Press), pp. 251–290, June, https://doi.org/10.1017/CBO9780511803970, accessed January 9, 2021.

26 Voltaire, https://www.brainyquote.com/quotes/voltaire_124855, accessed February 16, 2021.

27 Perkins, S. (2020), "The relationship between law and ethics," *Perkins Law Group*, March 7, 2020, https://www.ssplawgroup.com/the-relationship-between-law-and-ethics, accessed December 21, 2021.

28 MacDonald, E. (2011), "Goldman Sachs accused of misleading Congress, client," Fox Business, April 14, 2011, www.foxbusiness.com/markets/2011/04/14/goldman-sachs-accused-lying-congress/, cited in Zinkin, J. (2014), *Rebuilding Trust in Banks: The Role of Leadership and Governance* (Singapore: John Wiley & Sons), pp. 138–139.

29 Thurlow, E., *Oxford Essential Quotations*, https://www.oxfordreference.com/view/10.1093/acref/9780191826719.001.0001/q-oro-ed4-00010943, accessed January 2, 2021.

30 Thurlow, E. (1978), *The Oxford Dictionary of Quotations, Second Edition* (Oxford: Oxford University Press), p. 547.

31 Sison, A. J. G. (2000), "Integrated risk management and global business ethics," *Business Ethics: A European Review*, Volume 9, Number 4, October, 2000, https://onlinelibrary.wiley.com/doi/abs/10.1111/1467-8608.00203, accessed January 2, 2021.

32 Neuberger, D. (2016), excerpt from a speech given at the School of Law, Singapore Management University, August 19, 2016, sent in an email to the authors on December 29, 2021.

33 "CIMA Code of Ethics for Professional Accountants," CIMA, January 2020, https://www.cimaglobal.com/Documents/Ethics/Code%20of%20Ethics/CIMA%20Code%20of%20Ethics%202020%20V1.0.pdf, accessed December 28, 2021.

34 "Handbook of the International Code of Ethics for Professional Accountants (including International Independence Standards), 2021 Edition," IFAC, 2021, https://www.ifac.org/system/files/publications/files/IESBA-English-2021-IESBA-Handbook_Web.pdf, accessed December 28, 2021.

35 "NSPE Code of Conduct for Engineers," NSPE, July 2019, https://www.nspe.org/resources/ethics/code-ethics, accessed December 28, 2021.

36 Ibid.

37 "The Chartered Banker Code of Professional Conduct," *Chartered Banker Professional Standards Board*, January 2016, https://www.charteredbanker.com/static/uploaded/5e917c8b-7bc6-45ed-a43287ee7466612b.pdf, accessed December 29, 2021.

38 "SPJ Code of Ethics," *Society of Professional Journalists*, September 6, 2014, https://www.spj.org/ethicscode.asp, accessed December 29, 2021.

39 Ibid.

40 "Model rules of professional conduct: Preamble and scope," American Bar Association, 2000, https://www.americanbar.org/groups/professional_responsibility/publications/model_rules_of_professional_conduct/model_rules_of_professional_conduct_preamble_scope/, accessed December 28, 2021.

41 Ibid.

42 Riddick, F. A. (2003), "The Code of Ethics of the American Medical Association," *The Ochsner Journal*, Spring, Volume 5, Issue 2, 2003, p. 7, https://www.ncbi.nlm.nih.gov/pmc/articles/PMC3399321/, accessed January 7, 2022.

Chapter 2
The Ethics Continuum

Behaving *ethically* and *consistently* is difficult.[i]

"Ethical" decision-making depends on the circumstances and context within which the decisions are made.

The difficulties experienced in practice arise from five causes:

1) Ethics are usually considered to reflect what *"ought to be"* not *"what is."*
2) Reconciling "duty-based" with "consequential ethics" can be impossible.
3) Different religious and cultural axioms lead to different ethical conclusions.
4) Individuals and organizations have multiple ethical personas and reference groups, whose salience depends on circumstances and context.
5) Rewards and punishments have an impact.

The choices made vary depending on the interaction of these five factors and the context. Inconsistencies inevitably result. If the inconsistencies are too frequent or too great, they result in "moral damage" leading to a loss of self-esteem and respect.

"Ought" Versus "Is"

The "ought" approach to ethics has been to build an ethical edifice based on how the world and human behavior *ought* to be.

This view was first challenged by the Sicilian Arab philosopher Ibn Zafar al-Siqilli writing in 1159,[1] and then more thoroughly by Machiavelli in *The Prince*,[2] writing in 1513. The Scottish philosopher David Hume was perhaps the first writer to argue why we cannot derive *ought* from *is* in his *Treatise of Human Nature*, published in 1739, and in *Enquiry concerning the Principles of Morals*, published in 1751.[3] Hume's contribution is that there is a difference between what *ought to be* and what *is;* and that *ought* cannot be derived from *is.* He also observed that there are two types of moral sentiments: "natural" and "artificial." *Natural* moral sentiments are based on the positive (approval/approbation) and negative feelings (disapproval/disapprobation) they engender.[4] Approval/approbation is a positive emotion akin to pleasure, whereas disapproval/disapprobation is uneasiness or pain. These sentiments are experienced when we observe people or their actions and resulting emotions. If the emotions aroused are pleasant then we approve; if unpleasant we disapprove.

---

i This chapter is based on Chapter 8: "Business Strategy Implications" of the companion volume, Zinkin, J. and C. Bennett (2022), *Criminality and Business Strategy: Similarities and Differences* (Berlin/Boston: Walter de Gruyter).

https://doi.org/10.1515/9783110780871-002

Artificial moral sentiments according to Hume "are some virtues, that produce pleasure, and approbation by means of an artifice or contrivance, which arises from the circumstances and necessities of mankind." These artificial virtues derive ethical merit from the presence of rules designed to achieve the common good. They include honesty with respect to property, keeping one's promises, allegiance to one's government,[ii] conformity to the laws of nations for kings and princes, chastity, and modesty.[5]

Hume argued that what engendered the sentiments people felt was the effect on them of "sympathy," or in today's parlance empathy. Empathy is the ability to feel what others do by observing their reactions and behaviors. In a sense, Hume anticipated the discovery of "mirror neurons,"[iii] which explain how we can experience the feelings of others and incorporate them into our own behavior:

> According to Hume's associationism, *vivacity of one perception is automatically transferred to those others that are related to it by resemblance, contiguity, and cause and effect.* Here resemblance and contiguity are primary. All human beings, regardless of their differences, are similar in bodily structure and in the types and causes of their passions. The person I observe or

---

ii "The duty of allegiance to our present governors does not depend upon their or their ancestors' divine right to govern . . . but rather on the general social value of having a government. Rulers thus need not be chosen by the people in order to be legitimate. Consequently, who is the ruler will often be a matter of salience and imaginative association; and it will be no ground for legitimate rebellion that a ruler was selected arbitrarily. *Rulers identified by long possession of authority, present possession, conquest, succession, or positive law will be suitably salient and so legitimate, provided their rule tends to the common good. . . . A government that maintains conditions preferable to what they would be without it retains its legitimacy and may not rightly be overthrown. But rebellion against a cruel tyranny is no violation of our duty of allegiance, and may rightly be undertaken.*" [Emphasis ours]

Cohon, R. (2018), "Hume's moral philosophy," *The Stanford Encyclopedia of Philosophy*, edited by Edward N. Zalta, Fall Edition, https://plato.stanford.edu/archives/fall2018/entries/hume-moral/, accessed June 17, 2021.

iii "The idea is that thanks to mirror neurons, we are able to first observe an action ('What is being done?'), then understand the intention of that action ('Why is it happening?') and finally, to reproduce the same action in order to achieve similar results (the motor component).

Both our understanding of an action and the ability to then mirror that same action is of great significance to learning, speech perception, and emotional intelligence. One argument is that *since mirror neurons are responsible for both the 'what' and the 'what for' of a particular action, they are strongly linked to our ability to show empathy.*

If we see a person crying, we must be able to identify the action and then positively correlate it with the feeling of sorrow. *The mirror neuron system also teaches children to cry to show their discontent.*

Similar arguments had been made in favor of the mirror neurons' role in language learning and, in fact, in the way that our civilization had evolved over centuries [as well as our moral sentiments]." [Emphases ours]

Anderton, K. (2019), "What are mirror neurons?", *News Medical Life Sciences*, February 27, https://www.news-medical.net/health/What-are-Mirror-Neurons.aspx, accessed June 23, 2021.

consider may further resemble me in more specific shared features such as character or nationality. Because of the resemblance and my contiguity to the observed person, the idea of his passion is associated in my mind with my impression of myself, and acquires great vivacity from it. *The sole difference between an idea and an impression is the degree of liveliness or vivacity each possesses. So great is this acquired vivacity that the idea of his passion in my mind becomes an impression, and I actually experience the passion.*[6]   [Emphases ours]

The key points are the significance of "resemblance," "contiguity," and "cause and effect."

Resemblance and contiguity may explain why membership of different collectives and salience determines our most likely reactions to ethical dilemmas. They explain why we respond differently to the same issues when dealing with family, clan, nation, and ethnic group, or as members of a team, department, division, and company as a whole. Appreciating the implications of cause and effect is the basis of consequential ethics (about which more later).

Following Hume, it seems to us that there are moral laws that are generally accepted regardless of culture. This phenomenon has been described by C. S. Lewis in a more modern context.[7] Lewis noted the difference between how people feel they *ought* to behave and how they *actually* behave. This distinction between what people feel they ought to do and what they actually do enables them to judge in a practical way whether they are behaving ethically or not. We need to be clear here that we do not necessarily take Lewis's position on all matters of morality – but we do find his position that some things are universally recognized as "wrong" persuasive as a practical guide.

No leader, in our experience, says with pride, "I am a thief" or "I am corrupt" or "I damaged the environment." When they do such things, they add a justification to themselves and others; "If I didn't do it, someone else would" or "It is the local cultural practice to give gifts." The fact that behavior is justified by claiming that "it isn't really what it appears to be" is the giveaway. When people behave ethically, they feel positive emotions and do not need to justify their actions to themselves or others! When they behave unethically, they feel negative emotions and need to explain why their actions are not what they appear to be.

We can illustrate the concept by imagining "Negative Manifestos." Picture candidates for political office or people being interviewed to become CEO who state explicitly that they will be more corrupt, steal more, murder more, break the law more often, lie more, abuse human rights, and bully people more ruthlessly than their opponents. How likely do you think are they to be chosen? The reason they are unlikely to be chosen is best explained by Hume's argument that the influence of negative sentiments engendered by behaving in a vicious manner leads us collectively to experience painful emotions that we wish to avoid and therefore would vote against.

In the world *as it is*, as opposed to the world *as it ought to be*, people routinely engage in unethical acts.[8] Reflecting power of ethical ideas of how the world *ought* to be, people try to refrain from behaving in ways that violate their own moral standards.

When faced with conflict between "ought" and "is" people find ways to reduce the resulting cognitive dissonance. They do this in one of two ways: a) either by changing their behavior to bring it back into closer alignment with their beliefs, or b) by changing their beliefs to reduce the pain of cognitive dissonance, through "moral disengagement":

> Moral disengagement may take any of the following forms: by *portraying unethical behavior as serving a moral purpose, by attributing behavior to external cues, by distorting the consequences of behavior, or by dehumanizing victims of unethical behavior.* Together, these ways to morally disengage explain how individuals recode their actions to appear less immoral and, as a result, shift ethical boundaries.[9]   [Emphasis ours]

The first way is Machiavelli's justification in *The Prince* that "the ends justify the means" and that there is no point in being ethically or ideologically pure, but powerless to do anything, if changing the world and how it operates is the objective – the justification for *Realpolitik*.[iv] The second is to shrug one's shoulders and say that that is how the world is and we have neither the power nor the authority to do anything about it. The third is to appeal to "alternative facts," conspiracy theories, and untruths to justify unethical outcomes. The fourth is to do what all racial and religious supremacists do: treat "others" as inferior beings unworthy of equitable treatment.

"Moral disengagement" has a longer-term impact on ethical behavior. It can lead to "motivated forgetting" of both the original unethical behavior and the code that it is violating. It becomes a "slippery slope" leading to ever more unethical behavior. Strong reminders of ethical codes and enforcement are needed to prevent this slippage. Some evidence suggests that nudging works best when people are required to sign up explicitly to honor codes or codes of conduct, as the act of signing reduces the sense of ethical permissiveness in their environments.[10]

Duty-based Versus Consequential Ethics

Approaches to ethics can be considered under two broad headings: duty-based where the ethics of an action are considered (focus on the means) and consequential ethics where the results of the action are evaluated (focus on the ends).[v]

---

iv "Realpolitik, politics based on practical objectives rather than on ideals. The word does not mean 'real' in the English sense but rather connotes 'things' – hence a politics of adaptation to things as they are. Realpolitik thus suggests a pragmatic, no-nonsense view and a disregard for ethical considerations. In diplomacy it is often associated with relentless, though realistic, pursuit of the national interest."

The Editors of Encyclopaedia (2017) "Realpolitik," *Encyclopedia Britannica*, April 28, https://www.britannica.com/topic/realpolitik, accessed June 21, 2021.

v Much of the material in this section is based on Zinkin, J. and Bennett, C. (2021), *The Principles and Practice of Effective Leadership*, Chapter 11: Ethical and Effective Decision-making (Berlin/Boston: Walter de Gruyter), pp. 300–319.

In Table 2.1 we compare and contrast duty-based (deontological[vi]) and consequential ethics.

Table 2.1: Duty-based and consequential ethics compared.

Duty-based ethics	Consequential ethics
Doing the "right thing" has priority over achieving a desirable outcome: 1. Do the right thing because it is the right thing to do. 2. If an act is wrong, it must not be undertaken, regardless of the good it could do.	*Whether an act is right or wrong depends only on the outcome:* 1. The greater number of good consequences an act produces, the better or more right it is. 2. People should choose actions that maximize good consequences.
Advantages 1. One set of rules regarding behavior for everyone regardless of the circumstances. 2. Clarity and simplicity; individuals know what they are expected to do and not do. 3. Easy to apply codes of conduct, rewarding, or punishing behavior, based only on what happened, without allowing for intent, purpose, and outcome. 4. Predictable outcomes and speedy decisions.	*Advantages* 1. Each decision considers current circumstances and its likely consequences. 2. Actions are justified by the overall good they achieve. 3. Behaviour can be flexible provided it results in a good outcome; intent, purpose and outcome are considered. 4. Allows for particular circumstances to be considered.
Drawbacks 1. May fail to recognize differences between cultures and value systems, creating unnecessary misunderstanding between groups. 2. May cause problems in cultures where relationships matter more than rules. 3. Addresses form rather than substance in ambiguous situations. 4. Rigidity and rash decisions based on simple assumptions unsuited to the complexity of prevailing circumstances. 5. Can lead to ethical paralysis in situations where "ethical" actions will lead to "unethical" outcomes.	*Drawbacks* 1. In a complex, interconnected world with tightly coupled systems, often extremely difficult to establish what the consequences are going to be. 2. Can create uncertainty and lack of predictability. 3. Often difficult to decide on suitable time horizons and appropriate cut-off point after which the consequences are no longer relevant to the decision. 4. Takes time; undesirable analysis paralysis can result, when quick decisions are needed, based on incomplete or conflicting data.

Source: Zinkin, J. and Bennett, C. (2021), *The Principles and Practice of Effective Leadership* (Walter de Gruyter GmbH: Berlin/Boston), pp. 300–301.

---

vi "Deontology falls within the domain of moral theories that guide and assess our choices of what we ought to do. Within the domain of moral theories that assess our choices, deontologists – those who subscribe to deontological theories of morality – stand in opposition to *consequentialists*."

"Deontological Ethics," *Stanford Encyclopedia of Philosophy*, October 17, 2016, https://plato.stanford.edu/entries/ethics-deontological/ accessed May 23, 2020.

Different Axioms, Different Choices

Below, we review very briefly the development of ethical theory and the six different ethical approaches that can result – Virtue, Effectiveness, Predictability, Mutuality, Utility, and Self-Image – each with a role to play in making ethical and effective decisions, discussed in Chapter 6.

Virtue

Virtue-based ethics are the earliest form of ethics, associated with Aristotle and Plato in the West, and Confucius and Mencius in the East:

> Virtue ethics is currently one of three major approaches in normative ethics. It may, initially, be identified as the one that emphasizes the virtues, or moral character, in contrast to the approach that emphasizes duties or rules (deontology) or that emphasizes the consequences of actions (consequentialism).[11]

1. Aristotle's Virtue Ethics: Three concepts define a virtuous person according to Aristotle: excellence or virtue (*arête*), practical or moral wisdom (*phronesis*), and happiness or flourishing (*eudaimonia*):

   a) *Excellence or virtue (arête):* a trait of character that defines how people behave. A virtuous person is one who acts and feels as he or she should:

   > An honest person cannot be identified simply as one who, for example, practices honest dealing and does not cheat. *If such actions are done merely because the agent thinks that honesty is the best policy, or because they fear being caught out, rather than through recognising "To do otherwise would be dishonest"* . . . *they are not the actions of an honest person.*[12]   [Emphasis ours]

   b) *Practical or moral wisdom (phronesis):* the caveat that people who only behave with *arête* could be virtuous to a fault – for example being too generous or too honest:

   > Someone's compassion might lead them to act wrongly, to tell a lie they should not have told, for example, in their desire to prevent someone else's hurt feelings. It is also said that courage, in a desperado, enables him to do far more wicked things than he would have been able to do if he were timid. *So it would appear that generosity, honesty, compassion and courage despite being virtues, are sometimes faults.*[13]   [Emphasis ours]

   Practical or moral wisdom considers context. It appreciates that "the right thing to do" in one set of circumstances may not be in another. It reconciles practising virtuous excellence with the need to foresee consequences. It addresses the overlap of virtue ethics and consequential ethics, recognizing the difficulty of adopting virtue ethics without considering potentially adverse consequences of an intended virtuous action.

c) *Happiness* or *flourishing (eudaimonia):* actions are defined by their contribution to the individual's happiness or flourishing/well-being. Plato and the Stoics believed that virtuous behavior on its own was sufficient to yield happiness. Aristotle argued that luck and the possession of material things also mattered:

> According to eudaimonist virtue ethics, the good life is the *eudaimon* life, and the virtues are what enable a human being to be *eudaimon* because the virtues just are those character traits that benefit their possessor in that way, barring bad luck.[14]

2. Confucius's Virtue Ethics: Different cultural backgrounds lead to different behaviors in similar circumstances; for example, Confucius and Mencius prioritize relationships above rules. They recommend morality based on the five cardinal virtues of benevolence, filial piety, trustworthiness, loyalty, and righteousness, with hierarchically defined interactions.[vii,viii]

a) *Benevolence (ren):* requires rulers and leaders to care for others and the examples used in Confucius's *Analects* are of treating people in the street as if they were guests; common people as if they were important attendants at sacrifices; being reticent and not dominating conversations; being respectful of where the person lived; revering fellow workers; and being loyal in dealings with others.[15] In summary, it concerns having empathy and humility and being unselfish out of consideration of the needs of others – in contrast to Aristotle's definition of a "magnanimous man" who looked down on his social inferiors; spoke his mind regardless of the pain he caused; and was not humble,[16] but self-centred.

b) *Filial piety (xiao):* entails loyalty and deference to one's parents, ancestors, and by extension, to one's country, its leaders, and one's superiors.[ix]

---

vii The five cardinal Confucian relationships are ruler to subject, father to son, husband to wife, elder brother to younger brother, and friend to friend.

viii "*Morality among Chinese people is traditionally defined by relationally determined norms grounded in Confucian precepts that are shared by persons bound by particularistic ties rather than by reference to some abstract standards applying to autonomous individuals.* For instance, in seeking to be the ideal moral character, a junzi or cultivated gentleman in Confucian terms, a person must demonstrate a considerable number of desirable qualities, plus the five cardinal virtues of benevolence (ren), filial conduct (xiao), trustworthiness (xin), loyalty (zhong), and righteousness (yi), *in interactions with particular others in a highly defined hierarchical social order.*" [Emphases ours]

Tan, D. and Snell, R. S. (2002), "The third eye: Exploring Guanxi and relational morality in the workplace," *Journal of Business Ethics,* December, 2002, p. 362; *Journal of Business Ethics,* Volume 41, p. 366, https://doi.org/10.1023/A:1021217027814; accessed December 27, 2021.

ix "In general, filial piety requires children to offer love, respect, support, and deference to their parents and other elders in the family, such as grandparents or older siblings. Acts of filial piety

c) *Trustworthiness (xin):* Confucius taught that this is the most valuable quality when advising a ruler. It qualified a gentleman to give advice to a ruler and a ruler or official to rule over others. Trustworthiness was more important than weapons or food for a ruler and more effective than strength or the ability to flatter an individual.[x] If the ruler could not be trusted, the state would fall:

> If the people do not find the ruler trustworthy, the state will not stand.[17]

d) *Loyalty (zhong):* Confucius regarded loyalty as a mutual obligation that required subordinates to speak up.[xi,xii]

e) *Righteousness (yi):* related to public responsibility of officials as stewards who were not corrupt, emphasizing fairness and integrity in dealings. Confucius was clear that corruption was not to be tolerated, insisting it was better to eat coarse rice, drink water, and sleep without a pillow than to achieve wealth and power corruptly.[18] However, Confucius saw righteousness as contextually determined:

---

include obeying one's parent's wishes, taking care of them when they are old, and working hard to provide them with material comforts, such as food, money, or pampering.

... [P]arents give life to their children, and support them throughout their developing years, providing food, education, and material needs. *After receiving all these benefits, children are thus forever in debt to their parents. In order to acknowledge this eternal debt, children must respect and serve their parents all their lives* ... *The tenet of filial piety also applies to all elders – teachers, professional superiors, or anyone who is older in age – and even the state.* The family is the building block of society, and as such the hierarchical system of respect also applies to one's rulers and one's country. *Xiào means that the same devotion and selflessness in serving one's family should also be used when serving one's country.*" [Emphases ours]

Mack, L. (2019), "Filial piety: An important Chinese cultural value," ThoughtCo, August 15, 2019, https://www.thoughtco.com/filial-piety-in-chinese-688386, accessed May 24, 2020.

x "*If your words are sincere and trustworthy and your actions are honorable and respectful, you will get on in the world even among the barbarian tribes.* If your words are insincere and untrustworthy, if you act without honor and respect, how can you possibly get on in the world even in your own village? When you stand, you should always have this principle in front of you. When you drive you should have it carved upon the yoke of your carriage; only then will you truly be able to move ahead." [Emphasis ours]

Confucius, *Analects,* Volume 15, p. 6, cited in Brown, R. (2015), "Analects of Confucius: On loyalty," *BrownBeat,* August 30, 2015, https://brownbeat.net/2015/08/analects-of-confucius-on-loyalty/, accessed May 24, 2020.

xi "Ji Kangzi asked: 'What should I do to make the people respectful, loyal, and eager to follow me?' Confucius said: 'Treat them with dignity, and they will be respectful. Show you are a good son and a loving father, and they will be loyal. Promote the good and teach those who lack ability, and they will be eager to follow you.'"

Confucius, *Analects,* Volume 2, p. 20, quoted in ibid.

xii "Confucius said: 'Can you truly love someone if you are not strict with them? How can you be truly loyal to someone if you refrain from admonishing them?'"

Confucius, *Analects,* Volume 14, p. 7, quoted in ibid.

In regulating one's household, kindness overrules righteousness. Outside of one's house, righteousness cuts off kindness. What one undertakes in serving one's father, one also does in serving one's lord, because one's reverence for both is the same. Treating nobility in a noble way and the honorable in an honorable way, is the height of righteousness.[19]

[Emphasis ours]

The common threads in the Aristotelian and Confucian approaches to virtue ethics are apparent. Differences in resulting behavior result because the Aristotelian approach is essentially individualistic, whereas the Confucian is communitarian. The Aristotelian "magnanimous man" comes across as more self-centred than the Confucian "benevolent man."[20]

Four, disguised, Singaporean case studies (Tables 2.2–2.5), with their predominantly Confucian ethical frame of reference, illustrate dilemmas caused by the conflict between rules-based and relationship-based approaches (discussed in Chapter 1). How you react to the four dilemmas will depend on whether you are a Universalist, putting respect for rules regardless of circumstances first, or you are a Particularist, recognizing that different circumstances created by *Guanxi*[xiii] require different reactions on the grounds that "in this particular case, we should waive the rules."

Universalists argue that in the dilemma caused by trust, (Table 2.2), the fact that the contractors do high-quality work at reasonable prices does not justify breaking the rules, because once buyers are used to overlooking the rules, there is nothing to stop them granting contracts to organizations that bribe and do substandard work. Particularists will counter that given that these contractors do high-quality work at reasonable prices, they should be given a heads up since "there is nothing wrong with doing work with friends who do a good job."

Organizational cultures that profess a commitment to lifetime employment overlook temporary failures to perform because they assess performance over the

---

xiii *"Guanxi loosely translates as personal connections, relationships or social networks. It implies trust and mutual obligations between parties, and it operates on personal, familial, social, business and political levels.* Having good, bad or no guanxi impacts one's influence and ability to get things done . . .

[One is] better served by understanding . . .:

1.   Guanxi is an ingredient to business success, but varies by sector and even geography . . .
2.   Consider guanxi on three levels: personal, corporate and governmental . . .
3.   Understand and manage the downsides of guanxi

The downside of guanxi is that it is often associated with corruption and can lead to dangerous reciprocal obligations and collective blindness." [Emphases ours]

Wenderoth, M. C. (2018), "How a better understanding of guanxi can improve your business in China," *Forbes*, May 16, 2018, https://www.forbes.com/sites/michaelcwenderoth/2018/05/16/how-a-better-understanding-of-guanxi-can-improve-your-business-in-china/?sh=61fb02645d85, accessed June 24, 2021.

Table 2.2: Dilemma caused by trust *(xin)*.

Situation	Approaches	Dilemma
Chung, a new executive in the purchasing department, has just become "one of the boys" and is told over lunch by his seniors that their standard practice is to release confidential tender information to a few favored suppliers. *The contractors do high-quality work, at reasonable prices.* The practice violates the company code of conduct. **What should Chung do?**	**Rules-based:** Chung must report the release of confidential information because it is corrupt behavior, violating company policy and the law. **Relationship-based:** To report the practice would be a violation of the trust placed in him by his seniors, getting them into trouble when no harm has been done to the company.	**Which matters more?** Adhering to a policy that applies to everyone regardless of their seniority and whether they are members of a close group. **Or,** Respecting and protecting long-term relationships and a sense of communal/in-group identity and trust?

Based on: Tan, D. and Snell, R. S. (2002), "The third eye: Exploring *guanxi* and relational morality in the workplace," *Journal of Business Ethics*, Volume 41, p. 366, https://doi.org/10.1023/A:1021217027814, accessed June 18, 2021.

Table 2.3: Dilemma caused by benevolence *(ren)*.

Situation	Approaches	Dilemma
Mark is responsible for turning around the performance of the sales division. He inherits a deputy he likes and who is regarded by Mark's superiors as a "high flier" with potential to become a key leader in the near future. His deputy knows this and has not worked hard to meet Mark's standards, despite having been personally coached and *repeatedly* shown how to improve. **What should Mark do?**	**Rule-based:** Mark should terminate him for a failure to perform, given that he has been repeatedly told that his performance is not up to the desired standard, regardless of whether he has potential and his straitened family conditions. **Relationship-based** Benevolence requires he should do nothing, given that his deputy has already been identified as a "high flier" and he has a wife, two young children, and an ailing mother to support.	**Which matters more?** Adhering to a policy that applies to everyone regardless of their seniority to ensure that career development is based on fair performance evaluation that applies in the same way for all, based on recent performance. **Or,** Considering past performance (basis for being identified as a "high flier"), overlooking failure to perform because of his straitened family circumstances?

Based on: Tan, D. and Snell, R. S. (2002), "The third eye: Exploring *guanxi* and relational morality in the workplace," *Journal of Business Ethics*, Volume 41, p. 366, https://doi.org/10.1023/A:1021217027814, accessed June 18, 2021.

Table 2.4: Dilemma caused by filial conduct (*xiao*).

Situation	Approaches	Dilemma
Meng is instructed by his boss to "ensure the quarterly business report looks good when presented to the board of directors." Meng had always been on good terms with his boss. He realized his forthcoming bonus depends on his boss's evaluation of his performance. Including the latest research-based statistics in the report would definitely cast doubt on the viability and continuity of the joint venture project and make his boss look bad. His performance review and bonus assessment are due. **What should Meng do?**	**Rule-based:** Meng includes the statistics to give the board an accurate picture of the project's viability, even if it may make his boss look bad. **Relationship-based:** Filial conduct requires Meng to make his boss look good, and so he omits the statistics that cast doubt on the project's viability and make his boss look bad.	**Which matters more** Providing up-to-date and accurate information to the board so that they can make informed decisions. **Or,** Delaying bad news to make his boss look good and protect his bonus, in the hope that either the report will prove to be wrong, or that submitting it at the following board review will not have a material impact on decision-making and so the board will not make a mistake as a result of the delay?

Based on: Tan, D. and Snell, R. S. (2002), "The third eye: Exploring *guanxi* and relational morality in the workplace," *Journal of Business Ethics*, Volume 41, p. 366, https://doi.org/10.1023/A:1021217027814, accessed June 18, 2021.

lifetime of an employee, whereas organizations whose personnel culture is "you are only as good as your last progress review" find it easy to terminate an employee.

Deceptive behavior starts small and escalates over time until it consumes the integrity of the senior management, as in the case of Enron, which suggests that the motivation for such behavior exists equally in Aristotelian and Confucian cultures.

Effectiveness

Although not the first,[xiv] the most famous proponent of ethics focusing on effectiveness of rulers was Machiavelli, who analyzed what made rulers effective. Effectiveness is consciously amoral, concerned with what works in different contexts.

---

xiv The *Sulwan Al-Muta' Fi 'Udwan Al-Atba* (Consolation for the Ruler During the Hostility of Subjects) by the Sicilian Arab Muhammad ibn Zafar al-Siqilli focuses on the need to be effective and was written in the twelfth century.

Table 2.5: Loyalty (*zhong*).

Situation	Approaches	Dilemma
Pang's immediate boss – his mentor – received a summons from the traffic police for beating the lights at a busy junction while driving a company-registered car. He was charged with not stopping the car when the lights changed from amber to red. His boss was prepared to pay the fine but could not bear the penalty of six demerit points because that would result in his losing his driving license that he needed for work. His boss asks Pang to confess to being the driver, as he has a clean license. **What should Pang do?**	**Rule-based:** Pang should not agree because he was not the driver and his boss should in any case bear the consequences of breaking the law; otherwise he may be encouraged to do the same again. **Relationship-based:** Pang should agree to confessing to something he has not done out of loyalty to his boss, friend, and mentor as required by loyalty because the cost to his boss is severe and that since his boss is paying the fine and he can afford the six demerits, the cost to him is negligible.	**What matters most** To ensure that the law applies to all regardless in order to maximize safe driving **Or,** To live by the precepts of loyalty regardless of what the law says?

Based on: Tan, D. and Snell, R. S. (2002), "The third eye: Exploring *guanxi* and relational morality in the workplace," *Journal of Business Ethics*, Volume 41, p. 366, https://doi.org/10.1023/A:1021217027814, accessed June 18, 2021.

The Prince makes it clear that a ruler's goals and objectives are determined by historical antecedents and current political contexts. Constraints to action should be recognized and the "art of the possible" practiced.

A ruler establishing his rule will have to behave differently from one who is secure. Difficulties prospective rulers face when taking over a state depend on whether it was a well-established republic where its people value their freedom; or a principality where people are used to being ruled by a monarch. In either case, Machiavelli made it clear that *what matters first is to get and hold on to the levers of power by whatever means* and to exercise that power by using situational leadership skills. Amoral behavior is justified for "reasons of state."

Mutuality

The concept of mutuality (or reciprocity) is to be found in all major ethical systems as the "Golden Rule":

> "Do unto others as you would have them do unto you" is the idea (also called the *law of reciprocity*) that may be the most universally applauded moral principle on Earth – the Golden

Rule. Something like it appears in every major religion and ethical philosophy. The wording above is from the King James *Bible*, Matthew 7:12, however Hindu, Jewish, Buddhist, Confucian, and Zoroastrian versions of it appeared 3,000-500 years earlier . . .

. . . Similarly, around 500 BCE, Confucius wrote "What you do not want done to yourself, do not do to others." In contrast to the statement in Leviticus, which is found in the middle of a long list of rules, the Confucian rule has always been emphasized, as a foundation of Confucian society.[21]

As far as ethics for decision-making is concerned, we are interested in the social contract ethics expressed in the "Golden Rule," which Rousseau re-interpreted as:

The essential point remains the same: that only where all are equally affected by the policy adopted can an equitable solution be expected:

"*The undertakings which bind us to the social body are obligatory only because they are mutual; and their nature is such that in fulfilling them we cannot work for others without working for ourselves . . .* this admirable agreement between interest and justice gives to the common deliberations an equitable character which at once vanishes when any particular question is discussed, in the absence of a common interest to unite and identify the ruling of the judge with that of the party".

Provided this condition is met, nobody will deliberately vote for a burdensome law because it will be burdensome to him too: this is why no specific limitations on the "general will" are needed . . . Among the various policies which would affect everyone in the same way, each person has to decide which would benefit himself the most – and, since everyone else is similarly circumstanced, he is automatically deciding at the same time which would benefit everyone else the most.[22]   [Emphases ours]

The concept of mutuality makes foreseeable where there will be resistance to the imposition of rules. People are more likely to agree to decisions that limit their freedoms if they are perceived to be equal in application and beneficial to the group as a whole. This has become apparent in the UK[23] and other places during the COVID pandemic where rules strictly applied to the public were flouted by ministers and their advisers, causing resentment and a breakdown of trust.

Predictability

Decision-makers should provide clarity and predictability for those affected by their decisions. A mix of laws, regulations, rules, and operating procedures are needed to let people know what they can and cannot do; how they are expected to act; the penalties they face for breaking laws and rules; and guidance on the best ways to do what is asked of them.

The German philosopher Immanuel Kant provided a comprehensive framework for setting rules, recognizing the need for predictability that satisfied the demands of fairness. He divided rules into two types: *maxims* and *imperatives*. He argued that since humans are rational, actions always aim at some sort of end or goal, captured by a *maxim* – a subjective rule or policy of action explaining what a person is doing and why.[24]

Kant's *hypothetical imperatives* describe how people *ought* to behave and are the basis of standard operating procedures. *They are customized to suit the context and circumstances.*

Kant also provided a predictable set of rules called *categorical imperatives*. These are formal rules describing how people *should behave without making any reference to their actions*. Categorical imperatives are those that all should adopt, regardless of the circumstances involved. Categorical imperatives apply to people no matter what their goals and desires may be, unlike hypothetical imperatives that apply to people only if they have desires that they want to satisfy, defining how to satisfy those specific desires. *The categorical imperative to help others in need does not apply to people only if they desire to help others in need, and the duty not to steal is not suspended if they have some desire that they could satisfy by stealing.*

Utility

Building on Hume's ideas[25] Utilitarianism focuses on actual, direct, and indirect consequences of decisions by attempting to measure the pleasure and pain created. It views the most important goal for humanity as maximizing pleasure and minimizing pain. However, that does not mean it is enough for a majority to want something that harms the minority; if it did, it would justify persecution of minorities. The pain or loss of the minority may be much greater than the pleasure or gain of the majority and so outweigh it:

> These claims are often summarized in the slogan that an act is right if and only if it causes "the greatest happiness for the greatest number." This slogan is misleading, however. An act can increase happiness for most (the greatest number of) people but still fail to maximize the net good in the world if the smaller number of people whose happiness is not increased lose much more than the greater number gains. *The principle of utility would not allow that kind of sacrifice of the smaller number to the greater number unless the net good overall is increased more than any alternative.*[26]
>
> [Emphasis ours]

Self-image

Personalistic ethics (or self-image) ethics are subjective. They reflect the inner values and purpose of each individual. They matter a great deal when people agree to do something that conflicts with their inner values and purpose. Violating their values and purpose will discredit them in their own eyes and those of their colleagues and friends. Equally, harmony with inner values and purpose will reinforce self-image, reputation, and authenticity, making it easier to implement a similar decision in the future. The fact that people's values and purposes change depending on how they categorize themselves socially[27] in any given situation makes achieving consistent alignment of individuals' purposes and values with the purpose and values of organizations to which they belong difficult.

Multiple Ethical Personas

People do not have a single, integrated set of values, and/or purpose. We do know that despite the fact that we behave and dress in different ways for different occasions, there remains an identifiable common thread that makes us recognizably who we are and differentiates us as individuals from one another. Our behavior reflects our biological, experiential, and ethical underpinnings: "who we are and what we believe in." It changes over a lifetime as "nurture" impacts "nature," always in an interaction with our life experiences.

The same applies to our ethics. They are affected by the different circumstances, conditions, and contexts in which we find ourselves, the choices we made in the past, and their conditioning impact on the acceptability (to us and others) of our choices in the present and future. This explains why it is not easy to align employees' personal values and purpose with the purpose and values of their employers.

Often discussions of the importance of achieving alignment between an organization's purpose and values and those of the individuals working for it, assume that individuals within an organization will all respond to its purpose and values in the same way every time. This is an oversimplification because when we "self-categorize" the group(s) we use to self-categorize depend on context.

For example, when siblings only consider themselves within the nuclear family, they are likely to focus on their points of disagreement and difference that define who they are and how they are unique. Yet when they are criticized as members of their nuclear family by members of their extended family, they will rally round a common identity and purpose and defend themselves as members of their nuclear family ingroup with an agreed monolithic purpose and values that differentiates them from their extended family outgroup. When their extended family ingroup is attacked by other extended family outgroups within their clan or tribe, they will forget their differences and rally round their more broadly redefined common identity, purpose, and values. When the clan or tribe is attacked as an ingroup by a different clan or tribe as an outgroup, the same process of coalescing around a more broadly redefined commonality of purpose and values takes place to defend the broader ingroup against the broader outgroup. This process of redefinition applies when the clans and tribes that make up a linguistic or ethnic group, nation, religion, or empire are attacked by clans and tribes that are members of a different linguistic or ethnic group, nation, religion, or empire.

In a similar way, people within organizations choose which of their many in-groups to which they belong at the moment of tension between what they are being asked to do by the organization and how they feel about it. They categorize themselves based on complex interactions between their education, income, life stage, occupation, social/economic class, affiliation, ethnicity, gender and religious beliefs, that reflect the immediate, salient tensions created by the monolithic purpose and values expressed in their organization's mission, vision, and values statements that are laid down and enforced in their codes of conduct. The way in which employees categorize themselves in a context affects the decision they make.

The human condition requires people to categorize objects, experiences, and one another (stereotyping) in order to make sense of the world using System 1 thinking (discussed in Chapter 3: Barriers to Ethical Behavior). There are two important differences in the process of social categorization that makes for greater uncertainty and ambiguity of outcome:

> The first key difference is that social categories, unlike object categories, are made up of people who *can choose to unite or divide*. Social categorization can help us not only to understand why other people are similar to each other and different from us but also to predict when they will be similar and different to us. The second key difference is that *when we categorize ourselves, we learn who we can cooperate with, who shares our goals and interests, and who we might cooperate with*. It is hard to imagine effective human functioning without the abilities that social categorization grants us.[28]   [Emphases ours]

This ability to choose to unite or divide is critical in enforcing organizational codes of conduct. All regulation requires somebody to report malpractice. Yet, in all cultures children are brought up not to tell tales on others. In every police film and TV show snitching is despised. We are culturally predisposed to make it difficult to enforce laws. Appeals to reporting misbehavior are always couched in terms of the greater good, the big picture, the values of the organization – in other words appealing to the values of a collective that is usually larger than the ingroup that people associate with directly every day as members of a team, department, or division – and we should not be surprised at conflicts between individuals' purpose and values and those of organizations:

> For example, in a context where it is fitting to do so (e.g., at work), a person, Jane, may self-categorize as a tax accountant, and thereby see herself as relatively similar to other tax accountants, but also as different from auditors who review the work of accountants (e.g., in terms of her interests and commitments). In a different context, it may be more fitting for her to self-categorize as an accountant (a more abstract, more inclusive self-categorization that includes auditors) . . . in her daily work, Jane may define herself as a tax accountant committed to achieving the best outcome for her clients, but at an accountancy conference (attended by accountants and auditors alike) she may define herself as a member of her profession, dedicated to upholding professional values and standards. *Dynamics of this form clearly have the capacity to create situations in which different groups' values and goals come into conflict.*[29]   [Emphasis ours]

Whistleblowing is justified by appealing to our desire to unite and protect the organization, or industry, and public from free-riding "bad apples," failing to recognize
that it is also asking people to divide themselves from their day-to-day ingroups
with whom they may identify more strongly than to the ever more distant purpose
and values of the organization, industry, and nation with whom they may not be
able to identify:[30]

> Group members are most likely to conform and/or remain silent in the face of problematic in-
> group behavior when there is no (or low) motivation to act, such as when they identify weakly
> with the superordinate group whose values have been violated.[31]

> It appears that being strongly identified with a social identity whose values have been violated
> by an offending ingroup's wrongdoing generally increases the likelihood of whistleblowing,
> whereas being strongly identified with the wrongdoer(s) generally reduces the likelihood of
> whistleblowing.[32]

Reward and Punishment

Extrinsic and intrinsic motivators affect calculations individuals make regarding
risks and rewards implied by different ethical choices.

It is natural for most of the attention to be directed at extrinsic carrot and stick
motivators because that has been how legislation, regulation, and social sanctions
are applied, particularly in systems that use forms of reward and punishment that
are extrinsic – bonus, extra time off, and better living and working conditions as
rewards; and fines, physical pain (including death), and the denial of physical freedom in the form of custodial sentences as punishments, reinforced by schemes of
"naming" and "shaming" malefactors or people who have failed to meet the targets
set. "Social death," the expulsion of individuals who fail to behave according to the
expectations of their relevant ingroup, is one of the most serious forms of extrinsic
punishment,[33] and it explains why bona fide whistleblowing is a) rare, and b) never
extrinsically rewarding, though it may be very rewarding intrinsically.

Often superiors reward results instead of ethical decisions because they focus on
outcomes, regardless of the assumptions and decision-making processes that went into
making the decision; and assume that if the outcome was financially beneficial, then
the decision-making process must have also been good and probably was ethical.[34]
The converse also applies; often subordinates are punished because a "good" decision
based on what was known at the time turns out to have a bad result.

The best warning signal that an organization is only concerned with outcomes, regardless of how they were achieved, is management demonstrating that
its priority is financial performance. Most companies do exactly that, without realizing it, that by rewarding people on the basis of results only, they run the risk of
long-run disaster because they encourage unethical behavior, since that is what

they actually reward – illustrated by the following examples and the difference in the judgments made of the individual behavior in each case, once the outcomes were removed:

> Both stories begin: "A pharmaceutical researcher defines a clear protocol for determining whether or not to include clinical patients as data points in a study. He is running short of time to collect sufficient data points for his study within an important budgetary cycle in his firm."
>
> Story A continues: "As the deadline approaches, *he notices that four subjects were withdrawn from the analysis due to technicalities. He believes that the data in fact are appropriate to use, and when he adds those data points, the results move from not quite statistically significant to significant. He adds these data points, and soon the drug goes to market.* This drug is later withdrawn from the market after it kills six patients and injures hundreds of others."
>
> Story B continues: "He believes that the product is safe and effective. As the deadline approaches, he notices that *if he had four more data points for how subjects are likely to behave, the analysis would be significant. He makes up these data points, and soon the drug goes to market.* This drug is a profitable and effective drug, and years later shows no significant side effects."
>
> After participants read one or the other story, we asked them, "How unethical do you view the researcher to be?" *Those who read story A were much more critical of the researcher than were those who read story B, and felt that he should be punished more harshly. Yet as we see it, the researcher's behavior was more unethical in story B than in story A. And that is how other study participants saw it when we removed the last sentence – the outcome – from each story.*[35]
>
> [Emphases ours]

The reason for the difference in evaluations before and after the outcomes were removed is that the good outcome blinded the participants to the fact that researcher B had *cheated and invented data* to make the case, whereas researcher A had merely *added back data* that had been excluded on a technicality, but not on their veracity.[xv] Outcomes need to be assessed both in terms of what they achieve, but also on how they were achieved in terms of the intentions and considerations of protagonists, and whether they were intent on "gaming the system." Legal and regulatory systems are likely to punish bad outcomes more severely than bad intentions.

> You will know them by their fruits. Do men gather grapes from thornbushes or figs from thistles? Even so, every good tree bears good fruit, but a bad tree bears bad fruit. A good tree cannot bear bad fruit, nor *can* a bad tree bear good fruit. Every tree that does not bear good fruit is cut down and thrown into the fire. Therefore by their fruits you will know them.[36]

Even though this quotation comes from the New Testament, it is an oversimplification in that, sometimes, good trees bear bad fruit as a result of climate change or pest-borne illness and often bad trees bear some good fruit. Moreover, if all bad

---

xv There are similar issues with Meng's dilemma earlier in the chapter in Table 2.4: "Dilemma caused by Filial Conduct (*xiao*)" where he omits to mention the results of a report to make his boss look good and protect his own bonus.

trees are cut down and thrown into the fire, there is no chance for redemption; and punishment can become compensation for victims at best and vengeful retribution, justified in the name of deterrence, at worst.[37] Moreover, intentions are a matter of conjecture, given that we have no reliable ways of "making windows into men's souls," as Queen Elizabeth the First put it, and so there are no alternatives to using outcomes as criteria other than to look for extrinsic mitigating circumstances.

Evaluating reward and punishment for behavior that is framed in the amoral terms of cost–benefit analysis can lead to tragic mistakes and serious reputational damage for organizations that set key performance indicators (KPIs) and reward/recognition systems in this way, as evidenced by the famous Ford Pinto case.

Ford Pinto Case

The Pinto was an affordable compact car sold in the United States in the 1970s. However, because of a deliberate design choice, if the car was hit from behind it could leak fuel and burst into flames. More than 500 people died in the resulting fires before the car was recalled eight years after its launch. After-the-fact investigation revealed that Ford's response to the competitive pressure from Volkswagen and other compact car makers had led the company to rush the introduction of the car, disregarding the discovery by engineers during pre-production tests that there was a potential danger of ruptured fuel tanks in these particular conditions. When this became public knowledge, there was outrage at Ford's apparent callousness, greed, lobbying, and lying over the years to protect sales.[38]

Was Ford in the 1970s populated by unethical, callous people who did not care about safety and their customers' lives? Probably not. Instead, the "ethical fading" that occurred that excludes ethical considerations, making it more likely that unethical behavior will ensue, was the result of framing the decision as a purely business decision with a formal cost–benefit analysis[39] that added up the costs of a redesign, delayed launch, potential lawsuits, the probability of deaths and attributed costs to settling any lawsuits. The rational, amoral, and unempathetic conclusion was that it would cost less for Ford to launch the Pinto unchanged.[40]

When people make decisions based on hard numbers, forgetting that these numbers represent people, lives, and physical pain, such ethical blindness is often the result. Add to that the fear of being the bearer of bad news to a hard-charging CEO and the likelihood of "being shot as the messenger," and the Pinto scandal is almost banal rather than the result of deliberate evil.

Nobody was prepared to "speak truth to power" and recommend redesigning the car because they feared being fired for delaying the launch of Lee Iacocca's baby:

But Iacocca's speed-up meant Pinto tooling went on at the same time as product development. So when crash tests revealed a serious defect in the gas tank, it was too late. The tooling was well under way.

When it was discovered the gas tank was unsafe, did anyone go to Iacocca and tell him? "Hell no," replied an engineer who worked on the Pinto, a high company official for many years, who, unlike several others at Ford, maintains a necessarily clandestine concern for safety. That person would have been fired. Safety wasn't a popular subject around Ford in those days. With Lee it was taboo. Whenever a problem was raised that meant a delay on the Pinto, Lee would chomp on his cigar, look out the window and say, "Read the product objectives and get back to work."[41]

In the years since the Pinto case, people have come to understand more about behavioral ethics, and we know that the extrinsic motivators and patterns of thinking that applied in the Pinto case are not unique to Ford. What we know now is

few [people] grasp how their own cognitive biases and the incentive systems they create can conspire to negatively skew behavior and obscure it from view.[42]

Boeing 737 MAX Case

Similar behavior appears to have been the cause of Boeing's 737 MAX disasters, as evidenced in the case brought against the Boeing board in the Court of Chancery in the state of Delaware on February 21, 2021.

Excerpts from the submission show that Boeing abandoned its safety engineering culture to become a company that was more interested in financial engineering:[43] In the mid-1990s, after its acquisition of McDonnell Douglas, Boeing switched from being a company focused on aircraft safety to one on cost-cutting. As a result, the board had no tools to oversee safety and there were no mechanisms to bring safety issues to the attention of the board. The board failed to evaluate safety until 2019, after the October crash of Lion Air in 2018 and the Ethiopian airlines crash in 2019.[44]

Shortly after the Lion Air Crash in 2018, the Board learned that new software on the 737 MAX, the Maneuvering Characteristics Augmentation System ("MCAS"), was a potential cause of the crash, that the FAA [Federal Aviation Administration] had concluded that MCAS posed an unacceptably high risk of catastrophic failure, and that the FAA had issued an emergency directive notifying pilots about the potential danger. The Board did not order an immediate investigation into the safety of the 737 MAX, how Boeing obtained FAA certification of MCAS, or why MCAS was not mentioned in the flight manual for the 737 MAX. *Instead, the Board supported the public relations campaign of then-Chief Executive Officer and Chairman Dennis A. Muilenburg to attack accurate media coverage respecting the 737 MAX.*

The Board compounded its lack of oversight by publicly lying about it. In May 2019, then-Lead Director, now-CEO David Calhoun led a public relations defense of Muilenburg and the Board in order to "[p]osition the Boeing Board of Directors as an independent body that has exercised appropriate oversight." . . . By paying Muilenburg, the Board sidestepped questions about the Board's culpability in supporting him and not exercising safety oversight. Calhoun failed upward. The Board named him the new CEO.

The misconduct – no Board-level safety reporting; ignoring red flags including the first 737 MAX crash; defrauding the FAA; frustrating the DOJ [Department of Justice] investigation; delaying disclosure to the FAA; no internal investigation or assessment of airplane safety; phony public relations campaigns; paying Muilenburg $38 million to which he was not entitled; promoting Calhoun despite all of the above – reflects the arrogance of Boeing's long-time fiduciaries. In January 2021, the president of. . . Emirates, gave an interview in which he stated that Boeing needs to make "fundamental structural changes" because *"there is a top-down culpability and accountability"* and *"[c]learly there were process and practices, attitudes – DNA if you like – that need[] to be resolved at the top down."* [Emphases ours][45]

Such antisocial and immoral behavior by legitimate businesses is the result of focusing on shareholder value at the expense of people's health and safety (physical and mental), either directly by selling them harmful products or indirectly through pollution created by operations.

Summary

Ethical decision-making depends on the circumstances and context within which the decisions are made. Its difficulties are caused by the fact that what *"ought to be"* is not *"what is"*; reconciling "duty-based" with "consequential ethics" can prove impossible; different religious and cultural axioms lead to different ethical conclusions; individuals have multiple ethical personas and reference groups, whose salience depends on circumstances and context; and there is an impact on decisions of rewards and punishments. If the resulting inconsistencies are too great or frequent, they result in "moral damage" and a loss of self-esteem.

In the world *as it is,* as opposed to the world *as it ought to be,* people routinely engage in unethical acts. Reflecting power of ethical ideas of how the world *ought* to be, people try to refrain from behaving in ways that violate their own moral standards. When faced with conflict between "ought" and "is" people find ways to reduce the resulting cognitive dissonance: either by changing their behavior to bring it back into closer alignment with their beliefs, or by changing their beliefs through "moral disengagement."

"Moral disengagement" has a longer-term impact on ethical behavior. It can lead to "motivated forgetting" of both the original unethical behavior and the code that it is violating. It becomes a "slippery slope" leading to ever more unethical behavior.

There are two types of ethics: duty based and consequential ethics. Duty-based ethics are where the ethics of an action are considered. Duty-based ethics focus on doing the right thing regardless of the consequences because it is the right thing to do; whereas consequential ethics focus on the results of actions to determine after the event whether they were good. They may sometimes conflict.

Ethics include six different schools of thinking – Virtue, Effectiveness, Predictability, Mutuality, Utility, and Self-Image ethics – each with a role to play in making ethical and effective decisions.

Virtue ethics are the earliest form of ethics, associated with Aristotle and Plato in the West, and Confucius and Mencius in the East. The Aristotelian approach has three components: excellence or virtue (*arête*), practical or moral wisdom (*phronesis*), and happiness or flourishing (*eudaimonia*). The Confucian approach comprises five components: benevolence (*ren*), filial piety (*xiao*), trustworthiness (*xin*), loyalty (*zhong*), and righteousness (*yi*).

Effectiveness ethics propose that the "ends justify the means." Machiavelli made it clear in *The Prince* that what matters first is to get and hold on to the levers of power by whatever means and to exercise that power by using situational leadership skills. Amoral behavior is justified for "reasons of state."

Mutuality (reciprocity) ethics exist in every major ethical system. Expressed as the "Golden Rule," it can be interpreted to mean social contract ethics where people are more likely to agree to decisions that limit their freedoms if they are perceived to be equal in application and beneficial to the group as a whole.

Predictability ethics provide clarity and predictability for people affected by their decisions through a mix of laws, regulations, rules, and operating procedures and are needed to let people know what they can and cannot do; how they are expected to act; the penalties they face for breaking laws and rules; and guidance on the best ways to do what is asked of them.

Utility ethics focus on actual, direct, and indirect consequences of decisions by attempting to measure the pleasure and pain created (the hedonistic calculus). It views the most important goal for humanity as maximizing pleasure and minimizing pain.

Self-Image (personalistic) ethics are subjective. They reflect the inner values and purpose of each individual. Personalistic ethics are affected by the fact that people do not have a single, integrated set of values and/or purpose. They are affected by the different circumstances, conditions, and contexts in which they find themselves, the choices they made in the past, and their conditioning impact on future choices.

Assuming individuals within an organization will all respond to its purpose and values in the same way every time is an oversimplification because "self-categorizing" reflects complex interactions between education, income, life stage, occupation, social/economic class, affiliation, ethnicity, gender, and religious beliefs. These interactions determine individuals' sense of unity and division. The choice to unite or divide is critical in enforcing organizational codes of conduct, as all regulation requires people to report malpractice.

Appeals to reporting misbehavior are couched in terms of the greater good, the big picture, the values of a collective that is usually larger than the ingroup that people associate with directly every day as members of a team, department, or division –

and this can create conflicts between individuals' purpose and values and those of organizations. Whistleblowing is justified by the need to protect the collective/community from "bad apples." It fails, however, to recognize that it asks people to divide themselves from ingroups with whom they may identify more strongly, which is why it is so difficult to do in practice.

The nature of rewards and punishment make a difference because extrinsic and intrinsic motivators affect calculations that individuals make regarding risks and rewards in different ways. Legislation, regulation, and social sanctions use extrinsic rewards and punishment. Within organizations, superiors often reward results instead of ethical decisions because they focus on outcomes, assuming that if the outcome was financially beneficial, then the decision-making process must have also been good and probably was ethical. The converse also applies; often subordinates are punished because a "good" decision based on what was known at the time turns out to have a bad financial result.

The best warning signal that an organization is only concerned with outcomes is management demonstrating that its priority is financial performance. Most companies do exactly that – and by rewarding people on the basis of results only, they run the risk of long-run disaster because they encourage unethical behavior. Legal and regulatory systems reinforce this as they are likely to punish bad outcomes more severely than bad intentions.

The Ford Pinto and the recent Boeing 737 MAX scandals demonstrate that behavior framed in the amoral terms of cost–benefit analysis can lead to tragic mistakes and serious reputational damage for organizations that set KPIs and reward/recognition systems designed to maximize shareholder value.

References

1 Ibn Zafar (1159), "Sulwan Al-Muta' Fi 'Udwan Al-Atba,'" cited in Kechichian, J. A. and Dekmejian, R. H. (2003), *The Just Prince: A Manual of Leadership* (Singapore and Kuala Lumpur: Horizon Books), pp. 327–328.

2 Machiavelli, N. (1999 [1513]), *The Prince* (Harmondsworth: Penguin Books), Chapter VI, p. 18, Chapter VIII, pp. 30–31, Chapter XVIII, pp. 56, 57.

3 Hume, D. (1739), *Treatise of Human Nature* and (1751) *Enquiry concerning the Principles of Morals*, cited in Cohon, R. (2018), Edward N. Zalta, E. N. (ed.), "Hume's Moral Philosophy," *The Stanford Encyclopedia of Philosophy*, Fall 2018 Edition, https://plato.stanford.edu/archives/fall2018/entries/hume-moral/, accessed June 17, 2021.

4 Ibid., section 6.

5 Hume (1739, 1751), quoted in ibid., section 9.

6 Ibid.

7 Lewis, C. S. (1941), "The reality of the moral law" (BBC Talk 2, *Mere Christianity*, Chapter 2) broadcast on August 13, 1941, YouTube, https://www.youtube.com/watch?v=LqsAzlFS91A&list=PL9boiLqIabFhrqabptq3ThGdwNanr65xU, accessed December 26, 2020.

8 Shu, L. L., Gino, F., and Bazerman, M. (2010), "Dishonest deed, clear conscience: When cheating leads to moral disengagement and motivated forgetting," *Personality and Social Psychology Bulletin,* Volume 37, Issue 3, October 2010, p. 331, October, DOI: 10.1177/0146167211398138, http://pspb.sage pub.com, accessed June 21, 2021.

9 Shu, Gino, and Bazerman, (2010).

10 Ibid, p. 333.

11 Hursthouse, R. and Pettigrove, G. (2018), "Virtue ethics," *Stanford Encyclopedia of Philosophy* (Winter 2018), https://plato.stanford.edu/archives/win2018/entries/ethics-virtue/, accessed May 24, 2020.

12 Hursthouse and Pettigrove (2018).

13 Ibid.

14 Ibid.

15 Csikszentmihalyi, M. (2020), "Confucius," *The Stanford Encyclopedia of Philosophy* (summer 2020 edition), https://plato.stanford.edu/archives/sum2020/entries/confucius/, accessed May 24, 2020.

16 Aristotle, quoted by Russell, B. (1947), *The History of Western Philosophy* (London: George Allen & Unwin), p. 198.

17 Confucius, *Analects,* Volume 12, p. 7, cited in Csikszentmihalyi, (2020).

18 Csikszentmihalyi, (2020).

19 Confucius, *The Rites of Record,* cited in Brown, "Analects of Confucius."

20 Nesbitt, R. E. (2003), *The Geography of Thought* (New York: Free Press).

21 "Golden Rule," *Philosophy Terms,* https://philosophyterms.com/golden-rule/, accessed May 28, 2020.

22 Rousseau, J-J. (1762), *Contrat Social,* cited in Barry, B. (1964), "The public interest" from the Proceedings of the Aristotelian Society, Supp. Volume 38 (1964), pp. 1–18, in Quinn, A., ed. (1967), *Political Philosophy* (Oxford: Oxford Readings in Political Philosophy), pp. 121–122.

23 Fancourt, D., Steptoe, A., and Wright, L. (2020), "The Cummings effect: Politics, trust, and behaviours during the COVID-19 pandemic," *The Lancet,* August 6, 2020, https://www.thelancet.com/journals/lancet/article/PIIS0140-6736(20)31690-1/fulltext, accessed January 1, 2021.

24 Rohlf, M. (2020), "Immanuel Kant," *The Stanford Encyclopedia of Philosophy* (spring 2020 edition), https://plato.stanford.edu/archives/spr2020/entries/kant/, accessed May 26, 2020.

25 Hume, *Treatise of Human Nature* and *Enquiry concerning the Principles of Morals,* section 9.

26 Sinnott-Armstrong, W. (2019), "Consequentialism," *The Stanford Encyclopedia of Philosophy* (summer 2019 edition), https://plato.stanford.edu/archives/sum2019/entries/consequentialism/, accessed May 28, 2020.

27 McGarty, C. (2018), "Social categorization: You know it makes sense," *Psychology,* March 28, 2018, https://oxfordre.com/psychology/view/10.1093/acrefore/9780190236557.001.0001/acrefore-9780190236557-e-308, accessed June 25, 2021.

28 McGarty, (2018).

29 Anvari, F., Wenzel, M., Woodyatt, L., and Haslam, S. A. (2019), "The social psychology of whistleblowing: An integrated model," *Organizational Psychology Review,* Volume 9, Issue 1, 2019, p. 46, https://journals.sagepub.com/doi/full/10.1177/2041386619849085, accessed June 25, 2021.

30 Ibid., p. 45.

31 Ibid., p. 49.

32 Ibid., p. 54.

33 Ibid., p. 51.

34 Bazerman, M. H. and Tenbrunsel, A. E. (2011), "Ethical breakdowns," *Harvard Business Review,* April, 2011, https://hbr.org/2011/04/ethical-breakdowns, accessed June 26, 2021.

35 Ibid.

36 Matthew: Chapter 7, Verses 16–20, New King James Version.

37 Tadros, V. (2017), "Punishment and the appropriate response to wrongdoing," *Criminal Law and Philosophy*, Volume 11, 2017, pp. 229–248, https://philpapers.org/rec/TADPAT, accessed June 27, 2021.

38 Dowie, M. (1977), "Pinto madness," *Mother Jones*, September/October issue, https://www.motherjones.com/politics/1977/09/pinto-madness/, accessed June 27, 2021.

39 Bazerman and Tenbrunsel (2011).

40 Dowie (1977).

41 Ibid.

42 Bazerman and Tenbrunsel (2011).

43 IN RE THE BOEING COMPANY: DERIVATIVE LITIGATION: Consol. C.A. No. 2019–0907-MTZ. In the Court of Chancery of the State of Delaware, EFiled: Feb 05 2021 03:53PM EST, Transaction ID 66314557.

44 Ibid.

45 Ibid.

Chapter 3
Barriers to Ethical Behavior

In *Criminality and Business Strategy: Similarities and Differences* we described the continuum of crime, the range of harms created, and the range of sanctions deployed in response, showing that strategic issues both organized crime and legitimate businesses deal with are so similar that differences in their responses to their external and internal environments are ones of degree rather than kind. The barriers to ethical behavior reinforce this convergence and also form a continuum.

Evolution

The human brain has evolved to minimize cognitive load:

> Cognitive load that learners experience can be intrinsic, extraneous or germane. . .The level of intrinsic load for a particular task is assumed to be determined by the inherent difficulty of a certain topic and the level of element interactivity of the learning material in relation a student's prior knowledge. *The more elements that interact, the more intrinsic processing is required for coordinating and integrating the material and the higher the working memory load . . .*[1]   [Emphasis ours]

Cognitive processes work harder to make sense of the environment if instructions or messaging are unclear or confused and can be distracted by outside influences irrelevant to do the task at hand.[2] Consequently, cognitive processes have split into two "systems," one fast and the other slower.

System 1 and System 2

People like to believe they make decisions objectively. This postulated approach is largely illusory. Heuristics (mental shortcuts), biases (prejudices based on experiences), and the salience (relevance) of particular situations are the boundaries of reality within which individuals and groups make decisions. Taking the time to evaluate threats and decide whether to "fight or flee" could make the difference between life and death. The human brain developed fast, economical, unconscious, instinctive processes (System 1) to respond immediately to a threat.[3] The unconscious mind (System 1) works independently of the conscious mind (System 2) and is in "always on" mode. The conscious mind only operates when it is asked to, as it were:

> Systems 1 and 2 are both active whenever we are awake. System 1 runs automatically and System 2 is normally in a comfortable low-effort mode, in which only a fraction of its capacity is engaged. System 1 continuously generates suggestions for System 2: impressions, intuitions, intentions, and feelings. *If endorsed by System 2, impressions and intuitions turn into beliefs,*

https://doi.org/10.1515/9783110780871-003

and impulses turn into voluntary actions. When all goes smoothly, which is most of the time, System 2 adopts the suggestions of System 1 with little or no modification.[4]   [Emphasis ours]

System 2's processing of facts, using logic and making connections between different data, is hard work,[5] which is why System 2 normally operates in low effort mode, endorsing outputs from System 1. This division between System 1 and System 2 is efficient and works well most of the time. However, there are times when novel contexts lead to inappropriate System 1 responses that System 2 needs to correct.

When System 1 cannot provide satisfactory answers because its assumptions are violated, System 2 switches into high-energy mode. This happens when a problem requires working out to get to an answer when an event is detected that does not fit with the unconscious expectations of System 1. For example, Bugs Bunny cannot be seen in Disneyland and gorillas do not cross basketball courts in the middle of a game:

> Yet when test subjects were shown mocked-up images of Bugs Bunny shaking hands with tourists in Disneyland, *some 40 percent subsequently recalled a personal experience of meeting Bugs Bunny in Disneyland.*[6]   [Emphasis ours]

> Researchers asked subjects to count the number of times ball players with white shirts pitched a ball back and forth in a video. *Most subjects were so thoroughly engaged in watching white shirts that they failed to notice a black gorilla that wandered across the scene and paused in the middle to beat his chest.* They had their noses so buried in their work that they didn't even see the gorilla.[7]   [Emphasis ours]

> The gorilla experiment demonstrates that some attention is needed for the surprising stimulus to be detected. Surprise then activates and orients your attention: you will stare, and you will search your memory for a story that makes sense of the surprising event. System 2 is also credited with the continuous monitoring of your own behavior – the control that keeps you polite when you are angry, and alert when you are driving at night.[8]

It is logically impossible for the test subjects to have shaken hands with Bugs Bunny in Disneyland and yet they could remember meeting him there, somehow rationalizing to themselves how that could be the case – a phenomenon called "cognitive dissonance." Similarly, in the case of the gorilla, System 2 focused on the complicated task of counting the number of times the ball was being pitched, leaving no "space" for watching out for the gorilla. The mental effort of focusing created the equivalent of tunnel vision, blocking out the gorilla.

Recent research explains why this happens.[9] We recognize and appreciate the role that misdirection plays when we watch magicians perform on stage. It applies equally in the gorilla experiment. Asking people to focus on the number of times the ball was thrown deliberately directs the attention away from the gorilla crossing the pitch. Just as we do not notice how the magician has misdirected our attention at the key moment, so it is with our ability to process a stream of conflicting information.

Rhetoric

Rhetoric does the same as magicians to persuade us.[i] It is not concerned with the truth of an argument; it applies techniques designed to direct mental processes of an audience to propositions that support a particular line of reasoning:

> *Where there are political parties there must be propaganda; and rhetoric and oratory become essential to the citizen of a democracy who wanted to compete for social or economic or political success.* Where rhetoric is supreme, the decision of the law-courts will be swayed by brilliant argument and appeals to the emotions; and so, *in the law-courts it was persuasion, not truth, which prevailed. A policy, a point of view, a moral principle or a religion came to be valued not for its truth, but for its popular appeal,* just as the goodness of an article in modern life is sometimes assessed by its sales. In the end the substitution of reason for tradition as the supreme criterion produced not freedom for the individual, as had been hoped, but power for the few individuals who were skilled in the arts of salesmanship . . .

> . . . *For rhetoric – like propaganda and advertising – was the art of making others agree to a point of view whether that point was right or wrong. Indeed, the falser it was the greater the rhetorical success in persuading someone else to accept it: and conversely, the sounder a doctrine or a legal case or a political judgement, the more skill required to make it look ridiculous. Rhetoric, in fact, was the technique of making the worse appear the better and the better the worse cause. . .and it rapidly became the most highly developed science in all Greece.*[10] [Emphases ours]

Rhetoric employs three basic approaches, appealing to:
1. *Ethos*: Here speakers seek to persuade the audience via their personal authority or credibility or through the endorsement of their point of view by popular celebrities.
2. *Pathos*: This approach seeks to generate emotional responses (positive or negative) in the audience, using passionate pleas or convincing stories that may or may not be true, as long as they excite the relevant emotions in the listener or reader.
3. *Logos*: This approach uses logic to persuade by using facts and figures to make the case.

The control and manipulation of attention is central to being able to determine what is perceived as true, or false. Three hypotheses have been advanced regarding why people are happy to spread misinformation. The first is that they cannot tell the difference between what is true and what is false. The second is that they do not care. The third is that people act on impulse, sharing information without checking its veracity.[11] The evolutionary imperative means that we rely mainly on System 1 (the unconscious mind) rather than System 2 (the conscious mind). Most of the time, this works well; but

---

i For a detailed discussion of legitimate and illegitimate rhetorical techniques, see Zinkin, J. and Bennett, C. (2021), *The Principles and Practice of Effective Leadership* (Berlin and Boston: Walter de Gruyter), pp. 240–244.

sometimes heuristics are applied in inappropriate situations. Consequently, we make wrong decisions and are unwilling to recognize our mistakes.

Volatility, Uncertainty, Complexity, and Ambiguity (VUCA)

Volatility, uncertainty, complexity, and ambiguity (VUCA) challenge our desire for simplicity. People default to simple solutions and codes of conduct to guide them, preferring instructions and cognitive processes that make it easy to decide what to do. Consequential ethics – considering the implications of decisions, based on things we cannot fully know – require System 2 thinking and are too much work for most people.

> The firehose strategy is simple: barrage ordinary citizens with a stream of lies, inducing a state of learnt helplessness where people shrug and assume nothing is true. The lies don't need to make sense. What matters is the volume – enough to overwhelm the capabilities of fact-checkers, enough to consume the oxygen of the news cycle. People know you're lying, but there are so many eye-catching lies that it feels pointless to try to sift for the truth. [12]

Maslow's Five Needs

The extent to which people have the mental energy to consider ethical dilemmas depends on circumstances. Maslow's five needs[13] provides a useful framework for evaluating people's ability and willingness to adopt System 2 thinking.

Survival

People who are concerned with survival face the existential challenges of having enough to eat and finding a roof over their heads to protect them from the elements. The focus of their mental energy is on how to get the next meal and where to sleep the night. The primal drive to survive overrides everything else.

Safety

People who are concerned with safety have something to lose and so they form a Hobbesian social contract to avoid the "warre of every man against every man" with the beginnings of socially defined notions of right and wrong, justice and injustice. In return for predictable law and order, they are prepared to consent to authority.

Belonging

Most people need to feel that there is more to life than just what they do by themselves. As the Covid-19 pandemic reminded us, people need the intimacy of friendly and family relationships; and at work many need to belong to organizations as opposed to being self-employed. In return for the sense of belonging, there is the obligation to adhere to the customs and rules of the collective.

This explains why people follow toxic leaders. Toxic leaders succeed initially because their followers crave authority, order, security, and a sense of belonging, and all effective leaders understand this. Toxic leaders[ii] exploit four basic emotional needs and two primal fears:

1. *Need for authority*: From infancy, we are acculturated into followership – doing what our parents, elders, and authority figures tell us to. "Getting along by going along" is an important social lesson learned early. Such behaviour is usually evolutionarily advantageous in immature individuals but can be disadvantageous in adults.
2. *Need for security*: Security is a basic human need:[14]
   a. The security of the family structure is gone, and [they] seek replacements for parental authority, often finding leaders who promise security. After the September 11, 2001, terror attacks, for instance, Americans traded the freedom of hassle-free travel for the security of baggage searches and long delays at airport X-ray machines.[15]
3. *Need to feel special*: People follow leaders who make them feel part of something bigger and more important or beautiful than they are.
4. *Need to belong*: People conform to, and accept, group norms of behavior even if they are pathological; vide the "Milgram experiment."[16] Although individuals want to be valued for themselves and recognized as special, they need to be part of a community finding meaning in group approval.

Leaders play on people's fears, the fear of ostracization, and the fear of powerlessness. The fear of "social death" inhibits speaking truth to power:

---

ii Toxic leaders lack integrity and honesty and lie to bolster a compelling vision; put their personal glory above the well-being of others; are narcissists and arrogant, fostering incompetence and corruption; intimidate, demoralize, demean, and marginalize others; violate opponents' and followers' basic human rights; retain power by undermining potential successors and fail to nurture other leaders; feed followers' illusions, mislead through untruths and misdiagnoses, based on fear; stifle constructive criticism and "shoot the messenger"; set constituents against one another, encouraging division; and subvert institutions, structures, and processes intended to generate truth, justice, and excellence.

Lipman-Blumen, J. (2004), *The Allure of Toxic Leaders: Why We Follow Destructive Bosses and Corrupt Politicians – and How We Can Survive Them* (Oxford: Oxford University Press), reviewed in "Get Abstract, Compressed Knowledge," p. 3, https://www.getabstract.com/en/summary/the-allure-of-toxic-leaders/4368, accessed March 30, 2020.

> Toxic leaders demand more fealty than benign leaders require, and they do not tolerate dissent or questions about their decisions. The psychological pressure makes it especially difficult for whistle-blowers . . . [to] alert leaders and outside authorities about problems within a company. [17]

For individuals, leaders satisfy needs for certainty, simplicity, and security. People follow leaders because the emotional or economic rewards are implied *and/or* costs of not following are high. Resistance creates confusion and uncertainty – the states most followers want to avoid.

Esteem

This reflects feelings of accomplishment, measured in terms of the prestige individuals acquire as a result. Esteem in its prestige manifestation poses five challenges to ethical behavior.

1. First, it creates social stratification with all the issues of distributive and economic injustice and inequality.
2. Second, it can create a culture where rulers feel they are above the law and it is only the ruled who have to obey – leading to a culture of hypocrisy and a sense of impunity in those at the top of society.
3. Third, it glorifies competition between individuals and collectives that can lead to dangerous conflicts and lies at the heart of the "Thucydides trap," when a rising nation challenges a declining hegemon.
4. Fourth, rising leaders of street gangs often vie with one another to behave in more cruel and unethical ways as a way of gaining respect from their followers.
5. Fifth, it promotes conspicuous consumption leading to behavior that is environmentally unsustainable.

Self-actualization

This describes individuals achieving their full potential. From an ethical perspective, self-actualizers are those rare individuals who create ethical codes by which others live.

Inappropriate Role Models

There has been a perceived decline in the behavior of democratic leaders, ignoring the results of fairly conducted elections, continuing in office after being indicted for corruption, behaving as if they and their cronies are above the law, and putting their citizens at risk by ignoring science during the Covid-19 pandemic, acting as totally inappropriate role models.

Leaders have violated treaties[iii] and murdered their citizens who were legally resident in other countries[iv] and have led murderous regimes engaged in killing their own people (Syria and Myanmar), and appear to have got away with it.

A culture of increasing impunity and declining accountability has been the result, caused in part by an unwillingness of governments to take effective punitive action because of economic self-interest, and in part the failure of the media to hold officials to account, treating politics as another episode of reality TV, lionizing charismatic and toxic leaders.

Increasing Impunity, Declining Accountability

On June 4, 1963, John Profumo, the Defence Secretary, in Harold Macmillan's Conservative government was forced to resign because he had lied to Parliament about having an affair with Christine Keeler, a call girl. Her relationship with Yevgeny Ivanov, the Soviet Naval Attaché in London, raised concerns about breaches in national security. There was no evidence of a security breach. However, the investigations by the Press into Christine Keeler, her friend Mandy Rice-Davies, and her mentor Stephen Ward uncovered upper-class sleaze, leading to Prime Minister Macmillan's resignation, who was replaced by Sir Alec Douglas-Home, who lost the 1964 election to Harold Wilson of the Labour party in a cleaning out of the "old order" that had been in government since 1951.[18] The consequences of misbehavior were clear for all to see.

In 1997 the Conservatives, under John Major, lost to Labour led by Tony Blair, after Margaret Thatcher had led them to victory in 1979. Once again, the smell of

---

iii Putin's Russian Federation annexed Ukraine's Crimea March 18, 2014 in violation of the December 5, 1994 Budapest Memorandum on Security Assurances where Russia was a co-guarantor with the US and UK of the Ukraine's territorial integrity, in return for the Ukraine giving up nuclear weapons the former USSR had installed in the Ukraine.

Memorandum on Security Assurances in connection with the Republic of Belarus'/Republic of Kazakhstan's/Ukraine's accession to the Treaty on the Non-Proliferation of Nuclear Weapons, signed on December 5, 2019, Budapest, Hungary.

Xi Jinping's People's Republic of China imposed the "Law of the People's Republic of China on Safeguarding National Security in the Hong Kong Special Administrative Region on Hong Kong" on June 30, 2020 in violation of provisions agreed in "The Basic Law of the Hong Kong Special Administrative Region of the People's Republic of China" that came into effect on July 1, 1997, that was tabled as an internationally binding treaty at the United Nations.

iv Alexander Litvinenko was poisoned by the Komitet Gosudarstvennoy Bezopasnosti (KGB) using polonium on November 1, 2006 while living in London. There was a failed attempt by Main Intelligence Directorate (GRU) officers to poison Sergei Skripal and his daughter using Novichok in Salisbury on March 4, 2018. Only limited sanctions were imposed on Russia, because the UK wanted to preserve London as a haven for Russian oligarchs and their money, and Germany was not prepared to close the Nord Stream natural gas pipeline from Russia being built to serve German energy needs.

sleaze was in the air, contributing to their defeat. A number of obscure MPs were having affairs that would in previous years have been the end of their careers, and some 30 per cent were "taking cash for questions" to promote business interests in Parliament, which prompted Parliament to establish a committee on standards in public life that came out with the Nolan Report on May 1, 1995 with "Seven Principles."[v, 19] However, these principles have not been upheld; the Boris Johnson Conservative government and former Prime Minister David Cameron, who resigned after Brexit, have behaved in ways that have undermined the British public's belief in the process of government: Cameron by an inappropriately intrusive lobbying effort to get Treasury funding to prevent the Greensill organization going bust, where he stood to gain £60 million from his options in the company had he been successful:

> "We all know how it works. The lunches, the hospitality, the quiet word in your ear, the ex-ministers and ex-advisers for hire, helping big business find the right way to get its way." That someone was Mr Cameron, speaking shortly before he became prime minister, when he predicted that "the far-too-cosy relationship between politics and money" was "the next big scandal waiting to happen", though he failed to foresee that he would be at the core of it.[20]

A surprisingly strongly worded article by Bernard Jenkin, the Conservative MP who is the Chair of the Government Liaison Committee to whom members of the cabinet are answerable, documents the worrying decline in standards of behavior:

> After the dust settles over the Greensill affair, I suspect we will find that *the lack of judgment over David Cameron's approaches to ministers is less important than the general failure to address what has become a casual approach to conflicts of interest amongst many in government and politics.*
>
> . . . produced a series of reports over 15 years about *the failure of successive governments to manage the relationships between business and government in a more transparent way. There is nothing wrong with a private citizen wanting to make money, but we have a system that has allowed the lines between public service and private gain to become blurred. This is both shameful, and unfairly shaming of the majority in public office and in politics who do have good values and attitudes, but who are all tarred by the same brush.* Much of the wrongdoing is exaggerated, but the worst instances of people using public positions to enrich themselves are utterly corrosive of public trust in government. This must end . . .
>
> This does not just concern "lobbyists". . . . Of much more concern are those in public office who are being lobbied, and whose control over funding of outside organisations, and over contracts and regulation, the outsiders are seeking to influence. *All can now see the general inability of the various codes and systems of oversight, such as the toothless advisory committee on business appointments, to provide sufficient transparency and accountability,* which is why even its chair, Lord Pickles, wants reform.

---

v For details regarding the "seven principles," see *The First Report of the Committee on Standards in Public Life*, May 1, 1995, pp. 1–2, https://www.gov.uk/government/publications/mps-ministers-and-civil-servants-executive-quangos, accessed June 7, 2021.

> There are of course high-minded principles set out, and there are rules, but *what matters most is not whether someone under scrutiny can say, "I have not broken any rules" but whether they are demonstrating integrity, honesty, selflessness and openness in all they do in their life of public service.*[21]   [Emphases ours]

Illustrating further the decline in ministerial accountability is the reaction of the Cabinet Office to having lost a case in the High Court brought against Michael Gove, the minister in charge of the Cabinet Office, over the awarding of a contract "showing apparent favouritism."

In 2008, Benjamin Netanyahu called for the immediate resignation of the then Prime Minister of Israel, Ehud Olmert, who had been indicted for corruption.[22] Yet when he was indicted for corruption in 2019 Netanyahu did not resign but rather remained in power and fought four elections in the space of two years to try to avoid the consequences of the indictment,[23,24] getting away with it because sufficient numbers of the voters did not care about holding him to the standards he himself had demanded must be observed eight years earlier.

The central propositions of the Brexit campaign were based on falsehoods and contradictory promises Boris Johnson knew he could not keep, and has not kept.[25] This did not appear to hurt his popularity with his supporters:

> Johnson's deceit is "priced in". *The public has accepted he plays fast with the facts, and yet support him anyway* – look at the 2019 general election, when he won a big majority, and the 2016 EU referendum. *He is an entertainer, rather than a norm-bound politician, the argument goes, a soap opera character who exists in a half-real, half-fictional realm.*[26]   [Emphases ours]

The UK Ministerial Code resulting from the 1995 Nolan Review has no teeth in practice.

When accused of being slippery with the truth, Boris Johnson's defence has been that the narrative – the story he is telling to encourage people to be optimistic and adopt a 'can do' mentality – is more important than the facts.[27] While there are times when that may be true, it ignores the damage done to the concept of accountability – an essential component of good governance.

Media and Reality TV

An excellent explanation of the importance of a free press and of independent investigative journalism can be found on the Charles Koch Institute's website, parts of which are worth quoting verbatim:

> Freedom of the press is important because it plays a vital role in informing citizens about public affairs and monitoring the actions of government at all levels. . .

> Media-bashing is as old as the nation itself. George Washington once referred testily to the "infamous scribblers" who covered his administration. But our revolutionary forefathers knew that *when the press examines the actions of government, the nation benefits. News organizations*

expose corruption and cover-ups, deceptions and deceits, illegal actions and unethical behavior –
and they hold our leaders and our institutions accountable . . .

"Republics and limited monarchies derive their strength and vigor from a popular examination
into the action of the magistrates," Benjamin Franklin declared. By sharing knowledge and
sparking debate, a free press invigorates and educates the nation's citizens. *Freedom will be 'a*
short-lived possession' unless the people are informed, Thomas Jefferson once said. To quote
John Adams: 'The liberty of the press is essential to the security of the state."

Journalists are watchdogs – not cheerleaders. They ignite dialogue on essential issues. They
share the truths that powerful people would rather conceal. They are the force that holds our
leaders accountable for their actions.

When our leaders threaten journalists, they are threatening the First Amendment, along with
our most basic rights. *"Our liberty depends on the freedom of the press,"* said Jefferson, *"and*
that cannot be limited without being lost."[28]   [Emphases ours]

The article explains the importance of the First Amendment:

That means the government cannot punish you for your views, thoughts, or words, even if they're
unpopular save for very narrow limits. But we the people can say what we think – and the *press*
can perform its essential role: To agitate, investigate, and scrutinize our leaders and institutions.
That freedom is the difference between a democracy and a dictatorship.   [Emphasis ours]

It also points out that nearly half of Americans believed the press was doing "a
poor or very poor job" of supporting democracy according to a Knight/Gallup report
in 2017. This suggests that in some important ways the media are failing to:

1. *Act as watchdogs* and have become cheerleaders instead for polarizing points
   of view;
2. *Educate and inform* rather than entertain and mislead, turning politics into a
   modern-day "bread and circuses," trivializing issues and oversimplifying them
   into ephemeral soundbites;
3. *Agitate, investigate, and scrutinize thoroughly and persistently* leaders and the
   institutions of government;
4. *Hold people accountable for their words and actions*, instead of lionizing the behavior of extremists and conspiracy theorists;
5. *Provide platforms for civilized discussion based on balanced advocacy and in-*
   quiry instead of turning debates into competitions for share of voice designed
   to maximize the level of outraged engagement and ratings;
6. *Get questions answered* rather than allowing interviewees to stick to scripts designed to provide boilerplate non-answers or to change the subject.

Several factors may explain why the media have promoted a culture of impunity
and diminishing accountability.

First, is the concentration of ownership of the mainstream media at national levels, in individuals who are not interested in the socio-political health of the countries whose media they dominate.

Second, the decline of local media redirects the attention of viewers/readers from local issues to distant ones where viewers/readers do not have the experience to know when they are being manipulated.

Third, the advent of 24/7 news channels means they have become reality TV events to maintain the interest of viewers. If the news has to be repeated twenty-four times a day, it must be spiced up to keep it interesting for both the newscasters and the audiences.

Fourth, and most damaging, has been the rise of social media with its polarizing echo chambers.

Vested Interests

Vested interests exist in every collective; they are to be found in government, in legitimate and criminal organizations, in academia, the professions, the media and entertainment; and among stakeholders (who represent specific vested interests). Their aim is to defend the status quo with which they (the few) are comfortable (despite its defects) and resist change in order to protect the emotional and economic benefits they have acquired at the expense of those (the many) who are disadvantaged; or to expand the interests of their members.

The dynamics of the interactions over time between different vested interests within and between organizations, communities, nations, and cultures frame their "sustainable basins of attraction,"[vi] agree their superordinate goals, define their values, determine their priorities and ability to achieve their objectives successfully or not.

---

vi "Narratives serve as social attractors toward which behavior, society, and culture self-organize . . . *guided by an overall narrative(s), the complex self-organization dynamics between the collective mind of a society with its information-processing tools and the dynamics of a society's environment – the adaptive dance of the cognitive and the environmental domains – coevolves and shapes basins of attraction. As a result, some of these basins remain shallow and easy to change, while others become deep, persistent, and difficult to move out of.*

All human groups operate around shared narratives, which create identity, meaning, and core values and shape the epistemology through which they interact with the broader environment. All these are deeply anchored in the minds of its members, and frame their outlook, their opinions, and their decisions, consciously or unconsciously. Some examples of such more or less persistent systemic narratives that have shaped society, culture, and civilization are Christianity in Western Europe, Communism in the USSR and Eastern Europe, Manifest Destiny in the USA, indigenous cosmologies among the original inhabitants of the Americas, Sunni and Shiite Islam in many parts of Asia, and Fascism in twentieth-century Western European and South American countries. Of course, these are examples at the most general level for large numbers of people. Narratives adhered to by

Machiavelli explained how vested interests work:

The innovator makes enemies of all those who prospered under the old order, and only lukewarm support is forthcoming from those who would prosper under the new. Their support is lukewarm partly from fear of their adversaries, who have existing laws on their side, and partly because men are generally incredulous, never really trusting new things unless they have tested them by experience. In consequence, whenever those who oppose changes can do so, they attack vigorously, and the defence made by the others is only lukewarm. But to discuss this subject thoroughly we must distinguish between innovators who stand alone and those who depend on others, that is between those who to achieve their purposes can force the issue and those who must use persuasion. In the second case, they always come to grief, having achieved nothing; when, however, they depend on their own resources and can force the issue, then they are seldom endangered. That is why all armed prophets have conquered, and unarmed prophets have come to grief.[29]   [Emphasis ours]

Machiavelli's observations apply not just to the privileges created by vested interests in positions of power, they also apply to identity politics (another form of vested interest), where social conservatives or aggressive liberals use their clout as lobbyists to preserve traditional values, such as the prohibition of abortion and gay marriage,[30] or use gerrymandering and other ways of making it more difficult for people with different political opinions to make themselves heard at the ballot box.[31] When it comes to lobbying done by particular vested interests, the persistent vigor of the voices of the few for whom the issue is of vital importance (for example, the steel industry lobbying for tariff protection,[32] fossil fuels lobby denying climate change,[33] or the National Rifle Association (NRA) defending the US second amendment right to bear arms[34]) drown out the "lukewarm" voices of the many who would like to see changes but who only benefit at the margin from those changes, compared with the minority for whom the issue is vital.

The same conditions apply within organizations where vested interests reflect levels of seniority; departmental differences, priorities, and resources; cultural differences resulting from differing ethnic and religious backgrounds; and different economic interests driven by job class and responsibility. They also apply to trade unions and professional associations, such as lawyers, doctors, and engineers, where ethical standards and technical qualifications are barriers to entry, set to limit membership, justified on the grounds of maintaining standards, but often designed to raise the price of their members' goods and services to their clients, in the same way as all cartels do.

---

smaller subsections of such populations are often embedded in these larger narratives, such as Protestant, Catholic, and Orthodox narratives among the Christian populations of Europe, or, at an even lower level, the narratives of the various evangelical sects in North America.

. . . *an observed change in narratives is a central driver as well as a signal of the likelihood of a transition between basins of attraction, whether driven by exogenous or by endogenous dynamics, or a combination thereof.*" [Emphases ours]

van der Leeuw, S. and Folke. C. (2021), "The social dynamics of basins of attraction," *Ecology and Society*, Volume 26, Issue 1, 2021, p. 33. https://doi.org/10.5751/ES-12289-260133, accessed June 5, 2021.

Inappropriate Regulation?

It is worth restating why regulations are needed, given the prevailing view in some groups that a bonfire should be made of regulations.[vii] At its simplest, we need laws to feel safe from arbitrary action.[35]

Sometimes in markets, regulations are viewed as an opportunity for patronage, bribery, and corruption. In the case of patronage, regulations may be used to channel business opportunities to cronies by giving them unfair advantages.[viii] In the case of bribery and corruption, some rules provide an opportunity for a negotiated workaround and payoff to the officials responsible for enforcing the rules. So why do we need regulations? Perhaps the best answer comes from looking more carefully at what Adam Smith actually thought:

> According to Adam Smith, markets and trade are, in principle, good things – provided there is competition and a regulatory framework that prevents ruthless selfishness, greed and rapacity from leading to socially harmful outcomes. But competition and market regulations are always in danger of being undermined and circumnavigated, giving way to *monopolies that are very comfortable and highly profitable to monopolists and may spell great trouble for many people.* In Smith's view, political economy – as an important, and perhaps even the most important, part of a kind of master political science, encompassing the *science of the legislator* – has the task to fight superstition and false beliefs in matters of economic policy, to *debunk opinions that present individual interests as promoting the general good and to propose changing regulatory frameworks for markets and institutions that help to ward off threats to the security of society as a whole and provide incentives such that self-seeking behaviour has also socially beneficial effects.*[36]　　　　　　　　　　　　　　　　　　　　　　　　　　　[Emphases ours]

We need regulations to protect society and markets from the harmful effects of unscrupulous individuals and organizations and from rent-seeking by monopolies and oligopolies. We need regulations to distinguish between the interests of vested interests and the needs of society as a whole, and to define the "rules of the game" to create level competitive playing fields and honest markets. This must be the role

---

vii For an excellent discussion of the case for and against government regulations, see "More regulation or less?", Letters to the Editor, Sunday Dialogue, *The New York Times,* June 1, 2013, https://www.nytimes.com/2013/06/02/opinion/sunday/sunday-dialogue-more-regulation-or-less.html, accessed June 15, 2018.

viii "The dynamics of corruption in the public sector can be depicted in a simple model. The *opportunity* for corruption is a function of the size of the rents under a public official's control, the *discretion* that official has in allocating those rents, and the *accountability* that official faces for his or her decisions. Monopoly rents can be large in highly regulated economies and, as noted above, corruption breeds demand for more regulation. In transition economies economic rents can be enormous because of the amount of formerly state-owned property essentially 'up for grabs.' The discretion of many public officials may also be large in developing and transition economies, exacerbated by poorly defined, ever-changing, and inadequately disseminated rules and regulations."

World Bank, *Helping Countries Combat Corruption: The Role of the World Bank,* http://www1.worldbank.org/publicsector/anticorrupt/corruptn/cor02.htm, accessed June 15, 2018.

of government as arbiter of last resort.[ix] Regulations are often written without paying sufficient attention to how people who are being regulated will respond to the rules. On the one hand, some people will always try to "game the system," aided by lawyers and consultants using lacunae in "black letter law" to argue that if it has not been expressly forbidden, behavior is legal, even if it is "unethical" and goes against the spirit and intentions of the law. On the other hand, there is evidence that people respond to the level of permissiveness in their environment and that what helps to get them to behave more ethically is to a) draw their attention to moral codes, and b) get them to sign up to such codes to eliminate their tendencies to be dishonest.[37]

> *Signing a moral code can completely eliminate dishonesty. That a simple signature following an honor code can drastically change behavior points to the malleability of moral self-regulation. Determinants of honesty do not lie completely within the individual; seemingly innocuous factors outside the individual can dramatically affect the decision to behave honestly or dishonestly.* Many real-world decisions require self-regulation of ethical behavior (e.g., punching time cards, citing sources, preparing one's resume when applying for jobs, claiming tax deductions), and it is important not to underestimate the role of situational cues in encouraging ethical behavior. *If a situation permits dishonesty, then one should expect to observe dishonesty. At the same time, a simple intervention, such as merely reminding actors about established moral codes, could counteract the effect of a permissive situation.*[38]   [Emphases ours]

In his interview with Piers Morgan on CNN, when asked how he became a criminal, Jordan Belfort, nicknamed "The Wolf of Wall Street," replied that it was a gradual process:

> You don't lose your soul all at once. You lose it a little bit at a time incrementally, you know, when I lost my ethical way, it did not start off and I'm sure we'll go [into] that later. But, it's sort of like these tiny imperceptible steps over the line and before you do it, see each time you let him around and moves a bit, and before you know it, you're doing things, you thought you never do and it seems perfectly OK.[39]

Jordan Belfort was describing the fact that morality and memory are not fixed; they exist along a continuum of "motivated cognition" where moral disengagement or indifference is a reliable predictor of spiralling unethical behavior:

> [B]ad behavior motivates moral leniency and leads to the strategic forgetting of moral rules. Combining our finding that moral disengagement is a consequence of behavior with established work on unethical behavior as a consequence of moral disengagement, we suggest *people could set off on a downward spiral of having ever more lenient ethics and ever more unethical behavior. In alignment with social cognitive theory, we believe the moral disengagement we observe in our studies serves to reduce cognitive dissonance and alleviate guilt after cheating.*[40]   [Emphasis ours]

---

ix For a more detailed discussion on regulations, see Zinkin, J. (2019), *Better Governance across the Board: Creating Value through Reputation, People and Processes* (Boston/Berlin: Walter de Gruyter), pp. 31–36.

Deception

The same dynamic occurs in the way deception escalates in organizations. Once an individual and/or group have misbehaved and remain undetected, increased incentives and rationalization make it easier for them to repeat the deception until it colors the thinking of influential individuals, as happened with Arthur Andersen, Enron, and WorldCom in 2001.[41] The individuals concerned did not set out to be unethical, and yet were destroyed by deceptions that fed on themselves and grew over time. The escalation of deception can occur at individual, interpersonal, and organizational levels. If the deception is one-off or caught early enough it can be corrected, but if the initial deception remains unaddressed

> certain factors will make it easier to tell more lies, which over time can increase in severity and pervasiveness until deception becomes an organization level phenomenon. We highlight the importance of organizational complexity in amplifying this escalation process, and identify a positive feedback loop between organization level deception and each of the escalation stages.[42]

There are two types of lies: commission and omission. The first is where we tell an untruth that we know to be untrue in order to mislead others into believing what we ourselves do not believe; the second is the withholding of information – "being economical with the truth" – that leads others to wrong conclusions. As individuals, we all tell lies and understand the motives, as individuals, for lying. The motives for organizations to lie are similar – initially stretching the truth a little. Often, the spiralling cycle of deception begins with commission – a lie is told deliberately – and then is backed up by people omitting to correct the record, only to lead to having to tell increasingly complicated stories to cover up the initial and perhaps insignificant misdemeanor.

How do organizations get into such a condition? Once an individual or group within an organization has lied, it becomes easier to lie the next time. Moreover, the severity of the deception increases because of the need for more lies to cover up the original lie; a deteriorating underlying condition gets worse because there has been no appropriate corrective action to address the original conditions that prompted the lie; and people's attitude to risk changes as they get away with lying. Not only must the original deceit be hidden, but now the cover-up lies must also be justified, affecting more people as the situation gets more complicated, to the point where the cover-up lies are more damaging to the organization than the original lie itself.[43] As the consequences of the deteriorating situation become more serious, so do the likely punishments for the perpetrators, forcing them to take ever greater risks to delay the discovery of their malpractice. Prospect theory suggests that this downward spiral will become more serious as the risk-taking becomes more extreme.[44] This is because people are generally risk averse when considering gains but will become risk takers in order to avoid losses.[45]

There are three reasons why deception is contagious within organizations, as more and more people get involved in supporting cover-ups, as they outstrip individual spans of control. First, it may be ordered or condoned by people at the top, making participation non-negotiable in terms of personal safety. Second, the language used to describe what is in fact unethical may be deliberately designed to disguise the truth of the matter, making the actions seem respectable and natural. Third, individuals may find themselves drifting along to a point where there is no retreat from being asked to do something seriously wrong and so

> [a]s the deceit gets increasingly serious and becomes part of unofficial operating procedure, it moves from a case of destructive deviance, where one person lies in contrast to the norm of honesty, to destructive conformity where deceit is the organizational norm.[46]

"Bad Apples"

Once deception is systemic, organizational complexity increases the propensity to lie and cover up by:

1. *Breaking the deception down into its component atomistic parts*, making it easier for people to misbehave because they can dissociate themselves from the consequences of the overall outcome – for example, subprime derivatives traders who brought the financial system to its knees in 2008 were only looking at numbers on screens with no emotional connection with the real world and the consequences of their calculations on the people affected by their decisions. In a sense they could hide behind the fact (rationalize to themselves) that their decisions taken individually were not that important, even though collectively they represented serious malpractice.

2. *Amplifying a lie many times over into the future*, implicating other parts of the organization, thus increasing its pervasiveness. Complex structures transmit deception as different departments or sub-units deal with contaminated information when conducting their day-to-day operations invalidating future reporting so that even if the reporters were honest, they could only produce "garbage out" as a result of "garbage in."[47]

3. *Creating destructive deviant conformity* once it becomes the norm (that is, the barrel is rotten rather than "just a few bad apples"). At the point when lying becomes institutionalized it directly and indirectly affects day-to-day operations and processes through ready-made organizational "scripts" justifying malpractice, reinforced by peer pressure, and fear of missing out because others are doing it and being rewarded for their bad behavior. The resulting momentum implicates previously honest players in the lies of others (as it did in the subprime crisis), and failing to lie will then lead to censure from others and negative peer appraisal[48] and, worse still, negative comments by analysts when comparing

an honest organization's results with those of a dishonest one, as happened to Angelo Mozilo of Countrywide Financial, and force them to adopt dishonest practices leading to bankruptcy.[x]

> If lying is an unofficial norm in the organization that is integral to its everyday functioning, then individuals and/or groups are more likely to rationalize via the denial of responsibility. Moreover, when deception is an organization level phenomenon, the incentive to lie again is greater. This is because the malfeasance is so fundamental that its discovery will jeopardize the very survival of the organization. Indeed, many of the corrupt individuals at Enron portrayed themselves as "heroes" committed to rescuing the company.[49]

Finally, organizational deception becomes system-wide, relying on external enablers with conflicts of interest: the entire financial services industry including rating agencies, investment bankers, hedge funds, insurers, lawyers, and auditors colluding to create the subprime crisis.

As long as the deception is confined to a few individuals, as opposed to having infected the organization as whole, the "bad apple" defence may be justified. However, skepticism of the "bad apple" defence is warranted. What matters is whether senior levels in the organization were aware of the existence of "bad apples" and condoned their misbehavior because of either their seniority or their impact on the bottom line. For example, whereas the boards of leading financial institutions in New York and London insisted that the banking malpractices that led to the Global Financial Crisis (GFC) of 2008 were the actions of only a few "bad apples," a survey of 500 senior managers in Wall Street and London by Labaton Sucharow carried out in 2012, found:

1. *Thirty-nine percent* believed their competitors had behaved unethically or illegally.
2. *Twenty-six percent* said they had first-hand experience of unethical or illegal behavior.
3. *Twenty-four percent* believed they had to be unethical to succeed in financial services.
4. *Sixteen percent* would engage in insider trading if they thought they could get away with it.
5. *Thirty percent* said this was because of remuneration.[50]

---

x Countrywide Financial's CEO Angelo Mozilo was forced by shareholders and analysts to transform his company from being the leading and respected prime mortgage broker into a subprime broker as a result of losing market share to Ameriquest, which was accepting subprime business that Countrywide turned down because it was too toxic. This was a clear case of the capital market rewarding bad behavior by Ameriquest and other subprime brokers who were employing unscrupulous methods funded by Wall Street investors, at Countrywide's expense, signalling to Mozilo that he must follow suit. He finally gave way with devastating results as he too adopted the deceptive practices he had warned against.

Madrick, J. (2011) *Age of Greed: The Triumph of Finance and the Decline of America, 1970 to the Present* (New York: Alfred Knopf), p. 367.

The fact that four years after the Global Financial Crisis thirty percent were still saying that these unethical attitudes were specifically caused by remuneration demonstrates the existence of a systemic problem in the institutions whose senior managers were surveyed. Such high percentages do not suggest a "few bad apples" but rather rotten barrels, ones that would be rejected as being unfit for consumption if they really were barrels of apples.

Together with the University of Notre Dame, Labaton Sucharow repeated the exercise in 2015, surveying 1,153 professionals in financial services and investment banking in the US (925) and the UK (298) from all levels of seniority and accountability.[51] Their findings were a serious cause for concern that, despite all the legislation and regulation brought in to prevent a repeat of misconduct in the GFC, the ethics within investment banking had deteriorated further from 2012:

> The answers are not pretty. Despite the headline-making consequences of corporate misconduct, our survey reveals that attitudes toward corruption within the industry have not changed for the better. To be sure, there are some encouraging statistics such as increased faith in law enforcement and in colleagues. Nevertheless, *there is no way to overlook the marked decline in ethics and the enormous dangers we face as a result, especially when considering the views of the most junior professionals in the business. Most concerning, is the proliferation of secrecy policies and agreements that attempt to silence reports of wrongdoing and obstruct an individual's fundamental right to freely engage with her government* [as a whistleblower].[52]   [Emphasis ours]

The key findings make depressing reading. Of those surveyed:

a. *Forty-seven percent* believed their competition had behaved illegally or unethically (up from 39 percent in 2012), and among those earning more than $500,000 per year the figure was 51 percent.
b. *Twenty-seven percent* believed their industry did not put the needs of clients first, and in the UK, 42 percent of those with less than ten years' service disagreed that the industry put the client first.
c. *Thirty-three percent* did not believe the industry has changed for the better since the GFC, males (35 percent), females (28 percent), and among those earning more than $500,000 per year (38 percent).
d. *Nineteen percent* believe that misconduct is a key ingredient in success (up from 12 percent in 2012). [53]
e. *Thirty-two percent* believe that compensation/bonus structures incentivize employees to violate ethical standards or to break the law. Among those earning more than $500,000 per year, 23 percent had experienced pressure to compromise their values against 9 percent earning less than $50,000.
f. *Thirty-four percent* of those earning more than $500,000 had witnessed or had first-hand knowledge of wrongdoing in the workplace, compared to 21 percent who earned less than $50,000. Overall, this represented 22 percent (a drop from 26 percent in 2012); unlike in the US where there was no drop in the percentage of people who had witnessed or had first-hand knowledge of wrongdoing, there was a drop in the UK from 30 percent in 2012 to 25 percent in 2015.[54]

g. *Twenty-three percent* of all respondents believe it is likely that their colleagues have engaged in illegal or unethical activity in order to get ahead in their company; nearly 25 percent of employees with less than ten years of service believe that their colleagues engage in illegal or unethical behavior to get ahead, compared with 20 percent in employees with more than 21 years.

h. *Twenty-five percent* admitted they would engage in insider trading to make a quick $10 million if they thought they could get away with it – 32 percent of employees with less than ten years' service, compared with 14 percent with more than 21 years. Males (27 percent) were more likely than females (22 percent) to do insider trading.[55]

Based on these numbers, senior managers and bank boards cannot credibly maintain that misconduct is confined to "only a few rotten apples" and are unrepresentative of the industry's culture and values. It would appear they preside over "barrels of rotten apples."

Barbara Kellerman explains how people come to accept bad behavior by dividing them into three groups, each with its own rationale for putting up with malpractices:[56]

1. *The silent majority*: who go along with what is being done because it is too much effort or too risky to disagree, but they do not believe in what is being proposed. They neither participate in, nor oppose it.

2. *The doers*: who follow orders because that is what they are supposed to do as efficiently and effectively as possible, because they are being measured and rewarded accordingly, or because personal costs of not complying are too great.

3. *The acolytes*: who support the vision – because they believe it is the right thing to do, or because they will obtain social, psychological, or emotional benefits from enthusiastic alignment.

Perhaps the decline in the foundational principles of the liberal capitalist system (discussed in Chapter 6) was a consequence of the emphasis on deregulation in search of greater profits of the past fifty years, given that it was accompanied by moral disengagement and its consequent increase in unethical behavior.

Rules-based and Principles-based Regulation

Rules-based regulations are not mentally taxing, requiring regulatees to only use System 1 thinking unless they are in conflict with other rules. Principles-based regulations may be short documents, but they are mentally taxing because they require System 2 thinking and assessment of unknown consequences. Compliance officers prefer rules-based regulations because they are simple to enforce and reduce the personal risk to the enforcers, even though they may lead to all the defects attributed to regulations by libertarians: burdensome; over-complicated to implement; easy for clever lawyers to get around by finding loopholes in the wording; and, more seriously, ignoring the ethical issues at stake:

> *The greater the number of laws, rules and regulations, the more people ignore the ethical consequences and focus on compliance only* . . . The legalistic culture of the US gives people a strong motive to shuffle off responsibility to others and cover their back.[57]   [Emphasis ours]

There are also issues of culture, weak enforcement, inappropriate KPIs, and inappropriate rewards and punishments.

Cultural Complications

Regulators compare their rules and regulations with those applied in other jurisdictions, on the idea of benchmarking and adopting "leading edge" practice. This only makes sense if, and when, the framers of the rules and regulations have spent enough time understanding the context in which those rules and regulations have been drawn up (the problems they were trying to prevent, and the cultural axioms and behavioral norms of the regulatees). If the context is different, then such a "cut and paste" approach is likely to fail. Culture matters and finding the best ways to reconcile differences in behavior is essential if the relationship between international organizations and their foreign host countries is to be mutually beneficial. It also matters if employees from diverse cultures are to give their best when working for an organization whose cultural foundations are different from their own.

> Culture is difficult to define, I think it's even more difficult to mandate – but for me *the evidence of culture is how people behave when no-one is watching.*[58]   [Emphasis ours]

Most legitimate organizations have a written code of conduct. It is the result of its history and the myths that bind its people together, answering the questions of "Who are we?" and "What do we believe?" and "How should we behave toward each other and our customers?" It reflects domestic laws and regulations that apply to its industry and, where relevant, international agreements, laws, and regulations of other jurisdictions, if the organization operates in more than one country.

Developing codes of conduct is seen as being relatively straightforward. In theory, all it requires is to look at past business practices, the history of the organization, and all laws and regulations that could apply to its operations. In practice, however, it is much more complicated. Cultural differences (national, religious, ethnic, age, class, and occupational) come into play, requiring great cross-cultural sensitivity when developing and applying codes of conduct.

Weak Enforcement

Many people assume that obeying the law is a must. Yet many organizations choose to break the law by disregarding environmental, health and safety, and consumer protection regulations and pay the resulting fines. Enforcement may be ineffective for a number of reasons.

First, the prevailing culture may be particularist so that people prioritize relationships over rules and find excuses why in the given particular circumstances, enforcing the rules need not apply.

Second, regulators may find that proving malfeasance beyond a reasonable doubt is too difficult and that the judiciary are not sufficiently expert in the application of the law in areas like white-collar crime, and the juries find the arguments too difficult to follow. In such circumstances, prosecutors often settle out of court, getting the company to pay a large often arbitrary fine without admitting to any wrongdoing. This sends the wrong signal for three reasons: a) if there was no wrongdoing, then how is the fine justified; b) companies often do not take the penalty seriously and are repeat offenders, reinforcing the idea that it does not matter – it is just the cost of doing business, whereas if there had been a custodial sentence, the perpetrators would have felt the consequences of their malfeasance personally; c) usually the fine is paid by the company out of its profits, punishing the shareholders rather than the originators of the malpractice. In some jurisdictions, this is less of a problem, because the financial services regulations stipulate that senior officers and directors of financial institutions must meet the standard of "the specific burden of proof" for serious white-collar crimes (for example, Malaysia[xi]) where they have to prove they are innocent rather than the prosecution having to prove they are guilty.

Third, the judiciary may be unqualified, and may also be corrupt and be bought off by the malefactors or their patrons. In some countries, regulators do not have the power to prosecute but have to hand the case over to other agencies. Often in

---

xi "**Offences by bodies of persons and by employees and agents**

367. (1) Where an offence against this Act or any regulations made there under has been committed by a body corporate, any person who at the time of the commission of the offence was a director, a chief executive, an officer or a representative of the body corporate or was purporting to act in such capacity, *is deemed to have committed that offence unless he proves that the offence was committed without his consent or connivance and that he exercised all such diligence to prevent the commission of the offence as he ought to have exercised, having regard to the nature of his functions in that capacity and to all the circumstances.* (2) Where a person who is an employee of another person contravenes any provision of this Act, the person for or on behalf of whom the employee is acting shall be deemed to have contravened such provision." [Emphasis ours]

Capital Markets Services Act 2007, section 367, p. 285, Securities Commission Malaysia, https://www.sc.com.my/api/documentms/download.ashx?id=d15d8121-57ce-44f9-a3e1-36da0191b965, accessed June 19, 2021.

such cases, malefactors may believe they can buy their way out of trouble before the case ever gets to court.

Fourth, there may be a lack of independent, qualified investigation that follows the money regardless of where it leads. This is important because so often it is a news story that uncovers malpractices.

Fifth, the pecuniary and social penalties may not be heavy enough to act as effective deterrents.

Sixth, as with Prohibition in the United States, the "crime" is not viewed as such by the public and as a result, effective enforcement becomes almost impossible, because even when perpetrators are found guilty, there are no social sanctions.

Inappropriate KPIs

Ever since Milton Friedman argued in 1970 that the role of business is to maximize shareholder value (MSV), legitimate businesses have adopted an almost single-minded focus on return on equity to ensure that so called "activist investors" and other shareholders get the maximum benefit from financial engineering, as opposed to a) investing in the long-term future by ploughing money back into research and development (R&D) and investing in brand equity, b) ensuring that their investments maximized the return on assets by focusing on improving productivity, or c) considering the externalities their activities impose on the environment and the communities within which they operate. Instead, this has led to "predatory value extraction" being interpreted as a license to maximize the short-term distribution of cash to shareholders and CEOs via dividends, buybacks, and stock options at the expense of sustainability and ignores the need to retain cash to perform R&D, develop innovative programs, invest for the future, pay for mistakes, buy new equipment, launch new products, and have reserves to carry the company through hard times. The late Jack Bogle, founder of Vanguard and an icon of investing on behalf of ordinary people, had this to say about shareholders:

> We are a *rent*-a-stock industry, a world away from Warren Buffett's favorite holding period. Forever.

> But while a fund that *owns* stocks has little choice but to regard proper corporate governance. One that *rents* stocks could hardly care less.[59]

As renters, shareholders have little interest in the long-term viability of the business. The fact that banks and fund managers lend their clients' securities to activist investors who are looking to short shares[60] makes these players behave even less like owners.

This is a huge market[xii] and its existence undermines the concept of ownership – essential to good governance and a focus on sustainable value creation. As a result, activist shareholders mean something quite different when they talk about extracting value:

> Since the late 1970s, *the richest American households have increased their power to extract value that the American working class has helped to create.* This change . . . has manifested itself in an *ever-increasing gap between the growth of labor productivity and the rate of growth of real wages, with wage growth falling further and further behind productivity growth.* . . . The prime cause . . . was the abandonment of the "retain-and-reinvest" regime, in which CWOC ["career-with-one-company"] was rooted, and the transition to the "downsize-and-distribute" resource allocation regime, characterized by contingent employment relations.

> *Under the retain-and-reinvest regime senior executives made corporate resource allocation decisions that, by retaining people and profits within the company, permitted reinvestment in productive capabilities that could generate competitive . . . products.* . . . The retain-and-reinvest regime, combined with the CWOC norm, enabled both white-collar and blue-collar workers to join a growing middle class.[xiii] In sharp contrast, *under downsize-and-distribute, a company is prone to downsize its labor force and to distribute to shareholders, in the form of cash dividends and stock buybacks,[xiv] corporate cash that it might previously have retained.*[61]   [Emphases ours]

The fact that many US organizations have chosen to change the allocation of cash from investment in the business to maximizing return on equity has made matters worse since 1988 when there has been an unprecedented "reallocation of rents" to shareholders at the expense of real value creation:

> From the beginning of 1989 to the end of 2017, 23 trillion dollars of real equity wealth was created by the nonfinancial corporate sector. *We estimate that 54% of this increase was attributable to a reallocation of rents to shareholders in a decelerating economy.* Economic growth accounts for just 24%, followed by lower interest rates (11%) and a lower risk premium (11%). *From 1952 to 1988 less than half as much wealth was created, but economic growth accounted for 92% of it.*[62]   [Emphases ours]

---

xii Lenders earned $9.16 billion in securities lending revenues in 2016: $4.67 billion in North America; $2.64 billion in Europe; $1.67 billion in Asia Pacific; and $182 million in the rest of the world. The value of securities made available for borrowing was $16 trillion, up $2.75 trillion year on year. More than 45,000 unique securities are available for loan worldwide.

Walsh, P. (2017), "Global securities lending hits $2 trillion mark," *Global Custodian*, March 13, 2017, https://www.globalcustodian.com/global-securities-lending-hits-2-trillion-mark/, accessed on May 14, 2022.

xiii It also provided workers with job security, in-house promotion possibilities, health insurance, and defined benefit pensions.

xiv The buybacks in the United States have been huge. In the period 2008–2017, S&P 500 corporations have repurchased $4.0 trillion, equal to 53 percent of net income – on top of the 41 percent of net income paid in dividends. The benefits went to senior management through their exercising of stock options at times of their choosing and to hedge funds and investment bankers, in the business of influencing stock prices and timing the sale and purchase of stock. Lazonick, W. and Shin, J-J. (2019), *Predatory Value Extraction* (Oxford: Oxford University Press), pp. 2–3.

In the period 1989–2017, "reallocation of rents" represented 54 percent of equity gains. Only 24 percent came from economic growth – that is, new value creation; whereas in the period 1952–1988, 92 percent of equity gains came from real growth – that is, new value creation. Only 8 percent came from a "reallocation of rents." This is one of the reasons for the unsustainable rise in inequality.

Summary

The human brain evolved fast, economical, unconscious, instinctive processes (System 1) to respond immediately to a threat. The unconscious mind (System 1) works independently of the conscious mind (System 2) and is in "always on" mode. System 2's processing of facts, using logic and making connections between different data, is hard work, which is why System 2 normally operates in low effort mode, endorsing outputs from System 1.

When System 1 cannot provide satisfactory answers because its assumptions are violated, System 2 switches on. However, inappropriate heuristics, misdirection, or rhetorical tricks may cause this process to fail, creating cognitive dissonance because the mental effort needed to correct the System 1 process proves too great. Consequently, people make the wrong decisions and are unwilling to recognize their errors.

VUCA challenges the evolutionary desire for simplicity, leading people to prefer instructions and cognitive processes that make it easy to decide what to do. Maslow's five needs (survival, safety, belonging, esteem, and self-actualization) provides a useful way of evaluating people's ability to adopt System 2 thinking.

Inappropriate role models have set bad examples encouraging a culture of impunity and declining accountability caused in part by government unwillingness to take effective punitive action and in part by the media's failure to hold officials to account, treating politics as reality TV.

This is a reflection of the role played by vested interests. The dynamics of the interactions over time between different vested interests within and between organizations, communities, nations, and cultures frame their sustainability, agree their superordinate goals, define their values, determine their priorities and ability to achieve their objectives.

Regulations are needed to protect society and markets from the harmful effects of unscrupulous individuals and organizations and from rent-seeking by monopolies and oligopolies. Regulations are required to distinguish between the interests of vested interests and the needs of society as a whole, and to define the "rules of the game" to create level competitive playing fields and honest markets. Inappropriate regulations fail to recognize how people respond to being regulated: either to ignore them or to "game the system."

People respond to the level of permissiveness in their environments and they can be made to behave more ethically by drawing their attention to moral codes, and getting them to sign up to such codes. This is because morality and memory are not fixed; they exist along a continuum of "motivated cognition" where moral disengagement or indifference is a reliable predictor of spiralling unethical behavior.

This explains how deception escalates in organizations. Once an individual and/or group have misbehaved and remain undetected, increased incentives and rationalization make it easier for them to repeat the deception until it colours the thinking of influential individuals. Once an individual or group within an organization has lied, it becomes easier to lie the next time. Moreover, the severity of the deception increases because of the need for more lies to cover up the original lie; a deteriorating underlying condition gets worse because there has been no appropriate corrective action to address the original conditions that prompted the lie; and people's attitude to risk changes as they get away with lying.

As the consequences of the deteriorating situation become more serious, so do the likely punishments for the perpetrators, forcing them to take ever greater risks to delay the discovery of their malpractice. Prospect theory suggests that this downward spiral will become more serious as the risk-taking becomes more extreme. This is because people are generally risk averse when considering gains but will become risk takers in order to avoid losses.

As long as the deception is confined to a few individuals, as opposed to having infected the organization as whole, the "bad apple" defence may be justified. However, skepticism of the "bad apple" defence is warranted. What matters is whether senior levels in the organization were aware of the existence of "bad apples" and condoned their misbehavior because of either their seniority or their impact on the bottom line. Regular reviews of the financial services industry in New York and London since the subprime crisis suggest that the "bad apple" defense is incorrect; the percentages of people who behave unethically have proved too high.

Enforcing regulations is made more complicated by cultural differences, weak enforcement, inappropriate KPIs, and rewards and punishments.

References

1 Larmuseau, C. et al. (2019), "Combining physiological data and subjective measurements to investigate cognitive load during complex learning," *Frontline Learning Research,* Volume 7, Issue 2, 2019, p. 59, https://journals.sfu.ca/flr/index.php/journal/article/view/403, accessed September 1, 2020.
2 Ibid.
3 Kahneman, D. (2012), "Of 2 minds: How fast and slow thinking shape perception and choice [excerpt]," *Scientific American,* June 15, 2012, https://www.scientificamerican.com/article/kahneman-excerpt-thinking-fast-and-slow/, accessed August 31, 2020.
4 Ibid.

5 Sweller, J. (2010), "Element interactivity and intrinsic, extraneous and germane cognitive load," *Educational Psychology Review*, Volume 22, April 23, 2010, pp. 123–138.

6 Edelman, G. (2000), *Universe of Consciousness: How Matter Becomes Imagination* (New York: Basic Books), cited in Wind, Y., Crook, C., and Gunther, R. (2005), *The Power of Impossible Thinking: Transform the Business of Your Life and the Life of Your Business* (Upper Saddle River, NJ: Wharton School Publishing)), p. ix.

7 Wind, Crook and Gunther (2005).

8 Kahneman (2012)

9 Harford, T. (2021), "What magic teaches us about misinformation," *Financial Times Magazine*, May 6, 2021, https://www.ft.com/content/5cea69f0-7d44-424e-a121-78a21564ca35, accessed June 2, 2021.

10 Crossman, R. H. S. (1963), *Plato Today, 2nd edition* (London: Unwin Books), pp. 38–39.

11 Harford (2021).

12 Ibid.

13 Maslow, A. H. (1943), "A theory of human motivation," *Psychological Review*, Volume 50, Issue 4, 1943, pp. 370–396, http://psychclassics.yorku.ca/Maslow/motivation.htm, accessed April 23, 2020.

14 Ibid.

15 Lipman-Blumen, J. (2004), *The Allure of Toxic Leaders: Why We Follow Destructive Bosses and Corrupt Politicians – and How We Can Survive Them* (Oxford: Oxford University Press), reviewed in Get Abstract, Compressed Knowledge, p. 3, https://www.getabstract.com/en/summary/the-allure-of-toxic-leaders/4368, accessed March 30, 2020.

16 "Milgram experiment – Obedience to authority," Explorable, https://explorable.com/stanley-milgram-experiment#:~:text=Conclusion%20%2D%20Obedience%20to%20Authority,65%20%25%20Onever%20stopped%20giving%20shocks, accessed July 16, 2020.

17 Lipman-Blumen (2004), p. 4.

18 Harris, A. (2016), "Sex. lies and spies: The real history of the Profumo affair," *BBC History Revealed*, Christmas Issue, 2016, https://www.historyextra.com/period/20th-century/real-history-profumo-affair-christine-keeler-who-what-happened/, accessed June 7, 2021.

19 Committee on Standards in Public Life (1995) "Summary of the Nolan Committee's First Report on Standards in Public Life," May 1, 1995, p. 3, https://assets.publishing.service.gov.uk/government/uploads/system/uploads/attachment_data/file/336840/1stInquiry_Summary.pdf, accessed June 7, 2021.

20 Rawnsley, A. (2021), "David Cameron and the Greensill scandal is just the tip of the Fatberg," *The Guardian,* April 18, 2021, https://www.theguardian.com/commentisfree/2021/apr/18/david-cameron-greensill-scandal-tip-of-fatberg?utm_term=38e92d65c8b6af9906524601d559f20e&utm_campaign=BestOfGuardianOpinionUK&utm_source=esp&utm_medium=Email&CMP=opinionuk_email, accessed April 20, 2021.

21 Jenkin, B. (2021), "The line between public service and private gain is shamefully blurred," *The Guardian,* April 17, 2021, https://www.theguardian.com/commentisfree/2021/apr/17/the-line-between-public-service-and-private-gain-is-shamefully-blurred, accessed April 18, 2021.

22 TOI staff (2019), "PM 'cannot serve one more day': Calls for resignation multiply over indictment," *Times of Israel*, November 21, 2019, https://www.timesofisrael.com/calls-for-pm-to-resign-multiply-after-indictment-announcement/, accessed June 7, 2021.

23 Heller, A. (2019), "Netanyahu infuses campaign with anti-media incitement," *Times of Israel*, September 2, 2019, https://www.timesofisrael.com/netanyahu-infuses-campaign-with-anti-media-incitement/, accessed June 7, 2021.

24 Bachner, M. (2020), "Deputy AG likens Netanyahu's attacks on judiciary to Protocols of elders of Zion," *Times of Israel,* November 15, 2020, https://www.timesofisrael.com/deputy-ag-likens-neta nyahus-attacks-on-judiciary-to-protocols-of-elders-of-zion/, accessed June 7, 2021.

25 Smith, C. (2021), "Video exposing Boris Johnson's 'lies' to Parliament hits 20 million views," *The Big issue,* May 27, 2021, https://www.bigissue.com/latest/politics/video-exposing-boris-john sons-lies-to-parliament-hits-20-million-views/, accessed June 8, 2021.

26 Harding, L., Elgot, J., and Sparrow, A. (2021), "Accusations of lying pile up against Boris John-son. Does it matter?", *The Guardian*, April 30, 2021 https://www.theguardian.com/politics/2021/apr/30/accusations-of-lying-pile-up-against-boris-johnson-does-it-matter, accessed on September 2, 2022.

27 McTague, T., (2021), "The minister of chaos", *The Atlantic,* June 7, 2021, https://www.theatlan tic.com/magazine/archive/2021/07/boris-johnson-minister-of-chaos/619010/, accessed on June 8, 2021.

28 "Importance of a free press," Charles Koch Institute, May 3, https://charleskochinstitute.org/stories/importance-of-a-free-press/, accessed June 7, 2021.

29 Machiavelli, N. (1513), *The Prince* (Harmondsworth: Penguin Books, 1999), Chapter VI, p. 19.

30 Moreau, J. (2020), "States across US still cling to outdated gay marriage bans," NBC News, Feb-ruary 18, 2020, https://www.nbcnews.com/feature/nbc-out/states-across-u-s-still-cling-outdated-gay-marriage-bans-n1137936, accessed on June 19, 2021.

31 "Voting laws roundup: May 2021," Brennan Center for Justice, May 28, 2021, https://www.bren nancenter.org/our-work/research-reports/voting-laws-roundup-may-2021, accessed June 19, 2021.

32 Pfeifer, S. and Bounds, A. (2021), "Steels industry hits out at UK plans to remove tariff protec-tions," *Financial Times,* May 21, 2021, https://www.ft.com/content/5ea1b348-9fd6-4bcd-b679-dc166716ed9c, accessed June 19, 2021.

33 Pierre, J. (2021), "How decades of disinformation about fossil fuels halted US climate policy," NPR, October 27, 2021, https://www.npr.org/2021/10/27/1047583610/once-again-the-u-s-has-failed-to-take-sweeping-climate-action-heres-why, accessed February 20, 2022.

34 Tucker, J. (2019), "How the NRA hijacked history," September 9, 2019, https://www.washington post.com/outlook/2019/09/09/why-accurate-history-must-guide-coming-debate-about-guns-sec ond-amendment/, accessed June 19, 2021.

35 Baron de Montesquieu (1748), translated by Nugent, T. (1899), *The Spirit of the Laws,* Volume 1 (New York: The Colonial Press), p. 151.

36 Kurz, H. D. (2015), Abstract of "Adam Smith on markets, competition and violations of natural liberty," *Cambridge Journal of Economics,* Volume 40, Issue 2, March 1, 2015, pp. 615–638, https://academic.oup.com/cje/article-abstract/40/2/615/2605099, accessed June 15, 2018.

37 Shu, L. L., Gino, F., and Bazerman, M. H. (2011), "Dishonest deed, clear conscience: When cheating leads to moral disengagement and motivated forgetting," *Personality and Social Psychol-ogy Bulletin*, Volume 37, Issue 3, 2011, pp. 344–345, http://pspb.sagepub.com, accessed May 27, 2021.

38 Ibid.

39 Belfort, J. (2014), "Interview with Jordan Belfort," *Piers Morgan Live,* CNN, January 24, 2014, http://edition.cnn.com/TRANSCRIPTS/1401/24/pmt.01.html, accessed June 4, 2021.

40 Shu, Dino and Bazerman (2011).

41 Fleming, P. and Zyglidopoulos, S. (2006), "The escalation of deception in organizations," *Work-ing Paper Series,* 12/2006 (Cambridge: Judge Business School), presented at the 1st Organization Studies Summer Workshop: "Theorizing Process in Organizational Research," 12–13 June, 2006, Santorini, Greece.

42 Ibid., p. 3.

43 Ibid., p. 9.

44 Harley, A. (2016), "Prospect theory and loss aversion: How users make decisions," *NN/g, Nielsen Norman Group,* June 19, 2016, https://www.nngroup.com/articles/prospect-theory/, accessed June 19, 2021.

45 Thomas, C. W. (2002), "The rise and fall of Enron," *The Journal of Accountancy*, April 1, 2022, https://www.journalofaccountancy.com/issues/2002/apr/theriseandfallofenron.html, accessed June 5, 2021.

46 Fleming and Zyglidopoulos (2006).

47 Ibid., p. 13.

48 Ibid., p. 15.

49 Madrick, J. (2011), *Age of Greed: The Triumph of Finance and Decline of America, 1970 to the Present* (New York: Alfred Knopf), p. 367.

50 La Capra, Tara L. and Adler, L. (2012), "Many Wall Street executives say wrongdoing is necessary," Reuters, July 10, 2012, http://www.reuters.com/article/2012/07/10/us-wallstreet-survey-idUS BRE86906G20120710, accessed January 10, 2013, cited in Zinkin, J. (2014), *Rebuilding Trust in Banks: The Role of Leadership and Governance* (Singapore: John Wiley and Son).

51 Tenbrunsel, A. and Thomas, J. (2017), *The Street, The Bull and The Crisis: A Survey of the US & UK Financial Services Industry* (New York: Labaton Sucharow LLP), https://www.secwhistleblower advocate.com/pdf/Labaton-2015-Survey-report_12.pdf, accessed December 11, 2021.

52 Ibid., p. 2.

53 Ibid., p. 6.

54 Ibid., p. 5.

55 Ibid., p. 4.

56 Kellerman, B. (2004), *Bad Leadership: What It Is, How It Happens, Why It Matters* (Boston: Harvard Business School Press), pp. 25–27.

57 Persaud. A. and Plender, J. (2007), *Ethics and Finance: Finding a Moral Compass in Business Today* (London: Longtail Publishing, 2007), pp. 5–8.

58 Diamond, R. (2011), "Today business lecture 2011," BBC Radio 4, http://news.bbc.co.uk/today/hi/today/newsid_9630000/9630673.stm, accessed July 23, 2018.

59 Bogle, J. (2003), Speech given to 2003 National Investor Relations Conference, Orlando, Florida, June 11, 2003, *Bogle Financial Center*, https://www.vanguard.com/bogle_site/sp20030611.html, accessed on August 7, 2019 quoted in Zinkin, J. (2020), *The Challenge of Sustainability, Corporate Governance in a Complicated World*, (Berlin/Boston: Walter de Gruyter GmbH), p. 43.

60 Walsh, P. (2017), "Global securities lending hits $2 trillion mark," *Global Custodian,* March 13, 2017, https://www.globalcustodian.com/global-securities-lending-hits-2-trillion-mark/, accessed January 19, 2020.

61 Lazonick, W., and Shin, J-J. (2019), *Predatory Value Extraction*, (Oxford: Oxford University Press), pp. 2–3.

62 Greenwald, D. L. et al. (2019), "How the wealth was won: Factor shares as market fundamentals," NBER *Working Paper* No. 25769, May, 2019 (Cambridge, MA: National Bureau of Economic Research), https://www.nber.org/papers/w25769, accessed January 19, 2020.

Chapter 4
Handling Ethical Dilemmas

In our book *Criminality and Business Strategy: Similarities and Differences* we showed that what defines crimes and criminal behavior depends on who has the power to determine what constitutes a crime and that this changes over time.

Many struggle to accept that changes in circumstances, conditions, and scientific knowledge justify amending laws based in history or religion. Such resistance, and the inevitable lagging of laws behind changing social mores, means that "crimes" can only be defined in a narrow sense. In that sense, we are all criminals – a categorization we usually reject because we consider the levels and kinds of harm that we perceive arise from our conduct.

Establishing an Ethical Baseline

Harms and sanctions are continua and reflect circumstances, context, conditions, and our perception of consequences. Barriers to individual "ethical" behavior also exist on continua. Consequently, ethical and effective decision-making is complex, depending on contexts. There is only a difference of degree between the criminality of governments, non-state actors, organizations, and individuals. Unsurprisingly, individuals often experience stress, confusion, anger, and a sense of powerlessness when making choices that violate their values.

Choosing the best way for leaders to deal with so many factors is more complicated in practice than many recognize. We suggest an approach to decision-making that depends on circumstances and which of people's multiple ethical personas are in play and that recognizes the "moral injury"[i] they suffer as a result. In order to appreciate the extent to which they are susceptible to "moral injury," they need to establish a baseline that represents their beliefs and values. To establish their ethical baseline, they need to establish their personal "Moral Capital" and define their "kaleidoscopic ethical personas."

---

i "Moral injury is understood to be the strong cognitive and emotional response that can occur following events that violate a person's moral or ethical code. Potentially morally injurious events include a person's own or other people's acts of omission or commission, or betrayal by a trusted person in a high-stakes situation . . . morally injurious events threaten one's deeply held beliefs and trust."

Williamson, V. et al. (2021), "Moral injury: The effects on mental health and implications for treatment," *The Lancet,* Volume 8, Issue 6, June 1, 2021, pp. 453–455, https://www.thelancet.com/journals/lanpsy/article/PIIS2215-0366(21)00113-9/fulltext, accessed on July 11, 2021.

https://doi.org/10.1515/9783110780871-004

Establishing Personal "Moral Capital"

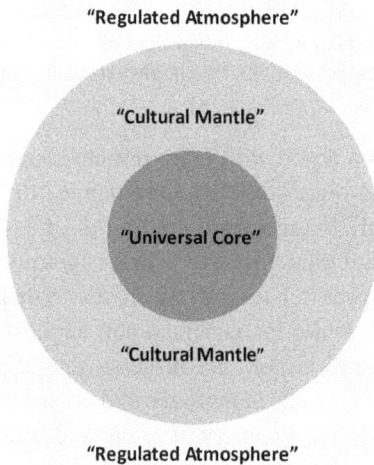

There are three stages to establishing personal "Moral Capital" that is based on values and beliefs. First in childhood people accept uncritically what they are told by parents and families, by educators and religious leaders, and by friends. Next, in adolescence, they challenge some things they have been taught, as part of a process of self-discovery. Finally, in adulthood, they are held accountable for their beliefs and resulting behaviors.

Personal "Moral Capital" can be represented in three circles of beliefs and values, using the planet as an analogy, shown in Figure 4.1.

"Moral Capital"

"Regulated Atmosphere"

"Cultural Mantle"

"Universal Core"

"Cultural Mantle"

"Regulated Atmosphere"

Figure 4.1: Moral Capital and circles of beliefs and values.

Just as Earth's centre is the permanent molten core, the foundation for all that happens to the planet, so humanity has a "Universal Core" of values that are the basis of ethics everywhere. Just as Earth's mantle is made up of shifting tectonic plates that crash and grind into one another, causing earthquakes and continental drift over time, so humanity has a "Cultural Mantle," representing its peoples' diverse histories, cultural beliefs, values, and axioms that can create tension when they come into contact with one another. Finally, just as Earth has a thin and changeable biosphere that provides the necessities of diverse life forms, so humanity has created a "Regulated Atmosphere" that provides for the different conditions required for law and order in different parts of the world. Although the boundaries between the circles is drawn as fixed frontiers, in reality, they are porous, allowing influences from each of the three circles to flow both ways into one another.

It seems to us that there are generally accepted moral laws, regardless of culture, as described by C. S. Lewis.[1] The circle at the center of Figure 4.1 reflects moral laws or the "Universal Core" of beliefs and values that major faiths endorse, summarized in the "Golden Rule." Moral relativists challenge the idea of a "Universal Core" of ethics because they assert that ethical systems are culturally bound and subjective.

Principles that are sometimes questioned or ignored belong in the second circle – the "Cultural Mantle." They are accepted on cultural or contextual grounds in specific contexts. We also need to recognize that some fringe philosophies and religions specifically reject the "Golden Rule" and we would also place their ethical arguments in the second circle, namely the "Cultural Mantle":

> In fact, there are a few traditions that actually *disdain* the Rule. In philosophy, the Nietzschean tradition holds that the virtues implicit in the Golden Rule are antithetical to the true virtues of self-assertion and the will-to-power. Among religions, there are a good many that prefer to emphasize the importance of self, cult, clan or tribe rather than of general others; and a good many other religions for whom large populations are simply excluded from goodwill, being labeled as outsiders, heretics or infidels.[2]

The interaction of cultures creates a world with more possibilities but also creates stresses and strains in polities and organizations. For example, differences in the "Cultural Mantle" have increasingly found expression in the United States, which appears to have broken into four different "tribes"[3] whose superordinate goals and desired destination for America appear to have become increasingly incompatible.

Leaders need to recognize that senior management and employees may belong to different cultures and consequently experience dissonance and disengagement when conflicts arise. Conflicts between goals of ingroups and outgroups are contextually conditional, making it hard to decide which set of values and beliefs has priority.

The outermost circle – the "Regulated Atmosphere" – incorporates legal issues that affect day-to-day lives as a result of regulation, legislation, and changing societal expectations, which individuals may find easier to ignore. Typical examples are rule- or- law- breaking where people pay the fines when caught and repeat the offence (for example, speeding, parking).

Ethics are Situational

Choosing between right and wrong poses little difficulty, if it is an obvious black-and-white choice. The real problem with ethics and personal integrity lies in the so-called gray areas where we are forced to choose between two rights or two wrongs. And how we make these choices is not so obvious because they depend on two different approaches to ethics, which, for simplicity, are classed as "duty-based ethics" and "consequential ethics." They are also affected by our cultural norms, beliefs, and values, and where we are in the organization, which makes ethics situational.

Although the philosophical difficulties created by the two different approaches have already been covered in chapter 2, they are worth repeating. Tables 4.1 and 4.2

Table 4.1: Duty-based and consequential ethics compared.

Duty-based ethics[4]	Consequential ethics[5]
1. Do the right thing because it is the right thing to do.	1. Whether an act is right or wrong depends only on the results of that act.
2. Don't do wrong, because it is wrong.	2. The greater number of good consequences an act produces, the better or more right that act.
3. Doing right has priority over doing good.	
4. If an act is in violation of doing right, it should not be undertaken, regardless of the good it could do.	3. A person should choose the action that maximizes good consequences.
	4. People should maximize good consequences.

Source: Zinkin J., and Bennett, C. (2021), *The Principles and Practice of Effective Leadership* (Walter de Gruyter: Berlin/Boston), p. 300.

Table 4.2: Relative merits of each approach.

Duty-based ethics[6]	Consequential ethics[7]
Advantages	**Advantages**
1. It is a straightforward system with clear, unambiguous commandments.	1. It is flexible.
	2. It takes into account context.
2. It applies in all circumstances regardless of context or outcome.	3. It allows for exceptions to the rule, based on consequences.
3. It is fair because it treats all people the same.	4. It focuses on outcomes and results: the more good outcomes, the better.
4. It is easy to teach.	
5. In principle it is easy to apply.	
6. What should be done is predictable.	
Drawbacks	**Drawbacks**
1. It ignores context and outcomes.	1. It is difficult to apply in practice.
2. How can we justify doing right when it leads to a bad outcome?	2. Every act must be assessed on its merits.
	3. We must understand the consequences correctly before we can make a choice.
3. It can create serious cognitive dissonance as a result.	4. Research required to do this may be costly.
4. It can undermine the very principles it sets out to promote.	5. Time to make decisions may be too long.
	6. May be bad for society as a whole:
	a. Outcomes are unpredictable.
	b. May destroy trust because of biased decision-making.
	c. Who decides how to assess the outcomes?
	d. Outcomes may be regarded as unfair.

Source: Zinkin J., and Bennett, C. (2021), *The Principles and Practice of Effective Leadership* (Walter de Gruyter: Berlin/Boston), p. 301.

compare, in a simplified way, duty-based ethics with consequential ethics as ways of deciding what to do.

Table 4.2 compares the relative merits of each approach.

How people, as individuals, reconcile the potential conflicts between duty-based and consequential ethics depends on the answers to two questions:

1. *Who is affected by the consequences?* A simple example of an ethical dilemma makes the point well – it is a variant of the famous "Trolley Case" first proposed by the British philosopher Philippa Foot in 1967.[8]

Imagine you are standing by the switch on the trolley track and a trolley car comes careering toward you totally out of control. You are in charge of the switch, determining whether the trolley car will go to the left or to the right. You must choose. If the trolley car goes to the left, it will kill one person; if it goes to the right, it will kill five people.

How do you decide what to do? We would guess you calculate the consequent loss of life and choose to send the trolley car to the left, killing only one person, instead of five. However, supposing that one person is a child with a great future ahead of her and the other five people are very old and sick, would that change your mind? What if the person on the left was your husband, your wife, your child, or one of your parents and the other five people were total strangers? Would you still make the same decision on the grounds that only one life would be lost as opposed to five?

All religions teach the equal sanctity of life in the eyes of God, so presumably one versus five should win because it is the right thing to do. Yet, based on our experience of teaching this case, we are willing to bet that you would choose to send the trolley to the right and kill five people if the one person on the left-hand track was a close relative. You would justify this on the grounds that we have a duty to look after family first – and society and the law would accept that argument.

Then there is the famous "Heart Transplant Case."[9] Imagine you are the administrator of a hospital and you are responsible for administering the organ donation program. A billionaire who needs an urgent heart transplant approaches you with the following offer: If you allow her to jump to the head of the line and replace an ordinary office worker (with a wife and two children) who has been waiting for the transplant heart that has just arrived, she will donate enough money to finance 50 dialysis machines and pay for 500 hip operations. You know that if you allow the billionaire to jump the queue, the office worker will die. What do you do and how do you justify your actions? Would it make a difference if the office worker was unmarried and had no children?

Whenever we have discussed this case, most people will not take the deal because they feel it is wrong to cause the death of the office worker and it creates an unfair society where only money matters, in violation of religious teachings that we are all equal in the eyes of God. Yet there is a substantial minority (15 to 25 percent) who will argue in favor of taking the billionaire's offer on the following grounds:

a. Look at the good the deal does: 500 people will have better lives because of the hip operations and thousands can live nearly normal lives because of the dialysis treatment.
b. The billionaire is obviously more valuable to society than the office worker.
c. You cannot be sure that the office worker will in fact die, as maybe another heart will arrive in time.

Perhaps the problem with their argument is that it turns the hospital administrator into a proxy for God. Also, it is not a big step from thinking like this to deciding that some human beings are less worth looking after than others. Once we discriminate between different types of people, it is a slippery slope that can all too easily lead to arguing for eugenics and even genocide. That is precisely the value of duty-based ethics – it allows us to draw a line we should not cross.

What about a relative who has made a living will, clearly indicating that if anything really serious happens she should not be resuscitated but allowed to die with dignity? What do you do when that person for whom you care very much has a serious stroke and the doctors say there is a 50:50 chance of recovery if she is put on life support? Do you listen to the doctors or to the wishes of the patient?

2. *Where are people in the organization*? Ethical dilemmas look different from the top of the organization and from the middle. This is why "tone at the top" must take into account "tone in the middle." The concept of compliance makes perfect sense to people at the top of the organization because it is about protecting the organization from itself to ensure there are no breaches of the law, of the organization's code of conduct. Yet for compliance to work, it is critical that breaches lower down in the organization be escalated upward. While this seems eminently uncontroversial when seen from the top, it may feel quite different lower down.

Escalating breaches of codes of conduct or reporting malpractices in the lower reaches of the organization means making profoundly difficult personal choices that affect real people with whom one has to work every day. This can lead them to being ostracized by their peers and being labeled as troublemakers by their immediate superiors and is often a career-limiting move. Few whistle blowers get promoted or get another job.

We forget at our peril that in every culture the idea of "snitching" is frowned upon. Parents bring their children up not to tell tales. The best case made against snitching is Lieutenant Colonel Frank Slade's impassioned defense (brilliantly enacted by Al Pacino) of Charlie in the 1992 film *Scent of a Woman*.[10] Yet we expect people to be comfortable with the idea of escalating misdemeanors and in effect snitching on the people they work with every day to protect abstract concepts like the ethical reputation of the organization that seem to be only of interest to the top management, every now and again.

We should not really be surprised that failures of compliance are so frequent when everybody at lower levels knows what is going on. It makes it all the more important that senior management follows Ronald Reagan's adoption of a Russian saying: "Trust, but verify."[11]

Determining "Kaleidoscopic Ethical Personas"

The ancient Greeks had an instruction, "Know thyself," inscribed over the entrance to the Temple of Apollo at Delphi. Not knowing what drives them, what their purpose in life is, what they believe in, and what their values are can be a source of stress, unhappiness, depression, even suicide. People have more than one ethical self. They have a kaleidoscope of ethical selves, depending on the circumstances in which they find themselves and the choices they have to make in those circumstances. Each choice can be prepared for by developing scenarios for challenges to their "Universal Core," "Cultural Mantle," and "Regulated Atmosphere" beliefs and values.

Dealing with the State

If people are faced with a situation created by the state where they have to choose between fundamental "Universal Core" beliefs and values and doing what they are commanded to do, they are likely to refuse, even if it means losing their lives, freedom, careers, or jobs. In extremis, if they do not wish to die, they can emigrate or become refugees (as demonstrated by Afghans who fled after the Taliban entered Kabul in 2021[12]).

Even though the "Cultural Mantle" reflects the relative moral nature of many of the most salient ethical choices, they can feel as agonizing as choices people make to defend "Universal Core" beliefs. The reason is that the differences in the "Cultural Mantle" relate to identities, to emotional definitions of who they are. They may be based on culture, gender, ethnicity, class, religion, education, or language. Violations of "Cultural Mantle" beliefs lead to similar levels of pain. As a result, they can feel more existential than challenges to "Universal Core" beliefs, and lead to strong reactions where people become willing to die for that which differentiates them.

The "Regulated Atmosphere" presents the least emotionally challenging environment that is brought to bear on people. After all, the "Regulated Atmosphere" is the manifestation of the laws, regulations, taxation, licensing systems, and enforcement. Whether to obey or to stand against what is required of them is a matter of legality as opposed to morality, or identity. The choices are transactional and economic. The choices they make are likely to be determined by weighing the convenience and economic benefits of disobeying against the penalties for being caught and being punished.

Whenever people find themselves resisting the state's demands, they need to remember that punishments can range from taking their lives, to taking away freedoms, to destroying livelihoods, or merely to making lives inconvenient and economically less attractive, depending on the nature of the conflict and on how existential the state deems it to be.

Dealing with Employees

Dealing with employees creates many of the same challenges to beliefs and values as dealing with the state. Employers have superordinate goals captured in their mission, vision, and values. Before joining any organization, it is prudent for employees to research its purpose, values, and practices.

The only difference between legitimate organizations and organized crime is that legitimate businesses are usually constrained by the legal and regulatory frameworks within which they operate, whereas organized crime chooses to operate outside the law and may require people sometimes to violate "Universal Core" beliefs and values, whereas legitimate businesses are unlikely to ask people to do things that represent a challenge to "Universal Core" values and beliefs.

What is more likely is that organizations ask people to do things that violate "Cultural Mantle" beliefs and values, leaving them to choose whether the violation to their sense of identity is existential, in which case refusal or resignation is the only course of action, or whether the negative consequences of refusal matter more than the "moral injury" caused by acquiescing. As for requests that violate "Regulated Atmosphere" beliefs and values, these are most likely to manifest in terms of violations of employers' codes of conduct, and so the "moral injury" is likely to be slight, making calculations ones that combine whether "Cultural Mantle" beliefs and values are in some way involved and evaluating the material cost–benefits of acquiescing, if not.

A couple of examples help illustrate the types of challenges employees can face that combine "Cultural Mantle" and "Regulated Atmosphere" issues when at work. We all face the challenge of finding the right work–life balance and it is not just a question of balancing protecting our mental health with maximizing our productivity. The Covid-19 pandemic has forced people, who can, to work from home and has further fueled the debate.

Chapter 2 explored four examples of dilemmas created by the Confucian values of *xin* (trust), *ren* (benevolence), *xiao* (filial conduct/piety), and *zhong* (loyalty). These illustrated once again the difficulties people may face as a result of different perspectives caused by "Cultural Mantle" values. As another example, take the case of a global professional services firm whose values were established in London and New York and where the client's needs always came first. The English partner in this case had an urgent request from a client requiring his high-performing Chinese senior associate to put in urgent extra work. The associate's grandmother was in hospital and when asked to do the work she declined. Upon being pressed by the partner, the associate offered her resignation rather than not spending time at the hospital with her grandmother, because filial piety demanded she should do so; her justification being that she had only one grandmother and she could always find another employer. Recognizing that this conflict reflected a profound difference in "Cultural Mantle" values between how Europeans and Americans would react in the same circumstances, the partner allowed her to see her grandmother and found another person to do the work – confronted, as he put it, with the reality that for the Chinese, "filial piety trumps everything."

Requests that violate the "Regulated Atmosphere" are most likely to manifest in terms of violations of employers' codes of conduct, and the "moral injury" is likely to be slight.

Dealing with Peers

Peer group pressure often places us in situations where we find ourselves doing things that make us feel uncomfortable, but our need to belong to a particular group leads us to override any ethical discomfort. This may lead to conflicts with our "Cultural Mantle" beliefs as well as our "Regulated Atmosphere" beliefs, such as drinking too much because getting drunk in certain cultures is a way of building rapport and trust between business associates, for example in China,[13] Japan,[14] or Korea,[15] and in certain occupational cultures. "Hazing" or bullying by the military of new recruits[16] or by university fraternities[17] and sororities[18] are other common examples:

> Those who undergo hazing often view the event as a demonstration of their high tolerance for psychological and physical pain . . .

> Hazing's original goal was to humiliate new members of organizations as a means of testing their devotion and helping them bond through a shared experience. But hazing changed at the turn of the century, when violence emerged as a central part of initiation.[19]

Kaleidoscopic Ethical Personas

The ethical challenges people face inform the choices they make and are the result of a range of different conditions, contexts, needs, and relationships. The choices they make reflect life experiences and lessons learned. They also depend on individuals' unique combinations of "nature versus nurture." In a sense every ethical choice is unique and depends on the context. Ethical choices accumulating, over time, determine who people are – they are their "Moral Capital."

We can use the kaleidoscope[ii] as a metaphor of how people make ethical choices: the coloured pieces of glass that tumble when the box is tapped or rotated, within which the pieces of glass always fall in a grouping that is never the same. The number of beautiful combinations and patterns are unlimited but mathematically related and grouped.

The coloured pieces of glass represent the unique choices people make as a result of calculations of the costs and benefits of each choice, justified by past experiences and reactions to prevailing conditions through their lives. The box represents them as individuals as they move through life from infancy to death, and the taps or rotations represent the incidents through life that forced them to make choices.

People can classify ethical choices as affecting their "Universal Core," "Cultural Mantle," or "Regulated Atmosphere." They can develop scenarios for dealing with conflicts depending on which beliefs and values are threatened. However, every ethical challenge is unique and reflects the conditions and context. Costs and benefits also reflect unique circumstances, and consequently every decision is unique, even though it belongs to a given category.

Confronting Ethical Dilemmas

Leaders at all levels in the organization, in their roles as superiors and subordinates, need help to make informed choices that they will not live to regret when confronted by ethical dilemmas created by the state and at work. A consequence of having kaleidoscopic ethical personas is that they may find themselves in many different areas of conflict.

We suggest that when confronting the ethical dilemmas leaders face at work, it helps people to 1) determine the potential areas of conflict beforehand; 2) determine the potential costs of any conflicts; 3) make appropriate decisions as a result; 4) apply a six-step ethical framework to ensure decisions are both effective and ethical; 5) assess the level of "moral injury" suffered as a result of the outcomes of their actions; and 6) re-assess their resulting levels of "Moral Capital" to see if they increased or diminished and how they feel as a result.

---

ii "A simple kaleidoscope consists of two thin, wedge-shaped mirror strips touching along a common edge or of a single sheet of bright aluminum bent to an angle of 60° or 45°. The mirrors are enclosed in a tube with a viewing eyehole at one end. At the other end is a thin, flat box that can be rotated; it is made from two glass disks, the outer one ground to act as a diffusing screen. In this box are pieces of coloured glass, tinsel, or beads. When the box is turned or tapped, the objects inside tumble into an arbitrary grouping, and when the diffusing screen is illuminated, the sixfold or eightfold multiplication creates a striking symmetrical pattern. The number of combinations and patterns is effectively without limit."

Editors of Encyclopaedia (2016), "Kaleidoscope," *Encyclopedia Britannica*, February 25, https://www.britannica.com/technology/kaleidoscope, accessed 29 July 2021.

Determining Areas of Conflict

There are numerous areas where superiors can experience conflict with subordinates, and as subordinates themselves with their superiors. They may relate to their purpose, mission, and vision and the priority they place on shareholder value maximization versus other stakeholder priorities; they may reflect the culture of the organization and the demands made by the organization on work–life balance; or they may reflect the organization's philosophy and treatment of employees in practice. These may or may not be ethical disagreements.

Should employees find upon joining the organization or at any stage in their careers that their individual purpose and values, defined by their own "Cultural Mantle" of beliefs and values, cannot align with those of the organization, and having calculated that they can live with the consequences of continuing refusal (loss of career advancement or being asked to leave), their personal values and purpose should have priority over doing what their employers require them to do that would violate their values and they should look for a job elsewhere.

Ethical superiors will understand this and empathize, even supporting conflicted subordinates by helping them find more suitable roles or employment elsewhere because if the reason for staying is only the money, John Ruskin, the Victorian social and art critic, had this to say:

> You cannot serve two masters; – you *must* serve one or other. If your work is first with you, and your fee second, work is your master, and the lord of work, who is God. But if your fee is first with you, and your work second, fee is your master, and the lord of fee, who is the Devil . . . Work first – you are God's servants; Fee first – you are the Fiend's.[20]

The reason why Ruskin is correct in his thinking is that there are likely to be two consequences. The first is that employees will not be able to "be their best" in performance terms, damaging their careers as a result, as the poet Khalil Gibran wrote:

> Work is love made visible.
>
> And if you cannot work with love but only with distaste, it is better that you should leave your work and sit at the gate of the temple and take alms of those who work with joy.
>
> For if you bake bread with indifference, you bake a bitter bread that feeds but half man's hunger.
>
> And if you grudge the crushing of the grapes, your grudge distils a poison in the wine.
>
> And if you sing though as angels, and love not the singing, you muffle man's ears to the voices of the day and the voices of the night.[21]

The second consequence, in part a reflection of the first, is that remaining in such an environment may ultimately lead to serious "moral injury" with resulting stress, unhappiness, ill-health, depression, and, in extremis, suicide.

People can avoid such misalignment by choosing organizations that do not believe that the sole purpose of business is to maximize shareholder value and find ones that believe and practice a purpose that is:

> To serve society's demands and the common good and to be rewarded for doing so.[22]

Professor Richard Shell of Wharton suggests that a good way to face ethical dilemmas for people as individuals is for them to be "people of conscience", and that this includes small, everyday challenges like honesty in recording expenses, using company assets for private purposes, and flagging major scandals:

> I deliberately chose that term, as opposed to the more alarming 'whistleblower' or anything that suggests that you have to be a moral hero or throw yourself over a cliff," he said. "To be a person of conscience – to bring your conscience to work, to bring your values to work and make a commitment to acting on them – is an essential leadership skill.[23]

He emphasizes the importance of "owning the conflict," even for small issues. We agree that this is critical because it combines peoples' need to take stock of their initial "Moral Capital," to articulate consciously what their "Universal Core," "Cultural Mantle," and "Regulated Atmosphere" beliefs and values are, with an ability to assess what is needed, defined by whichever of their kaleidoscope of ethical personas is involved in the immediate dilemma confronting them.

"Owning the conflict" and the approach provides a method for resolving dilemmas rather than getting outraged, depressed, or giving in to the temptation to ignore the problem. And it is the temptation to ignore the problem that does the "moral injury" that can be a significant cost because of the toll it takes on wellbeing and ability to do great work:

> A worker sees a systemic problem . . . and rationalizes inaction: Everybody does it. It's a little thing. Nobody will care. Don't make trouble.

> "Of course, it's when you don't make trouble for yourself that you've just denied your values. And whether you know it or not, you've left a little scar [indicating] that your values aren't worth speaking up for. . . . The next time it happens, that rationalization you listened to the first time becomes easier to follow. Then it gets harder and harder and harder to draw the line where action is required". . . . People of conscience bring their ethical standards to the office every morning, he said, so they can look themselves in the mirror at night. In addition, putting up with a toxic work culture inevitably takes its toll on wellbeing, as anxiety and fear replace the positive motivations that lead to great work.[24]

The obvious costs of standing up for values affect the ability to survive economically. Can people afford to lose their jobs? Can they find alternative employment that pays well enough to feed and house them and their dependents? If they cannot, can they plan an exit strategy and find alternative employment? The psychological costs of job loss can be considerable as often self-image and the respect others have for people depends on their jobs as much as, if not more than, on who they are.

Making Decisions

Making Individual decisions that are both ethical *and* effective requires leaders to consider six steps in a cycle,[iii] shown in Figure 4.2:

1. Leaders must establish their own opening balance in their "Moral Capital" account, as it were - ethical foundations or *Virtue*, which reflect their beliefs, values, and purpose. Once done, they should move to step 2.

2. The second step is to determine the *effectiveness* of proposed actions in achieving their purpose, namely whether the "ends justify the means." Only once they have verified that the proposed actions will deliver the desired ends should they move to step 3.

3. The third step is to make sure that actions are acceptably *mutual*, that they represent an equally fair burden on all affected. Only once they are sure their intended actions are generally acceptable should they move to step 4. It is most unlikely that unanimous consent can be obtained but significant dissent should be avoided. If significant dissent is likely, then they should think again.

4. The fourth step is to ensure they pass the *predictability* test and that they know what is expected of them in various circumstances. Without this step, implementing decisions will be ad hoc, often contradictory, and create confusion. Only once they have checked that they do not conflict with existing policies and procedures should they move to step 5.

5. A critical part of evaluation is to determine whether it delivers the maximum benefit for the maximum number of people affected by it – its *utility*. Once they have a reasonable belief that what they are proposing will deliver the greatest good for the greatest number, they should move to step 6.

6. Finally, they must decide whether they are personally comfortable with what they are proposing or what they are agreeing to, based on *self-image ethics*, considering the impact of their decisions on their "Universal Core," "Cultural Mantle," and "Regulatory Atmosphere" beliefs and values and whether the closing balance in their "Moral Capital" account has increased or diminished.

If at any step in the cycle there is an obstacle to moving to the next step, it is a red flag, a warning that the decision might be unethical, ineffective, or both. If such a red flag is detected, leaders must re-examine their assumptions, reasoning, and whether the risks are worthwhile.

[iii] The following discussion is taken from Zinkin J. and Bennett. C. (2021), *The Principles and Practice of Effective Leadership* (Walter de Gruyter: Berlin/Boston), pp. 311–318.

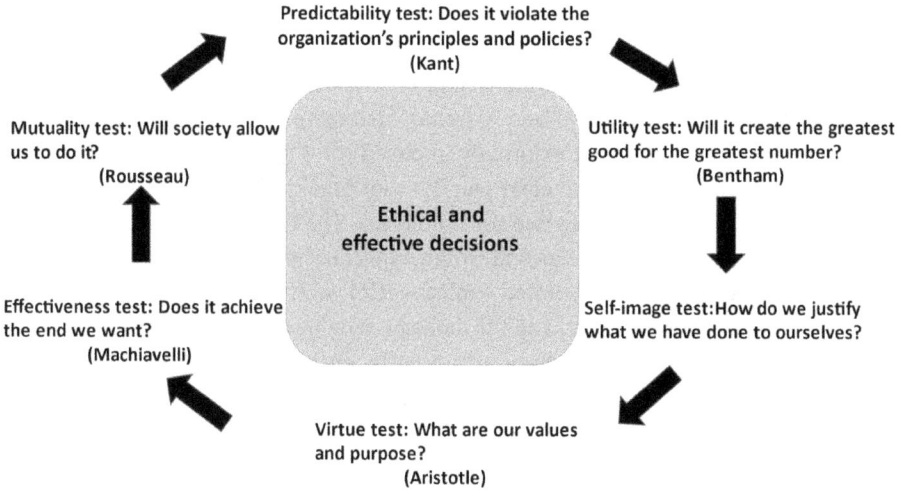

Figure 4.2: Six-step decision-making cycle.
Source: Zinkin, J. and Bennett, C. (2021), *The Principles and Practice of Effective Leadership*, (Walter de Gruyter: Berlin/Boston), p. 311.

Applying the Six-Step Ethical Framework

It is often said that business ethics are an oxymoron. We do not agree. We believe that the six-step ethical framework can be applied to business by combining the Self-image and Virtue tests into one test, using the "Five P" framework (discussed in Chapter 5) as a guide to ensure that business decisions are both ethical and successful, as follows:

Purpose

Choosing the mission and vision for any organization is both an ethical and commercial decision. Ethics are involved in deciding what kind of business the organization should do and in deciding what products or services are going to be offered. In making such decisions, leaders must consider the benefits they are proposing – answering the question, "What difference will they make in the lives of our customers?" The ethical answer to this question includes:

1. *Effectiveness test:* Will the products do what they are supposed to do and allow the organization to make a satisfactory return – the ends (creating and maintaining satisfied customers) must at least justify the means (allocating resources needed to do so).

2. *Predictability test:* When marketing products, organizations should provide clarity, predictability, and consistency of performance as part of branding. In addition, people in organizations need to know what they can and cannot do in their dealings with internal and external customers. This is the point of codes of conduct to complement externally imposed rules and regulations, with guidance on how to comply and clear penalties for breaking them.

3. *Mutuality test:* This includes two separate ideas. The first is based on the "Golden Rule" treating other people as you would expect to be treated. The second builds on this, dealing with implicit and explicit social contracts covering environment, safety, health, and equality, and the damage done by externalities to the environment (pollution, waste, congestion) caused by either legal but harmful behavior (such as the tobacco or junk food business) or illegal behavior, regarded as "the cost of doing business."

4. *Utility test:* At its simplest, this is stakeholder satisfaction. However, it becomes more complicated if satisfying stakeholders has unintended knock-on effects that harm other people. For example, there seems to be no issue with satisfying customers who want to eat junk food and confectionery or drink sugary drinks and alcohol or smoke. Surely, if they wish to harm themselves after having been advised of the risks that is their business? Yet, people who get diabetes or cancer put a burden on public health systems and increase the taxes for everybody.

5. *Virtue and Self-image tests:* This explains why some people do not wish to work for companies whose products are harmful, yet legal. They do not want to be associated with the products they offer, or the way they do business. Others have no qualms, as long as the business is legal. How people see themselves depends on their virtue ethics and whether there is internal conflict between the organization's purpose and values and their own (the Virtue test). People who ignore such conflicts risk losing their self-respect and the respect that other people have for them, thereby diminishing their "Moral Capital."

Principles

These define what business the organization is willing to do, with whom, and how. They need to pass the:

1. *Effectiveness test:* Here the question raised by the application of principles is what the impact will be on the viability of the business of sticking to declared principles. If sticking to principles means that it is impossible to do business (for example, because of corruption in a particular jurisdiction), some organizations violate their principles and justify their actions based on the impact on the bottom line. Others make the tougher decision to not get involved in such markets. What is clear is that declaring one thing, but doing another, leads to a breakdown of trust between the organization and its customers and between

the organization and its members. This applies with even greater force when people who violate the declared principles are excused either because of their seniority or because of their importance to the bottom line. In declaring principles of behavior by which the organization will be judged, it is essential that all are held to them, lest they become ineffective.

2. *Predictability test:* Principles pass the predictability test if they are spelled out clearly in codes of conduct and the consequences of failure to abide by them are understood by all. If there are many waivers or exceptions to the rules, they become discredited and a source of cynical disengagement. However, we should avoid "a foolish consistency" that "is the hobgoblin of little minds, adored by little statesmen and philosophers and divines"[25] and recognize that when circumstances change, appropriate solutions change as well.

3. *Mutuality test:* Society depends on businesses obeying the law and regulations designed to protect vested interests in the name of the common good as a minimum. Most organizations declare that they will obey the law and many go beyond that in their declarations of corporate responsibility. Some choose to break the law and pay the fines on the grounds that this is "the cost of doing business." While this may make sense for the individual organization, the costs to society of "free riding" are great.

4. *Utility test:* When deciding which principles to adopt and adhere to, leaders must recognize that sticking to principles incurs a cost, otherwise they would not be principles. This may mean that sticking to the principles makes it impossible to do certain kinds of business or to do business with certain types of regimes or customer. If that is the case, the consequent loss of business must be recognized explicitly and people should not be penalized for losing the business because they adhered to their principles. Equally, if espoused principles are undermined by exceptions being made because certain individuals are senior or too important for the bottom line, the principles cease to have value. Clearly articulated principles help build an organizational personality that allows suppliers, employees, customers, and regulators to know what behavior to expect.

5. *Virtue and Self-image tests:* If there is a serious divergence between the espoused values and purpose of the organization and those of individuals working within it, they will be disaffected and disengaged, reflecting the impact of the divergence on their personal values and purpose (the Virtue test), and thus how they feel about themselves.

Power

Power is a function of organizational design. It includes structural relationships between business units, divisions, departments, and teams; and reporting relationships within them. Their validity and duration depend on their ability to pass certain tests:

1. *Effectiveness test:* Once strategic objectives and priorities change, organizational designs must reflect the changed context to avoid misallocation of resources, putting people's futures at risk.
2. *Predictability test:* Organization designs change over time. The resulting impact on people in terms of remuneration, job scope, career, and reporting relationships should be understandable and transparent.
3. *Mutuality test:* This is particularly important when it comes to appraisals and development plans for individuals. Processes should be fair, transparent, and objective. Evaluations should reflect results achieved and how they were achieved including cross-departmental collaboration. It also matters when it comes to bullying, sexual harassment, and discrimination of all kinds, as these behaviors are the result of the power structure violating the "Golden Rule."
4. *Utility test:* Engaged employees lead to higher levels of productivity and innovation. Reporting relationships that treat subordinates with respect, allowing people to speak truth to power, help organizations avoid mistakes in execution, maximizing bottom-up, top-down flows of information. Some organizations choose to operate top-down, need-to-know styles of management; others choose to grant autonomy to employees, treating them as intelligent contributors, capable of solving problems on their own. Such organizations may be more adaptable and have lower levels of employee turnover, depending on operating context.
5. *Virtue and Self-image tests:* Here it is a case of whether employees are satisfied with their working conditions and their ability to contribute. It will reflect not just their working conditions but also the impact on their personal values and purpose (the Virtue test). The test is are they good ambassadors for their organizations?

People

Every organization consists of people. It must have the right number of people to meet current and future organizational design needs, with the right skills, attitude, and character. Such people should be able to feel comfortable with the mission, vision, and values of the organization, committing to achieving its goals. To do this, they must pass certain tests:

1. *Effectiveness test:* On all central key performance indicators (KPIs), they should perform on average at least up to benchmarked expectations regarding turnover,

gross margin, value added, and profit per capita; achieve high employee engagement measures; and have lower than industry/sector levels of attrition.

2. *Predictability test:* They are chosen and promoted on merit, not discriminated against on grounds of gender, race, or religion, and evaluated regularly based on objective assessments of their performance and how they have achieved their results in line with the agreed principles of the organization.
3. *Mutuality test:* People understand where they fit in the organization and have a clear "line of sight" between the organization's superordinate goals and their individual role and responsibilities in achieving them. They recognize how their career and personal development plans are built, regarding the process as equitable.
4. *Utility test:* As long as they perform according to the values of the organization and meet their targets, the system is the best for them as individuals and the organization.
5. *Virtue and Self-image tests:* They feel proud to be part of their work group and feel that they are respected by their friends and family as a result of working for the organization. The feeling of pride and belonging reflects the level to which their personal values and purpose (the Virtue test) are in harmony with those of the organization.

Processes

These ensure alignment with mission and vision. They include all feedback mechanisms, formal and informal, and should provide full, relevant, timely, accurate, and actionable information. They must pass certain tests:

1. *Effectiveness test:* All processes, including financial reports, management information, appraisal, reward and remuneration systems must be justified.
2. *Predictability test:* All processes and procedures, including standard operating procedures (SOPs) and service level agreements (SLAs), should be evaluated in terms of their ability to eliminate surprises and manage expectations of accurate and on-time, on-cost delivery. It is important that they allow timely progress tracking to allow timely corrective action to get back to plan.
3. *Mutuality test:* Every activity and department must have proper procedures and processes.
4. *Utility test:* This does not apply.
5. *Self-image test:* This does not apply.

Without the power to make things happen, there is little point in advocating change. We believe strongly that people can and should be *both* ethical *and* effective.

The ethical elements of decision-making are determined by the purpose and goals of decision-makers and their treatment of others on the journey to achieving desired objectives. We recognize:

> Making ethical decisions is easy when the facts are clear and the choices black and white. But it is a different story when the situation is clouded by ambiguity, incomplete information, multiple points of view, and conflicting responsibilities. In such situations which [people] experience all the time – *ethical decisions depend on both the decision-making process itself and on the experience, intelligence, and integrity of the decision-maker.*[26]   [Emphasis ours]

Responsible moral judgment cannot be transferred to decision-makers ready-made. Developing an ethical approach in business turns out to be partly an administrative process involving recognition of a decision's ethical implications; discussion to expose different points of view; and testing the decision's adequacy in balancing self-interest and consideration of others, its impact on future policy, and its consonance with the organization's traditional values.

Assessing Resulting "Moral Injury"

The best way is for people to check if they are comfortable with a decision and its likely results is to ask themselves if they would be able to sleep at night after making it; using the "newspaper headline test" or "newspaper test" to imagine how they and other people would feel about what happened when they read about the decision in the newspapers; and better yet to imagine how they would explain/justify what they had done to their eight-year-old child.

Reassessing "Moral Capital"

The state of individuals' "Moral Capital" account is best determined by using virtue ethics tests as the yardstick on a regular basis to assess whether the decisions they have made have increased or diminished the level of "Moral Capital" in their personal "Moral Capital" account:

> Virtue ethics places a strong emphasis on the pursuit of excellence in business. According to the virtue ethics tradition, *life is not fundamentally about achieving fame, power, wealth, or pleasure. It's about living happy, fulfilled lives in which we make the most of our talents and abilities. It follows from this that each of us has "an obligation to be the best that we personally can be at each and every thing that we do, across a broad range of interests and activities, given the legitimate constraints of our most basic natural endowments, the opportunities we've developed, and the other commitments it is equally good to have."*[27] This "ethical obligation of excellence"[28] applies to business as well as other spheres of human endeavor.

Finally, the most distinctive feature of virtue ethics is its focus on character and virtue. *Virtues are good habits – habits that perfect our powers of action and help us achieve our goal of leading happy, successful lives of overall excellence.*[29] According to virtue ethicists, no humanly successful life is possible without good character. *Having a good character means having virtues such as honesty, integrity, courage, generosity, caring, compassion, and self-discipline.* Among the most important virtues in business are traits such as *justice, fairness, honesty, trustworthiness, cooperativeness, helpfulness, loyalty, integrity, reasonableness, resourcefulness, toughness, diligence, persistence, sensitivity, dependability, civility, congeniality, cheerfulness and decency.*[30]

[Emphases ours]

If, as a result of their regular reassessment of their "Moral Capital" account, they find that they have fulfilled their *"ethical obligation of excellence,"* and if they find that they have exhibited the virtues and traits described above in their daily business dealings, then they should continue to do what they are doing. However, should they find that their choices and decisions have violated their values, and led them to failing to exhibit the virtues and traits described above, then they have to recognize they have not satisfied their *"ethical obligation of excellence"* and have diminished their "Moral Capital" account as a result.

Summary

Ethical and effective decision-making is complex. Unsurprisingly, individuals often experience stress, confusion, anger, and a sense of powerlessness when making choices that violate their values. In order to appreciate the extent to which they are susceptible to "moral injury," individuals need to establish a baseline that represents their beliefs and values. To establish their ethical baseline, they need to establish personal "Moral Capital" and define their "kaleidoscopic ethical personas."

There are three stages in life to establishing personal "Moral Capital": childhood, adolescence, and adulthood. Personal "Moral Capital" is based on three concentric circles (rings) of beliefs and values. At the center there is a "Universal Core" of values and beliefs that are shared by all of humanity. Next comes the "Cultural Mantle" representing humanity's diverse histories, cultural beliefs, values, and axioms that can create tension when they come into contact with one another. The outermost circle, the "Regulated Atmosphere," deals with the different regulatory and legal regimes in different parts of the world. The boundaries between the three circles are porous, allowing them to influence one another. The resulting interaction of cultures can create stresses and strains in polities and organizations.

Ethical decisions are situational because choosing between two rights or two wrongs – the so-called "gray areas" – pose real problems of ethics and integrity. Moreover, such choices depend on two different approaches to ethics, "duty-based ethics" and "consequential ethics." Each approach has its own advantages and drawbacks. They are also affected by cultural norms, beliefs, and values, and where people are in organizations, which makes ethical decisions situational. Reconciling the conflicts created by these approaches depends on the answers to two questions: who is affected by the consequences of any potential ethical dilemma, and where in organizations are those people, as the consequences can affect them differently as a result.

To make matters more complicated, people have "kaleidoscopic ethical personas" and how these manifest, depends on context. As leaders, are they dealing with ethical dilemmas created for them by the state, by their employees, or by their peers? Every ethical challenge they face reflects prevailing conditions and context and is unique, even though it belongs in a given category.

Every decision that comes in shades of gray requires confronting the resulting ethical dilemmas. When confronting the ethical dilemmas people face at work, it helps if they 1) determine the potential areas of conflict beforehand; 2) determine the potential costs of such conflicts; 3) make appropriate decisions as a result; 4) apply a six-step ethical framework to ensure their decisions are both effective and ethical, checking their impact on "Purpose," "Principles," "Power," "People," and "Processes"; 5) assess the level of "moral injury" suffered as a result of the outcomes of their actions; and 6) re-assess their resulting levels of "Moral Capital" and how they feel about themselves as a result.

References

1 C. S. Lewis (1941), "The reality of the moral law" (BBC Talk 2, *Mere Christianity*, Chapter 2), August 13, 1941, YouTube, https://www.youtube.com/watch?v=LqsAzlFS91A&list=PL9boiLqIabFhr qabptq3ThGdwNanr65xU, accessed December 26, 2020.
2 Anderson, S. L. (2009), "The Golden Rule: Not so golden anymore," *Philosophy Now*, https://phil osophynow.org/issues/74/The_Golden_Rule_Not_So_Golden_Anymore, accessed July 16, 2021.
3 Packer, G. (2021), "How America fractured into four parts," *The Atlantic*, July/August 2021 Issue, https://www.theatlantic.com/magazine/archive/2021/07/george-packer-four-americas/619012/, accessed July 12, 2021.
4 "Duty-based ethics," www.bbc.co.uk/ethics/introduction/duty_1.shtml, accessed December 27, 2012.
5 "Consequentialism," www.bbc.co.uk/ethics/introduction/consequentialism_1.shtml, accessed December 27, 2012.
6 "Duty-based ethics," www.bbc.co.uk/ethics/introduction/duty_1.shtml, accessed December 27, 2012.
7 "Consequentialism," www.bbc.co.uk/ethics/introduction/consequentialism_1.shtml, accessed December 27, 2012.
8 Costa, M. J. (1986), "The Trolley Problem revisited," *The Southern Journal of Philosophy*, Volume 24, Issue 4, 1986, pp. 437–449, https://philpapers.org/rec/COSTTP-2, accessed January 17, 2022.
9 Ibid.
10 *Scent of a Woman* (1992), Colonel Frank Slade Talking in Charlie Simm's Defense, Part 2, www.dailymotion.com/video/xrfqyj_frank-talking-in-charlie-s-defence-part-2-from-scent-of-a-woman-1992_shortfilms#.UNv5OeTqn48, accessed December 27, 2012.

11 Swaim, B. (2016), "'Trust but Verify': An untrustworthy political phrase" *The Washington Post,* March 11, 2016, https://www.washingtonpost.com/opinions/trust-but-verify-an-untrustworthy-polit ical-phrase/2016/03/11/da32fb08-db3b-11e5-891a-4ed04f4213e8_story.html, accessed on May 14, 2022

12 Baloch, S. M. (2021), "'Everyone is afraid': Afghans fleeing Taliban push for exit into Pakistan," *The Guardian,* August 27, 2021, https://www.theguardian.com/world/2021/aug/27/everyone-is-afraid-afghans-fleeing-taliban-push-for-exit-into-pakistan, accessed February 5, 2022.

13 Yoon, R. (2017), "Chinese 酒 – Alcohol in China," *ImmerQi,* 2021, https://immerqi.com/blog/chi nese-jiu-alcohol-china/, accessed July 25, 2021, https://immerqi.com/blog/chinese-jiu-alcohol-china/, accessed July 25, 2021.

14 Larsen, B. (2019), "Japan's toxic drinking culture no one talks about," GaijinPot Blog, Septem ber 27, 2019, https://blog.gaijinpot.com/japans-toxic-drinking-culture-no-one-talks-about/, ac cessed July 25, 2021.

15 Chao, S. and Gooch, L. (2016), "The country with the world's worst drink problem," Aljazeera, February 7, 2016, https://www.aljazeera.com/features/2016/2/7/the-country-with-the-worlds-worst-drink-problem, accessed July 25, 2021.

16 Miley, J. (2020), "Traditional hazing crosses line to sexual assault," US Army, December 22, 2020 https://www.army.mil/article/242011/traditional_hazing_crosses_line_to_sexual_assault, accessed July 25, 2021.

17 Reilly, K. (2017), "College students keep dying because of fraternity hazing. Why is it so hard to stop?", *Time,* October 11, 2017, https://time.com/4976836/fraternity-hazing-deaths-reform-tim-pi azza/, accessed July 25, 2021.

18 Breslaw, A. (2013), "The 13 most nightmarish stories of sorority hazing," *Cosmopolitan,* Septem ber 17, 2013, https://www.cosmopolitan.com/lifestyle/advice/g3457/sorority-hazing/, accessed July 25, 2021.

19 Freeman, V. (2021), "College hazing: What it is and how to stop it," *Best Colleges,* March 22, 2021, https://www.bestcolleges.com/blog/college-hazing/, accessed July 25, 2021.

20 Ruskin, J. (1866), "Essay on work," in *The Crown of Wild Olive* (London: Smith & Elder), pp. 31–32.

21 Khalil Gibran, *The Prophet* (1923), excerpt "On Work," www.katsandogz.com/onwork.html, accessed December 21, 2012, quoted in Zinkin, J. (2014), *Rebuilding Trust in Banks: The Role of Lead ership and Governance* (Singapore: John Wiley & Sons), pp. 58–59.

22 Solomon, R. C. (1992), *Ethics and Excellence: Cooperation and Integrity in Business* (New York: Oxford University Press), p. 110, quoted in Marchese, M., Bassham, G., and Ryan, J. (2002), "Work-family conflict: A virtue ethics analysis," *Journal of Business Ethics,* Volume 40, Issue 2, Special Issue on Work Ethics, October, p. 149.

23 Shell, G. R. (2021), "How to Bring Your Conscience to Work", *Knowledge at Wharton,* June 8, 2021, https://knowledge.wharton.upenn.edu/article/how-to-bring-your-conscience-to-work/, ac cessed on September 2, 2022.

24 Ibid.

25 Rosenzweig, P. (2013), Emerson, R. W. quoted in "A foolish consistency is the hobgoblin of little minds – the metadata stay," *Lawfare,* December 18, 2013, https://www.lawfareblog.com/foolish-consistency-hobgoblin-little-minds-metadata-stay, accessed July 23, 2021.

26 Andrews, K. R. (2003), "Ethics in practice," in *Harvard Business Review on Corporate Ethics,* 2003, (Boston, MA: Harvard Business School Publishing Corporation), p. 71.

27 Morris, T. (1994), *True Success: A New Philosophy of Excellence* (New York: Berkley Books), p. 225, quoted in Marchese, Bassham and Ryan, "Work-family conflict," p. 149.

28 Morris, T. (1997), *If Aristotle Ran General Motors: The New Soul of Business* (New York: Henry Holt & Company), p. 225, cited in ibid.

29 Ibid.

30 Morris, (1997), quoted in Marchese, Bassham, and Ryan, "Work-family conflict," p. 149.

Chapter 5
Building an Ethical Organization

Chapter 1 explained the legal concept that corporations have no conscience and that its ethical obligations are beyond legal purview. This may be why there is little recognition of the importance of ethics in business schools.

> In 2010, in *the Citizens United v. Federal Election Commission* case, the [US] Supreme Court granted corporations legal protections previously reserved for people. Since then, it's been hard to resist a natural question: If corporations are people, what *kind* of people are they? One answer, bleak but justifiable, is that they're psychopaths, devoted entirely to maximizing profits at the cost of everyone else, including their employees.[1]

It is the legal basis on which corporations are established and it is clear that they are not moral agents.[2] This has encouraged business academics to depersonalize business and finance and lump all companies and sources of capital together as economic abstractions of which *the market* is the biggest and most impersonal. And yet, those running modern corporations cannot escape the need to consider ethics.

> Insofar as the corporation resembles an individual person in the community, issues that arise are similar to those in classical moral philosophy: responsibility, integrity, conscience, virtue; duties to avoid harm and injustice; respect for the law; provisions for the needs of the least advantaged.[3]

Four factors determine whether an organization is perceived as ethical: the business it chooses to be in – its "purpose"; how it chooses to do that business – its "principles," "power," and "processes"; the "people" it employs; and the expectations of its stakeholders.

"Mission and Vision"

Defining mission and vision is the talk of founders and/or senior management and boards of directors.

The mission defines the business the organization is in and depends on four factors: first, the ethical choices made when defining the mission and deciding on its boundaries; second, the acceptability of the mission to communities they serve and within which they operate; third, the commercial viability of opportunities; and fourth whether they have appropriate resources and competencies to execute.

Far from being an oxymoron, business ethics are at the heart of a successful, sustainable enterprise. Ethical considerations have a critical role to play at every stage in establishing the sustainability of the mission, vision, and values of the enterprise.

https://doi.org/10.1515/9783110780871-005

This four-step evaluation process is summarized in Figure 5.1's four questions that must be answered in determining the mission, vision and values of any organization:

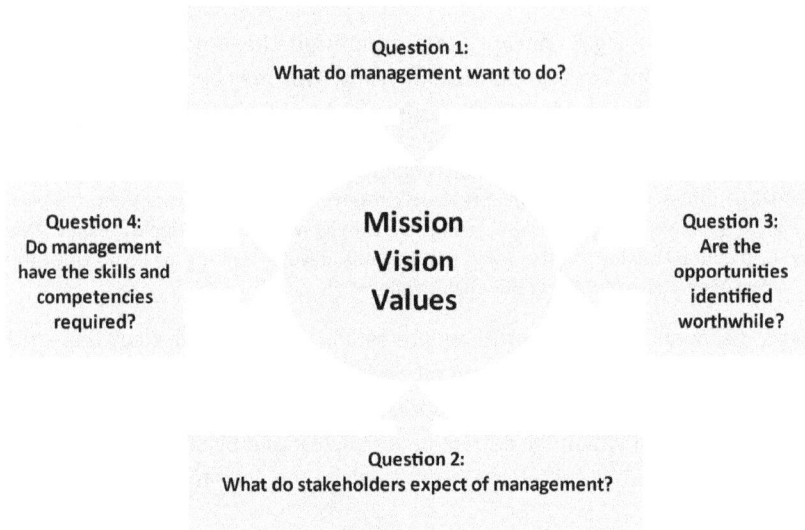

Question 1:
What do management want to do?

Question 4:
Do management
have the skills and
competencies
required?

Mission
Vision
Values

Question 3:
Are the
opportunities
identified
worthwhile?

Question 2:
What do stakeholders expect of management?

Figure 5.1: Four questions to be answered when determining Mission, Vision, and Values.
Source: Zinkin, J. (2022), "Redefining Encorp Berhad's Vision", Workshop 3, April 20, 2022.

Questions 1 and 2 have a strong ethical component dealing with both "what" is going to be done, and, equally important, with "how" it will be done and rewarded; in other words, the expectations by both management and the communities, in which they operate, of ethical behavior in their undertakings. Questions 3 and 4 deal with the commercial aspects of the decisions made in answer to questions 1 and 2. The combination of the answers to these four questions define the enterprise's mission, vision and values.

The critical success factor in achieving a sustainable mission and vision is to remember the primacy of the customer, adopting Peter Drucker's view that it is the customer who determines what value the enterprise offers:

> *It is the customer who determines what a business is. It is the customer alone whose willingness to pay for a good or service converts economic resources into wealth, things into goods.* What the business thinks it produces is not of first importance – especially not to the future of the business and to its success . . . *What the customer thinks he/she is buying, what he/she considers value, is decisive – it determines what a business is, what it produces and whether it will prosper.*[4] [Emphases ours]

Once the Mission and Vision have been agreed, for an enterprise to be ethical and successful it must achieve organizational alignment with the new Mission and Vision.[i] The easiest way to do this is to consider five factors.

1. *"Purpose"* – what the organization exists for
2. *"Principles"* – the values it lives by
3. *"Power"* – the organizational design and power structure it adopts
4. *"People"* – who make things happen
5. *"Processes"* – the systems and procedures governing its operations to hold it together.

These elements form the "Five P" performance framework that board and top management can use as a checklist, shown in Figure 5.2.

Aligning the organization to achieve the mission and vision

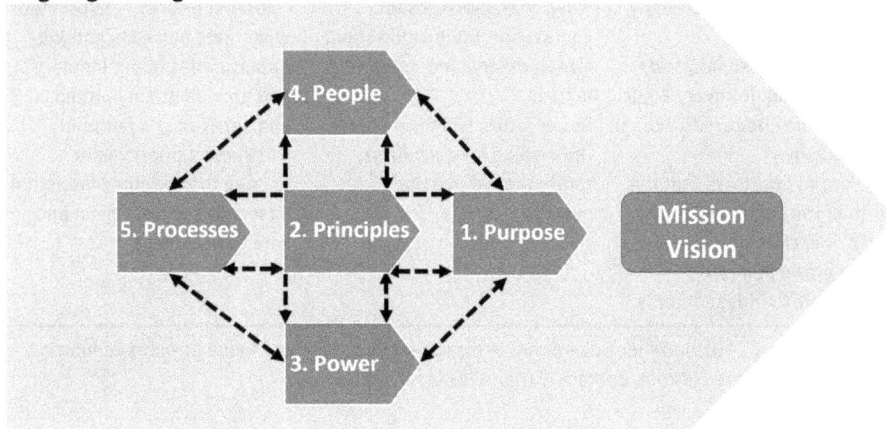

Figure 5.2: "'Five P' performance framework": aligning the organization.
Source: Zinkin, J. (2014), *Corporate Directors Onboarding Program* (Kuala Lumpur), April 16, 2014.

Purpose

Founders and top management need to define who are the organization's beneficiaries, the difference to be made in their lives, and the value they will derive from its products and services, and relate those to the costs of providing them, so as to establish expected rates of return. The appropriate rates of return depend on the risks

---

i Much of the material in this section is based on Zinkin, J. and Bennett, C. (2022), *Criminality and Business Strategy: Similarities and Differences:* Chapter 6: "The Criminal Internal Strategy Continuum" (Berlin/Boston: Walter de Gruyter).

involved in the type of organization and their different organizational purposes: whether it is a family firm, a publicly traded company, or a state-owned enterprise (SOE), as shown in Table 5.1.

Table 5.1: Differences in organizational purpose.

Family firm	Publicly traded firm	State-owned enterprise
Level 1	*Level 1*	*Level 1*
"The overall aim of our company is shared family wealth and work."	"The ultimate aim of the company is return on shareholder equity better than the return for firms with similar risk characteristics."	"The ultimate purpose of state ownership of enterprises should be to maximize value for society, through an efficient allocation of resources."[5]
Level 2	*Level 2*	*Level 2*
"Our first priority is the family stays together, with appropriate, satisfying, and rewarding work for every adult member who chooses to work in the company. Our second priority is that the worth of the company, and the worth of each family member's shares grows at a rate comparable to indexed funds."	"Risk characteristics for comparison will include similar size, industry, and maturity of market. Better return will mean above the median for such firms, rather than above the average."	"Our first priority is to promote and create business and job opportunities in our industry and provide quality products and services at a fair price. Our second priority is to enlarge the country's industrial base and ensure a clean and safe environment."

Source: Zinkin, J. (2019), *Better Governance across the Board: Creating Value through Reputation, People and Processes* (Berlin/Boston: Walter de Gruyter), p. 35.

The purpose for publicly listed firms has been "return on shareholder equity better than the return for firms with similar characteristics" since the 1970s.

A seminal article by Charles Handy in the *Harvard Business Review* in December 2002[6] explained that there are many ways to increase a company's share price of which increasing productivity and long-term profitability responsibly as stewards of the company is only one. The short-term ways of increasing the share price may not create long-term value. Cutting or delaying investment expenditure may increase immediate profits, but at the expense of the future. Buying and selling companies to boost the balance sheet appears easier than achieving organic growth, even though the evidence is that most mergers and acquisitions destroy value. The fact that so many executives are now rewarded with stock options means they are less willing to behave like true owners and are not prepared to wait for long-term results beyond the time limits of their options.

Johnson & Johnson's *Credo* written in 1943 by General Robert Wood Johnson expresses its business purpose with clarity and provides a view of the priorities it gives to its different stakeholders. (See Appendix 5.1: Two Approaches to Stakeholder

Engagement.) It provides a justification of the profit motive, articulating why profits are needed. The *Credo* is very clear and avoids ambiguities of priority between stakeholders. In the *Credo*, customers come first, then employees, then communities, and finally shareholders (stockholders). It makes it clear that shareholders are entitled to a fair return and not the maximum return. In 2019, the US Business Roundtable belatedly declared that the purpose of business was to satisfy stakeholders rather than just to maximize shareholder value (see Appendix 5.1: Two Approaches to Stakeholder Engagement). Unlike the *Credo,* The Roundtable Declaration does not set clear priorities between the different stakeholders:

> Each of our stakeholders is essential. We commit to deliver value to all of them, for the future success of our companies, our communities and our country.

Given the ambiguity regarding the ranking of stakeholders, the US Business Roundtable Declaration is unhelpful. Nevertheless, Larry Fink of BlackRock in his *2022 Letter to CEOs* argues that stakeholder capitalism is the essence of capitalism and not just "woke" whitewash:[7]

> Stakeholder capitalism is not about politics. It is not a social or ideological agenda. It is not "woke." *It is capitalism*, driven by mutually beneficial relationships between you and the employees, customers, suppliers, and communities your company relies on to *prosper*. This is the power of capitalism . . .

> Putting your company's purpose at the foundation of your relationships with your stakeholders is critical to long-term success. Employees need to understand and connect with your purpose; and when they do, they can be your staunchest advocates. Customers want to see and hear what you stand for as they increasingly look to do business with companies that share their values. And shareholders need to understand the guiding principle driving your vision and mission. They will be more likely to support you in difficult moments if they have a clear understanding of your strategy and what is behind it.[8]

Martin Wolf, writing in the *Financial Times*, asked important questions about the purpose of organizations:

> What am I as an influential individual, business leader and member of business organisations doing to increase the capacity of my country and the world to make sensible decisions in the interests of all? Am I mainly lobbying for special tax and regulatory treatment for our own benefit or am I supporting political action and activities that will bring the people of my divided country together? Am I prepared to pay the taxes that our success makes justifiable or am I exploiting every loophole that allows me to assign profits to tax havens that have contributed nothing to our success? What am I, my business and the organisations I am part of doing to discourage online harms, corruption, money laundering and other forms of dangerous and indeed criminal activity? What am I doing to support laws that will bring accountability to rogue business organisations and their leaders? What, above all, am I doing to strengthen the political systems on which successful collective action depends?[9]

The answers to these questions are determined by the personal ethical values of individuals and the principles of the organizations in which they work.

Principles

These reflect the ethical values of the organization. From a business perspective, ethical principles can be broken down into the following areas: *Caveat Emptor*, competition, ethical "fading," equal opportunity, information, marketing, pricing, and technology. They are exemplified in policy guidelines and codes of conduct.

Caveat Emptor

Caveat Emptor (buyer beware) is the legal doctrine that sellers are not obliged to inform prospective buyers about all the properties of the goods and services they are selling. When making a sale, sellers or advertisers provide information to prospective buyers that is designed to persuade them to buy. The ethical issue this raises is where is the line drawn between exaggeration (for example, advertising puffery) and salespeople overpromising, and deception. Deception, defined as "the act of causing people to have false beliefs," is not legally acceptable on the grounds that it is mis-selling. On the other hand, withholding information is not always illegal because if it does not *cause* the buyer to have false beliefs, it is not illegal but rather it is a case of failing to correct the buyer's false beliefs or assumptions about the performance of a good or service. *Caveat Emptor* permits the withholding of information, but does not permit lying or acts of active deception.[10] Buyers are often faced with asymmetrical information that makes it difficult for them to be good judges of the product's suitability. This is more of a problem with "credence" goods where the buyer has to take performance on trust because the time horizons over which the value of the product or service is assessed are so long that buyers have no effective recourse if the products they bought do not live up to their promise. There is an increasingly popular view that *Caveat Emptor* is no longer an acceptable ethical standard.[11]

Competition

Adam Smith pointed out that competition lies at the heart of innovation and is therefore to be welcomed; most societies recognize this and have regulatory systems in place to maximize competition.

> The essence of capitalism is competition. That has profound implications: *competitive profit-seeking entities are essentially amoral, even if they are law-abiding. They will not readily do things that are unprofitable, however socially desirable, or refuse to do things that are profitable, however socially undesirable.* If some try to do either of these things, others will outcompete them. Their shareholders may also revolt. *Being or pretending to be virtuous may bring benefits to a company. But others may do well just by being cheaper.*[12]   [Emphasis ours]

How organizations compete matters and past examples of very successful competitors are not the greatest examples of ethical behavior:

> Many of the great founders of American capitalism practiced very unethical competitive methods in their pursuit of increased market share. Diamond Jim Brady bribed customers with money, alcohol, and sex. William Hearst dragged the United States into the Spanish-American War to increase newspaper sales. Henry Ford was a cruel anti-Semitic employer. Henry Frick hired thugs who killed unruly employees. John Patterson and Tom Watson established dummy stores on both sides of a competitor and cut prices until the competitor went out of business. Charles Schwab, J. P. Morgan, Jay Gould, and Sam Insull were corrupt people who bribed well-placed sources to enhance their profits. *Firm survival in competitive battles over market share too often results in violations of common morality and the implicit morality of the marketplace. From the initial position of equality, all of these competitive activities are unethical.*[13]
>
> [Emphasis ours]

Part of the reason is the language of business competition, which uses metaphors devoid of ethical content. Words and metaphors matter because they create associations of ideas that go beyond the words used. Using jungles and military competition as analogies are inappropriate. Cooperating is more appropriate than "every man for himself" for business success, despite the popularity of reality shows like *The Apprentice*.

Consider the phrase "Business is war":[14]

1. *Customers are not territory to be conquered, occupied, and plundered.* Perhaps one of the reasons why banks lost their customer-centricity is that in the battle for market share they forgot what the objective was: not conquest and pillage but customer loyalty, achieved through customer satisfaction as opposed to brute force or capture through "sticky" customer relationship management (CRM) systems.

2. *Naïve interpretations of military perspectives and military language and thinking are nationalistic, alarmist, pessimistic, conservative, and authoritarian.*[15] None of which is good for innovation and creativity. Worse, they reinforce the win–lose mind-set, justifying extending win–lose thinking.

3. *Competition is not only about knocking out the other man, nor is it about winning the whole market for oneself.* As Supreme Court Justice Louis Brandeis put it:

> Competition consists in trying to do things better than someone else; that is, making or selling a better article at a lesser cost, or otherwise giving better service. It is not a competition to resort to the methods of the prize ring, and simply "knock the other man out." That is killing a competitor.[16]

No business succeeds in the long term by simply eliminating competitors. The bitterest battles in business end up as lose–lose, while the greatest success stories are not war stories at all.[17]

"Ethical Fading"

The language we hear affects how we think and can create ethical "fading" where people ignore the moral implications of their decisions:[18] the Ford Pinto and Boeing 737 MAX cases discussed in chapter 2 are examples of ethical "fading" where "anything goes." They were caused by people thinking in terms of impersonal numbers, lacking the empathy to realize that the numbers represent people, their lives, and their suffering. Ethical fading is prevalent in finance and accounting approaches to business because of their focus on the numbers.

Equal Opportunity

There are five ethical reasons why organizations should provide equal opportunities to employees:

1. There is a utilitarian reason, namely that organizations do better when their members are given an equal opportunity to be their best.[19] Another way of looking at it is that unequal opportunities are not just an issue of unfairness, but that they create inefficiencies caused by the mismatch between individuals' aptitudes and how roles are assigned to them – the reasoning used to justify diversity and inclusion, for example gender.
2. People benefit from broad points of reference by which to assess themselves and their performance objectively, in order to be able to expand their horizons and realize their potential is not limited by what they currently know.[20]
3. By virtue of being human, everyone deserves the right to equal opportunity, regardless of the economic costs or benefits involved. Restricting opportunity dehumanizes people and organizations.[21]
4. The "Golden Rule" and its requirement of reciprocity means that any opportunity we enjoy should be available to other people in the same way.[22]
5. The Bible asserts we are made in God's image and so:

   > Every human being is an image of God, and thereby an heir to certain privileges and opportunities that should not be arbitrarily restricted. Equal opportunity is every person's divine endowment which should be honored and protected with IMPARTIALITY.[23]

Impartiality matters, lest employees feel that that there is favoritism and people are treated unfairly – one of the swiftest ways of destroying morale.

Information

Information is a source of power and in organizations the flow of information reflects the power structure.[24] The way the information flows – "top down" on a "need to know basis" or "bottom up" encouraging people to "speak truth to power" – affects both the moral climate of the organization and its ability to deal with issues in a timely fashion. At the personal level there is the "right to privacy" and those at the top of organizations have been severely punished for "tracking" individuals through the use of emails, credit cards, and phone calls.[25,26,27]

Accuracy of information is an ethical issue:

> *There is a moral imperative to properly qualify the accuracy of information. Reports should distinguish between data, scientific prediction, and personal interpretation.* In some cases, the attempt to ensure accuracy has led to the creation of standards by professional association or law . . . A wrong choice of statistical method or an error in application can be a serious professional lapse. And where there is consequential harm (e.g., from reliance on financial reports), it can justify a claim of fraud or negligence . . . *In all cases where information is based on prior reports or studies, there is a duty to fully report the provenance of the information, and a failure to do so may be condemned as "plagiarism".*[28] [Emphases ours]

Advocacy and lobbying are both legitimate and necessary for organizations and other groups to get their issues and points of view understood, as long as they are based on truthful information and are not attempts to distract, delay, or deny the need for change through the propagation of falsehoods using "alternative facts" or accusing factual information of being "fake news."

As Facebook, Instagram, Twitter, and YouTube are discovering there is a change in attitudes of regulators who are less willing to regard them as neutral platforms for accessing and disseminating information with no responsibility for what is on their platforms. This recognizes that their algorithms favor baser instincts of humanity and resulted in propagation of hate and false information leading to division, undermining civil discourse, heightening the risks of violence and cyber-bullying.

Marketing

Marketing uses processes that can become unethical, while still remaining legal. Senior management decide where "red lines" are drawn and ensure their processes reflect the codification of agreed boundaries. Ethical companies will only sell products that are "fit for purpose" and that satisfy the legal "duty of care."[ii]

---

ii "A duty of care is the legal responsibility of a person or organization to avoid any behaviors or omissions that could reasonably be foreseen to cause harm to others . . .
Manufacturers
Those who manufacture products owe a duty of care to those who buy them. This means that the products must be reasonably safe for others to use. Products should also carry warnings about any potential dangers that can result from using the product.
For instance, while a chain saw is not exactly "safe" to use, it should be reasonably safe enough that it is not impossible to use. It should also have an obvious warning label informing the customer of how he can become injured and the steps he can take to prevent this.
Property owners

Segmenting markets to appeal to targeted groups with common psychographics and needs is a fundamental tool of marketing. It can lead to offering products that are harmful where the ethical, physical, or environmental harms caused by using the product are hidden when the advertising focuses on the emotional desirability of owning or consuming the products and fails to mention the physical or environmental harms created by using and disposing of the product:

> Socially controversial products like the "sin" categories of tobacco and alcoholic beverages and firearms, consistently are questioned from an ethical standpoint. The environmental compatibility or incompatibility of many products including all packaged goods, chemicals, plastics, and many others are being scrutinized by consumers and policy-makers.[29]

Given the importance of sales promotion and "hard selling" in marketing, there is always the risk of asymmetrical information being used to pressure uninformed buyers into buying products they do not need or that do not do what is claimed. In such circumstances, unscrupulous marketers can hide behind *Caveat Emptor* and the small print disclaimers, "hiding in plain sight" in language that most people cannot understand. What they are doing is legal, but unethical.

Effective marketers know that there is more to branding than just the functional performance of a product or service. Great brands have emotional appeal and create a sense of community among users with similar psychographics – the sense of affiliation and identification with like-minded people can be a powerful reason to buy. Recognizing this can lead marketers to behave unethically, persuading people to buy things they do not need, or cannot afford, or that are bad for their health.

Pricing

The profit motive is based on the idea that good business practice is to buy cheap and sell dear. This raises the ethical question of what is a fair price and can a price be too high? Common law focuses on consent to paying the price that is asked, and so, as long as the buyer consents to the price, under the principle of "willing buyer and willing seller," the law regards the agreed price as being fair and enforceable.

Deciding what constitutes a "fair" price from an ethical perspective can simply mean the market price. In these circumstances, even if a buyer agrees to pay a price that is way above the market price, it would be considered unfair and unethical. In

---

Those who own businesses and homes both have a duty of care to anyone who comes onto their property, to ensure there are no reasonably foreseen dangers. For instance, a clothing store has a duty of care to ensure a tear in the carpet does not remain to trip customers, who might then be injured."

Content Team (2017), "Duty of Care meaning in law," *Legal Dictionary*, March 17, 2017, https://legaldictionary.net/duty-of-care/, accessed January 24, 2022.

the eighteenth century and early nineteenth courts did not enforce prices that were significantly higher than market prices on precisely this ground because the market provided an objective standard by which to judge the fairness of the price. However, by the mid-nineteenth century, the idea of the market providing an objective external notion of value was dropped in favor of the view that the parties involved alone could decide the value of the item being traded.[30]

Deciding how to price is more complicated because price is not just a signal of value; it is also a signal of quality. Being willing to pay a high premium price can confer status and prestige on the buyer that is independent of the product's price-performance, when measured in terms of its functional benefits without considering the emotional rewards it provides. Pandering to people's envy and desire to show off may be good marketing and legal, but is it ethical?

So called "price-gouging" is caused by a sudden shortage of goods or services and common law allows the seller to charge the highest price that clears the market. As long as the buyer and seller consent to the price, it is fair in law.[31] In the court of public opinion, however, such behavior is regarded as unethical or immoral, and the increase in profits may not be worth the resulting reputational damage to the organization or the individual CEOs who raise prices dramatically "because they can." For example, Martin Shkreli, then CEO of Turing Pharmaceutical, raised the price of Daraprim from $13.50 to $750 without any economic justification.[32] He was ordered in 2022 to repay $64 million and banned from the pharmaceutical industry for raising the price of Daraprim, an essential life-saving drug for the human immunodeficiency virus (HIV).[33]

The final complicating factor in the ethics of pricing is that the poorest always pay more for their purchases in both absolute and relative terms and they cannot afford to buy long-lasting quality that the rich can, further impoverishing them according to the "Boots Theory" of money.[34] This is because they only have the cash to buy cheap goods that do not last, small sizes, or even just individual units such as cigarettes by the stick rather than the pack and do not have enough to pay for the larger pack sizes that offer better value for money. In such circumstances, they cannot benefit from economies of packaging or distribution and may end up paying more for the packaging rather than the contents.

Technology

The ethical issues involved with technology relate to risks that can be split into risks to the individual and risks to the community. Sometimes, as with the use of pesticides, they create risk to the individual and to the community. Individual risks are largely chosen voluntarily. The crux of the matter is whether individuals and communities were properly informed about the dangers, and whether having been advised, consented to using the products, and if unknowingly harmed, have been properly compensated. Risks posed to the community raise more difficult ethical questions because the victims have less choice about whether to accept them.[35,36]

Ethics relating to technology have a major role to play in environmental issues where most of the issues are the result of the adoption of technologies that harm the community. Ethics impact on terms of intergenerational ethical issues. The rewards of new technologies manifest immediately to the benefit of the generations that introduce them whereas the drawbacks take much longer to surface and affect later generations. Ethical organizations are aware of this and try to take this into account when considering sustainability, whereas organizations that focus on profit maximization in the short-term deny, delay, or ignore the need to consider intergenerational equity. Risk imposition across time is an important ethical consideration:

> One important criterion for risk imposition is the equity of distribution of risks and benefits associated with an activity. For example, Parfit argues that temporal differences among people/generations are not a relevant basis for discriminating against them with respect to risk . . . a technological risk is less acceptable to the degree that it imposes costs on the future but awards benefits in the present. Commercial nuclear fission, for example, benefits mainly the present generations, whereas its risks and costs – because of radioactive waste – will be borne primarily by members of future generations.[37]

This in turn raises questions about the appropriate way to judge technological risk. The European Union adopts the precautionary principle when dealing with new technological applications.[38] In contrast, the US, which does not apply the precautionary principle in environmental, health, and food safety, takes corrective regulatory action only when risks materialize, creating a very different approach to doing business and the taking of risk.

> The ethical issues associated with technology may be just as important as the scientific and safety issues. Once we understand the magnitude of these ethical issues, we are forced to ask about a technology, not only "how safe is safe enough?" but also "how safe is equitable enough?" or "how safe is voluntary enough?" or "how safe is compensated enough?"[39]

Power

This deals with questions regarding organizational design, job descriptions, roles and responsibilities, and reporting relationships, as well as how people are treated by their superiors. Appropriate structures are a function of whether they operate as "Incubators," "Family Firms," "Eiffel Towers," or "Guided Missiles."[40] The differences in operating philosophy of each determine employee relationships, attitudes to authority, ways of thinking and learning, ways of changing, and how to handle criticism and resolve conflicts, shown in Table 5.2.

Although the behavioral characteristics of the four organizational archetypes are different, as shown in Table 5.2, the ethical issues remain the same.

Table 5.2: Characteristics of the four organizational cultures.

Behavioral characteristics	"Incubator"	"Family Firm"	"Guided Missile"	"Eiffel Tower"
Employee relationships	*Diffuse,* spontaneous relations arising from shared creative processes	*Diffuse,* intuitive, holistic, lateral, and error correcting	*Specific*, problem-centered, professional, practical, cross-disciplinary	*Specific*, logical, analytical, vertical, and rationally efficient
Attitude to authority	Status *achieved* by individuals exemplifying creativity and growth	Status *ascribed* to parent figures who are close and powerful	Status *achieved* by project group members who contribute to targeted goal	Status *ascribed* to "superior" roles who are distant yet powerful
Ways of thinking and learning	*Diffuse*, process-oriented, creative, ad hoc, inspirational	*Diffuse,* intuitive, holistic, lateral, and error correcting	*Specific*, problem-centered, professional, practical, cross-disciplinary	*Specific*, logical, analytical, vertical, and rationally efficient
Attitudes to people	*Diffuse,* co-creators	*Diffuse,* family members	*Specific*, specialists and experts	*Specific*, human resources
Ways of changing	Improvise and attune	"Father" changes course	Shift aim as target moves	Change rules and procedures
Ways of motivating/ rewarding	*Management by enthusiasm* Participating in the process of creating new realities	*Management by subjectives* Intrinsic satisfaction in being loved and respected	*Management by objectives* Pay or credit for performance and problems solved	*Management by job description* Promotion to greater position, larger role
Criticism and conflict resolution	Must improve the idea, not negate it	Turn other cheek, save others' faces, do not lose power game	Constructive, task-related only, then admit error and correct fast	Criticism is accusation of irrationality, unless there are procedures to arbitrate conflicts

Source: Based on Trompenaars, F. and Hampden-Turner, C. (2006), *Riding the Waves of Culture: Understanding Cultural Diversity in Business,* 2nd edition (London: Nicholas Brealey Publishing), p. 178, in Zinkin, J. and Bennett, C. (2021), *The Principles and Practice of Effective Leadership* (Berlin/Boston: Walter de Gruyter), p. 174.

People

There are three questions directors must answer:

1. *Does the organization have the right number of people?* Directors and senior executives must consider the current business strategy and how they expect it to evolve over time and how that will affect the organizational design of the company.
2. *Do the people have the right skills and competencies to do the job properly?* Too often when people are recruited or promoted, the important criterion is their ability based on their past performance,[iii] without paying sufficient attention to whether the nature of the job is changing. This means the organization must insist there is an up-to-date competency dictionary used in assessing the current skills base of its key employees. Even if such a dictionary exists, management must recognize that yesterday's competencies may no longer be suited for today's responsibilities or for tomorrow.
3. *Do the people have the right character to work in line with our "principles"?* Too often organizations hire and promote people based on their ability to meet targets they are set, their past track record, or their apparent list of competencies, *without considering enough whether they have the right character to fit with the "principles" espoused by the organization.* Too often, organizations excuse people whose behavior does not fit with their values either on the grounds of their seniority or on their ability to make a positive impact on the short-term bottom line.

Integrity

Personal integrity demands loyalty and obedience, but with a clear conscience; and if there is a fundamental disagreement about "Purpose" and "Principles" it may necessitate being disobedient, disloyal, or resigning. If integrity is just about being true to oneself and one's values, it can be argued that Hitler had integrity, given that he laid out everything he intended to do in his book *Mein Kampf,* or that Vladimir Putin's, Donald Trump's, or Boris Johnson's behaviors were entirely predictable and in character; and they were being true to themselves. Integrity requires considering other people and their values and one's own social roles as well.

---

iii This explains the famous "Peter Principle," which states people are promoted to their level of incompetence.

Processes

The glue that binds the organization. "Processes" include strategic planning, budgeting, and financial reporting and board-approved policies and procedures, regularly inspected by internal audits reported to the audit committee on lapses and loopholes and the corrective action being taken. They also include all forms of internal formal and informal feedback mechanisms, covering reward, remuneration, and appraisal systems; the setting and review of key performance indicators (KPIs) and scorecards; as well as training and personal development schemes; career development and talent management; and appropriate documentation of standard operating procedures and service level agreements.

It is essential the measurement and remuneration processes align with the mission and vision and do not contradict the "principles" if the board is to avoid falling into the trap of "rewarding A while hoping for B," shown in Table 5.3.

Table 5.3: "Rewarding A while hoping for B".

What we hope for	What we often reward
1. Sustainable growth	1. Quarterly earnings
2. Teamwork	2. Individual effort; bell curve
3. Meeting challenging "stretch" objectives	3. Achieving goals; "making the numbers"
4. Maximizing productivity	4. Maximizing Hay points (a job evaluation
5. Achieving total quality	method)
6. Candor; welcoming the messenger	5. Shipping on time
of bad news	6. Agreeing with the boss; "shooting the
	messenger"

Source: Based on Kerr, S., "On the Folly of Rewarding A While Hoping for B", https://web.mit.edu/ curhan/www/docs/Articles/15341_Readings/Motivation/Kerr_Folly_of_rewarding_A_while_hoping_for_B.pdf, cited in Zinkin, J. (2019), *The Challenge of Sustainability: Corporate Governance in a Complicated World* (Berlin/Boston: Walter de Gruyter), p. 234.

Measuring the Right Things

Senior managers, as stewards of their organizations, need to recognize the importance of making the organization viable in the medium and long term as well as financially attractive in the short term. They are not merely answerable for results within the financial year. Financial measures do not always provide appropriate guidance for the medium-to-long-term, given that business is a continuous process with relationships that cross the artificial reporting deadlines of quarterly and annual results.

Ensuring medium- and long-term viability requires investment in "infrastructure" (systems, physical assets, and the levels of competence and skills of employees involved). Much of the impact of this investment is only measurable in terms of customer satisfaction, employee engagement and morale, and does not show up in ways immediately visible to shareholders looking at share prices, price-earnings multiples, stock buybacks, and dividends. Senior managers, acting as good stewards, recognize that relationships with customers, employees, and suppliers continue beyond the financial year-end and their needs are ongoing and require continuous investment.

Performance appraisals are a key measurement process and inevitably focus on financial numbers. However, if they are to measure the extent to which managers are effective stewards, they need to measure more than the financials. Evaluations should also measure the ability of individuals to reconcile the needs of the current year against those of the next, and the speed and effectiveness with which managers adapt and redeploy the resources for which they are responsible in the light of changing circumstances.

If appraisals are to help management ensure that people are aligned with the agreed mission, vision, and values they need to incorporate the "principles" (values) in a way that makes them actionable, observable, measurable, and suitable for setting standards for everybody as well as specific targets for individuals as part of their personal development plans. Appraisals should assess the capability of superiors in their development of subordinates, and provide effective measurements of investment in training and career development. They should track the types of training undertaken and the return on investment (ROI) achieved by such training; they should include assessments of the attention managers pay to developing their subordinates and to the effectiveness of succession planning and talent development and management.

Motivating People

The right "Tone at the Top" takes into account people's attitudes and belief systems, allowing employees to internalize the purpose and values of the organization as a whole and improves performance.[41] The main reason for this is that intrinsic motivators drive performance better than extrinsic motivators, at least in work that does not require repetitive mechanical skills. Once work requires rudimentary cognitive skills there is evidence that beyond a certain point, the more money people are paid, the less well they perform[42] because they are not tapping into their three powerful intrinsic performance motivators:

1. *The desire for autonomy* – being able to self-direct the work and how to solve problems;
2. *Learning and self-development* as part of achieving mastery and making progress, even if it is slow;
3. *The desire to make a difference*, which requires fitting into a bigger purpose.

Admittedly, money has to be eliminated as a hygiene factor – in other words people must feel that they are being paid fairly and that they have enough for their basic needs.

> But I like to think that a lot of managers and executives trying to solve problems miss the forest for the trees by forgetting to look at their people -- not at how much more they can get from their people or how they can more effectively manage their people. I think they need to look a little more closely at what it's like for their people to come to work there every day.[43]

Islam, for example, regards work well done as an act of worship (*Ibadah*), as does the Quaker saying, "Hearts to God, hands to work" and Aristotle wrote thousands of years ago:

> Pleasure in the job puts perfection in the work.[44]

These insights recognize the value of intrinsic motivators, which seem to have been forgotten in banking as a result of excessive focus on short-term deals or trades and unrealistic expectations of sustainable returns in banking by investors. The aggressive, violent language used on so many trading floors, described in *F.I.A.S.C.O*,[45] has not helped.

The other problem with extrinsic motivators is that they over-focus the brain's attention on the immediate, short-term goal, creating a kind of tunnel vision that inhibits creative problem-solving and encourages excessive risk-taking.[46] So, it is clear that any "Tone at the Top" that ignores the intrinsic drivers of human behavior and that relies too much on extrinsic motivators that are more appropriate in achieving compliance will create problems of the type that were evident in banking leading up to the Global Financial Crisis.

Why do organizations persist in focusing on bonus-based "pay for performance" systems? We agree with Jim Kouzes and Barry Posner,[47] and Daniel Pink[48] that it is in part the result of invalid assumptions about what motivates people. We believe that businesses need to treat people with respect; to reward and recognize people rather than compensating them for coming to work; to provide people with a "line of sight" so that every job matters; and to recognize that money and bonuses are not everything.[49] It is worth quoting Robert Solomon on the impact on behavior of how we think about business:

> How we do business – and what business does to us – has everything to do with how we think about business, talk about business, conceive of business, practice business. *If we think, talk, conceive, and practice business as a ruthless, cutthroat, dog-eat-dog activity, then that, of course, is what it will become. And so, too, it is what we will become, no matter how often (in our off hours and personal lives) we insist otherwise. If, on the other hand, business is conceived – as it often has been conceived – as an enterprise based on trust and mutual benefits, an enterprise for civilized, virtuous people, then that in turn, will be equally self-fulfilling. It will also be much more amiable, secure, enjoyable, and last, but not least, profitable.*[50]   [Emphasis ours]

Stakeholder Expectations

Any organization's mission and vision have to recognize the limitations placed on it by what society will allow it to do. This means getting stakeholders to agree to the "purpose" of the organization. This raises a number of problems when trying to ensure that stakeholder expectations are aligned with those of the organization – expressed in its mission and vision.

The first problem is for an organization to understand clearly who its stakeholders are and how they interact with the organization and its supply chain. Stakeholders can be divided into three groups:[51]

1. *Primary stakeholders have a direct impact on the fortunes of the organization.* They include all members of the value chain. Customers (sources of revenue); members of the company supply chain (determinants of costs); shareholders, investors; and creditors (sources of funding); past, current, and prospective employees (past and future sources of labour). Regulators impose costs on doing business.
2. *Secondary stakeholders are involved with the activities or consequences of organizational activity.* Often service providers, auditors, lawyers, consultants and advisers, they include three types of endorsers of the company's license to operate: *government*: enforcing regulation; *civil society*: community, non-governmental organizations (NGOs), and advocacy groups; *trade/industry associations:* lobbying for/against the company's actions. Secondary stakeholders provide early warning signals of change in the organization's strategic freedom.
3. *Tertiary stakeholders are the "commentariat"* who influence primary and secondary stakeholders by changing or reflecting the climate of opinion. They include analysts, rating agencies, academics, mainstream and social media, and, competitors.

The second problem is to realize that stakeholders are people as well as institutions and communities and that they have multiple, different expectations, objectives, and priorities that may prove difficult or impossible to reconcile. In our view, the Johnson and Johnson *Credo* is a sound guide to reconciling conflicting priorities, if long-term viability is the uppermost objective in defining success:

> *Stakeholder and shareholder interests do align in the long term. If you have happy employees, collaborative suppliers, satisfied regulators, and devoted consumers, then they will help you deliver higher benefits over a longer-term period. It is hard to satisfy everybody in the short term; you may have to make trade-offs, for example, between purpose and profit. But in the long term, we don't believe this trade-off exists . . .*

> *Ninety-two percent of people want corporations to promote an economy that serves everyone, but only 50 percent believe that large companies are delivering on that goal . . . Almost 40 percent of consumers today are boycotting a product or service, not because they are unhappy with the performance but because of that company's social stance.*[52] [Emphases ours]

The third problem is that not all stakeholders are interested in long-term success, but are interested in maximum short-term financial gain, which may come at the expense of long-term success, because they are not holding shares with a view to realizing long-term gains and sustainability, given that they only expect to hold the organization's shares for less than a year.[53] This can cause serious tension between investors, in particular activist investors, as exemplified by what happened to Unilever when it announced its failed bid for GlaxoSmithKline's (GSK's) over-the-counter consumer products division. Unilever was first accused of "having lost the plot" because of its focus on sustainability by Terry Smith, an activist shareholder[54] who argued that Unilever should focus on improving its financial returns to shareholders. Investors did not support the bid and Unilever had to abort the bid, only to find that another more important activist, Nelson Peltz, had taken a stake in the company with a view to forcing it to change its direction and focus more on short-term results.[55] Clearly there is a substantial disagreement in the investing community between those who support a stakeholder engagement that focuses more on environmental, social, and governance (ESG) issues in the name of sustainability and those who are only interested in short-term benefits. The issue is how best to reconcile the long-term with the short-term:

> The real issue is the trade-offs between short-termism and long-termism. *Eighty percent of CFOs [chief financial officers] tell us in surveys that they would reduce discretionary spending on potentially high-NPV [net present value] activities like R&D [research and development] and marketing to achieve short-term earnings targets. They are literally sacrificing the long term for the short term.* Yet research shows companies that think long-term – meaning five to seven years ahead – substantially outperform, achieving 47 percent higher revenue growth over a 15-year period, for example.[56] [Emphasis ours]

The fourth problem is that stakeholders may have a broad range of roles that may create conflict in their own minds, making it even harder to reconcile and prioritize stakeholder considerations. A customer has multiple desires and priorities attached to those desires, depending on which role applies when engaging with an organization:

> It is important to recognize the broad range of roles that a single customer may have. *Customers may narrow or broaden how they engage with you over time. They are also citizens and taxpayers. They may have someone in their household who is a member of your supply chain. They also look at your community engagement – particularly in times of crisis – and loyal customers can become dissatisfied with your policy on environment or community engagement.* So, it's important to recognize that any single stakeholder can be in multiple roles.[57] [Emphasis ours]

Given the nature of these problems, stakeholder engagement needs a comprehensive plan: identifying and assessing stakeholders, planning communications, engagement, and an understanding of the necessity of compromise. All stakeholders need to know "what is in it for them" – professionally in terms of career and personally in terms of extra work and personal risk. Stakeholders wear different hats at different times, so, when engaging stakeholders, leaders must understand which hats their audience is wearing. Effective engagement seeks to build trust and confidence, solicit support and build alliances, and create goodwill.[58]

Summary

The legal basis on which corporations are established makes it clear that they are not moral agents. Nevertheless, leaders of modern corporations must consider ethical issues. An organization's "purpose," "principles," "power," "people," and "processes" determine whether it operates ethically, and they depend on the mission and vision, established by its founder, senior management, and/or board.

Business ethics are at the heart of a successful, sustainable enterprise. The key to success in developing a sustainable mission and vision is to remember that it is the customer who determines what value the enterprise offers, and then to ensure that organization's "purpose," "principles," "power," "people," and "processes" are properly aligned with its mission and vision.

"Purpose" requires defining who are the organization's beneficiaries, the difference to be made in their lives, and the value they will derive from its products and services, and relate those to the costs of providing them, so as to establish expected rates of return. Appropriate rates of return depend on the risk involved and ownership structure – whether it is a family firm, public listed, or state-owned enterprise. Johnson & Johnson's *Credo* avoids ambiguity between its stakeholders by making it clear that customers come first, then employees, then communities, and finally shareholders (stockholders). Its shareholders are entitled to a fair return and not the maximum return. The personal ethical values of individuals and the "Principles" of the organizations in which they work determine the priorities set between different classes of stakeholders.

"Principles" reflect the ethical values of the organization. From a business perspective, ethical principles can be broken down into the following areas: *Caveat Emptor*, competition, ethical "fading," equal opportunity, information, marketing, pricing, and technology. They are exemplified in policy guidelines and codes of conduct.

"Power" deals with questions regarding organizational design, job descriptions, roles and responsibilities, and reporting relationships, as well as how people are treated by their superiors. Appropriate structures are a function of whether they operate as "Incubators," "Family Firms," "Eiffel Towers," or "Guided Missiles."

"People" must answer the questions of whether the organization has the right number of people to fulfill its "purpose," whether they have the desired skills and competencies to do the job, and whether they have the right character and integrity to live up to its "principles."

"Processes" include strategic planning, budgeting, and financial reporting and board-approved policies and procedures, regularly inspected by internal audits reported to the audit committee on lapses and loopholes and the corrective action being taken. They also include all forms of internal formal and informal feedback mechanisms, covering reward, remuneration, and appraisal systems; the setting and review of key performance indicators (KPIs) and scorecards; as well as training and personal development schemes; career development and talent management; and appropriate documentation of standard operating procedures and service level agreements. They should strike the right balance between extrinsic and intrinsic motivators, making due allowance for autonomy, self-development, and the desire to make a difference by individuals.

Any organization's mission and vision have to recognize the limitations placed on them by what society will allow it to do. Stakeholders must agree to its "purpose." Stakeholders wear different hats at different times, so, when engaging stakeholders, leaders must understand which hats their audience is wearing. Effective engagement builds trust and confidence, solicits support and builds alliances, and creates goodwill to be called upon in times of need.

Appendix 5.1: Two Approaches to Stakeholder Engagement

Johnson & Johnson *Credo* (1943)	U.S. Business Roundtable Declaration (2019)
We believe our first responsibility is to the patients, doctors and nurses, to mothers and fathers and all others who use our products and services. In meeting their needs everything we do must be of high quality. We must constantly strive to provide value, reduce our costs and maintain reasonable prices. Customers' orders must be serviced promptly and accurately. Our business partners must have an opportunity to make a fair profit. *We are responsible to our employees who work with us throughout the world.* We must provide an inclusive work environment where each person must be considered as an individual. *We must respect their diversity and dignity and recognize their merit.*	Businesses play a vital role in the economy by creating jobs, fostering innovation and providing essential goods and services. Businesses make and sell consumer products; manufacture equipment and vehicles; support the national defense; grow and produce food; provide health care; generate and deliver energy; and offer financial, communications and other services that underpin economic growth. *While each of our individual companies serves its own corporate purpose, we share a fundamental commitment to all of our stakeholders. We commit to:*

(continued)

Johnson & Johnson *Credo* (1943)	U.S. Business Roundtable Declaration (2019)
They must have a sense of security, fulfillment and purpose in their jobs. Compensation must be fair and adequate and working conditions clean, orderly and safe. We must support the health and well-being of our employees and help them fulfill their family and other personal responsibilities. Employees must feel free to make suggestions and complaints. There must be equal opportunity for employment, development and advancement for those qualified. We must provide highly capable leaders and their actions must be just and ethical.	– *Delivering value to our customers.* We will further the tradition of American companies leading the way in meeting or exceeding customer expectations.
	– *Investing in our employees.* This starts with compensating them fairly and providing important benefits. It also includes supporting them through training and education that help develop new skills for a rapidly changing world. *We foster diversity and inclusion, dignity and respect.*
We are responsible to the communities in which we live and work and to the world community as well. We must help people be healthier by supporting better access and care in more places around the world. We must be good citizens – support good works and charities, better health and education, and bear our fair share of taxes. We must maintain in good order the property we are privileged to use, protecting the environment and natural resources.	– *Dealing fairly and ethically with our suppliers.* We are dedicated to serving as good partners to the other companies, large and small, that help us meet our missions.
	– *Supporting the communities in which we work.* We respect the people in our communities and protect the environment by embracing sustainable practices across our businesses.
Our final responsibility is to our stockholders. Business must make a sound profit. We must experiment with new ideas. Research must be carried on, innovative programs developed, investments made for the future and mistakes paid for. New equipment must be purchased, new facilities provided and new products launched. Reserves must be created to provide for adverse times.	– *Generating long-term value for shareholders,* who provide the capital that allows companies to invest, grow and innovate. We are committed to transparency and effective engagement with shareholders.
When we operate according to these principles, the stockholders should realize a fair return. [Emphases ours]	*Each of our stakeholders is essential. We commit to deliver value to all of them, for the future success of our companies, our communities and our country.* [Emphases ours]

References

1 Romeo, N. (2022), "Can companies force themselves to do good?", *New Yorker*, January 10, 2022, https://www.newyorker.com/business/currency/can-companies-force-themselves-to-do-good?, accessed January 11, 2021.
2 Solomon, R. C. (1999), *A Better Way to Think about Business: How Personal Integrity Leads to Corporate Success* (New York: Oxford University Press), pp. xx–xxi.

3 Goodpaster, K. E. (1998), "Business ethics," in Werhane, P. and Freeman, R. (eds), *Encyclopedic Dictionary of Business Ethics* (Oxford: Blackwell Business), p. 52.

4 Drucker, P. (1955), *The Practice of Management* (Oxford: Butterworth Heinemann), p. 35, quoted in Zinkin, J. (2020), *The Challenge of Sustainability: Corporate Governance in a Complicated World* (Berlin/Boston: Walter de Gruyter), p. 258.

5 OECD (2015), *OECD Guidelines on Corporate Governance of State Owned Enterprises, 2015 Edition* (Paris: OECD Publishing), p. 17, https://www.oecd-ilibrary.org/docserver/9789264244160-en.pdf?expires=1542261379&id=id&accname=guest&checksum=29D7D3455C42A7989C3D141939B2AAC9, accessed November 15, 2018.

6 Handy, C. (2002), "What's a business for?" *Harvard Business Review,* December 2002, p. 50, https://hbr.org/2002/12/whats-a-business-for, accessed January 17, 2022.

7 Fink, L. (2022), "Larry Fink's 2022 letter to CEO's: The power of capitalism," *BlackRock,* https://www.blackrock.com/corporate/investor-relations/larry-fink-ceo-letter, accessed January 18, 2022.

8 Ibid.

9 Wolf, M. (2022), "Business leaders have a better political role to play," *Financial Times,* January 18, 2022, https://www.ft.com/content/4b844f8b-4906-46b4-81e5-059a4d8d4eb6?, accessed January 19, 2022.

10 Carson, T. L., "Bluffing and deception," in Werhane and Freeman, *Encyclopedic Dictionary of Business Ethics*, p. 42.

11 Werhane and Freeman, op. cit., p. 43.

12 Wolf (2022).

13 Collins, D. (1998), "Ethics of competition," in Werhane and Freeman, *Encyclopedic Dictionary of Business Ethics*, p. 258.

14 Crichton, M. (1992), *Rising Sun* (New York: Knopf).

15 Hartle, A. E. (1989), *Moral Issues in Military Decision-Making* (Lawrence, KS: University of Kansas Press, 1989), cited in Solomon, (1999), p. 15.

16 Chief Justice Louis Brandeis (1913), "Competition," *American Legal News*, Volume 44 (January), cited in Solomon, (1999), p. 15.

17 Solomon, (1999).

18 Beasley, B. (2022), "Keep ethics from 'fading' when you face a tough decision," Notre Dame Deloitte Center for Ethical Leadership, https://ethicalleadership.nd.edu/news/ethical-fading-dont-let-ethics-fade-from-view/, accessed January 22, 2022.

19 De Vries, "Equal opportunity," in Werhane and Freeman, Encyclopedic Dictionary of Business Ethics, p. 215.

20 Ibid.

21 Ban Ki-Moon (2015), *Universal Declaration of Human Rights* (New York: United Nations), https://www.un.org/en/udhrbook/pdf/udhr_booklet_en_web.pdf, accessed November 20, 2020.

22 Ibid.

23 de Vries, op. cit., p. 215.

24 Snapper, J. W. (1998), "Ethical issues in information," in Werhane and Freeman, *Encyclopedic Dictionary of Business Ethics*, pp. 235–236.

25 Agence France Presse (2006), "HP chairwoman to step down after spying scandal," *Industry-Week,* September 12, 2006, https://www.industryweek.com/the-economy/regulations/article/21938302/hp-chairwoman-to-step-down-after-spying-scandal, accessed January 22, 2022.

26 David, D. (2020), "Credit Suisse boss Tidjane Thiam quits after spying scandal," BBC News, February 7, 2020, https://www.bbc.com/news/business-51411640, accessed January 22, 2022.

27 Collinson, P. (2018), "Barclays CEO Jes Staley faces fine over whistleblower incident," *The Guardian,* April 20, 2018, https://www.theguardian.com/business/2018/apr/20/barclays-ceo-jes-staley-facing-fine-over-whistleblower-incident, accessed January 22, 2022.

28 Snapper (1998), pp. 236–237.

29 Murphy, P. E. (1998), "Ethics of marketing," in Werhane and Freeman, *Encyclopedic Dictionary of Business Ethics*, p. 262.

30 Ostas, D. T. (1998), "Ethics of pricing," in Werhane and Freeman, *Encyclopedic Dictionary of Business* Ethics, pp. 266–267.

31 Werhane and Freeman, op. cit.

32 Pollack, A. (2015), "Drug goes from $13.50 to $750, overnight," *The New York Times,* September 20, 2015, https://www.nytimes.com/2015/09/21/business/a-huge-overnight-increase-in-a-drugs-price-raises-protests.html, accessed January 24, 2022.

33 Katersky, A., (2022), Pharma Bro' Martin Shkreli ordered to pay $64 million for hiking cost of lifesaving drug, *ABC News*, January 15, 2022, https://abcnews.go.com/US/pharma-bro-martin-shkreli-ordered-pay-64-million/story?id=82272398, accessed January 24, 2022

34 Huffman, T. (2021), "Understanding the 'Boots Theory' of socioeconomic unfairness," *Money-Wise,* December 1, 2021, https://moneywise.com/managing-money/budgeting/boots-theory-of-socio economic-unfairness, accessed March 9, 2022.

35 McFall-Johnsen, M. (2019), "Over 1,500 California fires in the past 6 years – including the deadliest ever – were caused by one company: PG&E. Here's what it could have done but didn't," *Insider*, November 3, 2019, https://www.businessinsider.com/pge-caused-california-wildfires-safety-measures-2019-10, accessed January 25, 2022.

36 Carmichael, B. and Moriarty, B. (2018), "How Coca-Cola came to terms with its own water crisis," *The Washington Post*, May 31, 2018, https://www.washingtonpost.com/news/business/wp/2018/05/31/how-coca-cola-came-to-terms-with-its-own-water-crisis/, accessed January 25, 2022.

37 Parfit, D. (1983), "The further future: The discount rate," in Maclean. D. and Brown, P. (eds), *Energy and the Future* (Totowa, NJ: Rowman and Littlefield), pp. 31–37, cited in Shrader-Frechette, K. (1998), "Ethical issues in technology," in Werhane and Freeman, *Encyclopedic Dictionary of Business Ethics*, pp. 245–246.

38 Beyer, P. et al. (2004), "The precautionary principle in European environmental, health and food safety policy," *Ecologic*, March, 2004, https://www.ecologic.eu/1126, accessed January 25, 2022.

39 Shrader-Frechette, (1998), p. 246.

40 Trompenaars, F. and Hampden-Turner, C. (2006), *Riding the Waves of Culture: Understanding Cultural Diversity in Business*, 2nd Edition (London: Nicholas Brealey Publishing), p. 178.

41 Katz, D. and Kahn, R. L. (1996), *The Social Psychology of Organizations* (New York: John Wiley).

42 Pink, D. (2010), "Drive: The surprising truth about what motivates us," Talk given at the Royal Society of Encouragement of the Arts, Manufactures & Commerce, London, January 27, 2010, uploaded on March 10, 2010, http://www.youtube.com/watch?v=_mG-hhWL_ug; accessed December 21, 2012.

43 Ibid.

44 Aristotle, *The Nicomachean Ethics*.

45 Partnoy, F. (2009), *F.I.A.S.C.O: Blood in the Water on Wall Street* (New York: W. W. Norton).

46 Pink (2010).

47 Kouzes, J. and Posner, B. (1995), *The Leadership Challenge* (San Francisco, CA: Jossey-Bass).

48 Pink (2010).

49 Zinkin, J. (2010), *Challenges in Implementing Corporate Governance: Whose Business is it Anyway?* (Singapore: John Wiley & Sons), pp. 25—29.

50 Solomon (1999), p. xxii.

51 For a detailed discussion on Stakeholder Engagement, see Zinkin, J. (2019), *Better Governance across the Board*, pp. 272–280.

52 Simpson, B. (2022), quoted in Hunt, V. (2022) "Putting stakeholder capitalism into practice," *McKinsey & Co podcast transcript,* January 7, 2022, https://www.mckinsey.com/business-functions/

strategy-and-corporate-finance/our-insights/putting-stakeholder-capitalism-into-practice; empha-ses ours.

53 Chatterjee, S. and Adinarayan, T. (2020), "Buy, sell, repeat! No room for 'hold' in whipsawing markets," Reuters, August 3, 2020, https://www.reuters.com/article/us-health-coronavirus-short-termism-anal-idUSKBN24Z0XZ, accessed January 26, 2022.

54 Conchie, C. (2022), "Fund manager says Unilever has 'lost the plot' with focus on purpose over profit," *City A.M.*, January 12, 2022, https://www.cityam.com/fund-manager-says-unilever-has-lost-the-plot-with-focus-on-purpose-over-profit/, accessed January 26, 2022.

55 The Daily Upside (2022), "Nelson Peltz's Trian partners acquires a stake in Unilever," Nasdaq, January 23, 2022, https://www.nasdaq.com/articles/nelson-peltzs-trian-partners-acquires-a-stake-in-unilever, accessed January 26, 2022.

56 Simpson (2022) quoted in Hunt (2022).

57 Hunt (2022).

58 Based on 2018 Edelman Trust Barometer: The State of Trust in Business, http://cms.edelman.com/sites/default/files/2018-02/2018_Edelman_Trust_Barometer_State_of_Business.pdf, accessed August 13, 2018.

Chapter 6
Leading Ethical and Successful Organizations

Ethical foundations are the basis for long-term sustainable success:

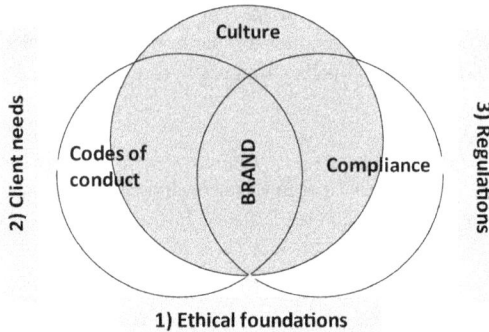

Figure 6.1: Ethical foundations: the basis of long-term sustainability.
Source: Zinkin, J. (2019), *Better Governance Across the Board: Creating Value Through Reputation, People, and Processes* (Boston/Berlin: Walter de Gruyter), p. 19.

Figure 6.1 shows how long-term sustainability depends on firm ethical foundations, encapsulated in the Mission, Vision, and Values (MVV). MVV are translated into ways of meeting and satisfying external and internal stakeholder needs. A written code of conduct describes acceptable and unacceptable behaviors for all employees. The code should reflect the founding values, and, over time, support the organization's culture.

Given that law and regulations create a defining element of sustainability, the organization must satisfy regulators, achieving this through compliance mechanisms that 1) reflect the MVV, 2) deliver what is needed to create and maintain satisfied stakeholders, and 3) ensure employees obey the law and regulations. From the outset, ethics play a critical part in determining the MVV that inform the code of conduct and the compliance mechanisms needed to ensure adherence and create long-term competitive advantage.

Ethical Obstacles

Once ethical foundations have been established, there remain obstacles to leading an ethical and successful organization, the law, maximizing profits, the effect of social media, decision-making difficulties, vested interests, cognitive dissonance, inappropriate regulation, deception, inappropriate KPIs, and investor expectations.

https://doi.org/10.1515/9783110780871-006

The Law

Chapter 1 explained that the law can only provide minimum guidance. In many circumstances there are conflicts between what is morally and what is ethically appropriate, and what is legal. This is not to deny that the law attempts to reflect the ideas of right behavior in a society's morality/ethics. For example, a basic principle of common law is that people are obliged to take care of their neighbors, and to avoid harming them, reflecting the moral injunction of reciprocity that exists in all moral codes, but in a restrictive form specifying particular instances to guide judges when considering the merits of a case:

> The rule that you are to love your neighbour becomes in law, you must not injure your neighbour; and the lawyer's question, Who is my neighbour? receives a restricted reply. *You must take reasonable care to avoid acts or omissions which you can reasonably foresee would be likely to injure your neighbour.* Who, then, in law is my neighbour? The answer seems to be – *persons who are so closely and directly affected by my act that I ought reasonably to have them in contemplation as being so affected when I am directing my mind to the acts or omissions which are called in question.*[1]   [Emphasis ours]

The legal opinion of Lord Thurlow that "corporations, have neither bodies to be punished nor souls to be condemned, they therefore do as they like"[2] and that though subject to law, they were beyond ethical claims, legitimizes the idea that organizations can be unethical and successful, for example, the tobacco companies. As Lord Thurlow said, "Did you ever expect a corporation to have conscience, when it has no soul to be damned and no body to be kicked?"[3] Furthermore, the law (because it is the codified response to incidents that have occurred) inevitably lags society's view of what is acceptable.

Maximizing Profits

Profit maximization as the sole purpose of business is, at best, a guide to achieving short-term success. It provides no goals capable of energizing people to "go the extra mile." The amorality of corporations with putting profit maximization as the goal of business means that decisions can be amoral and become ones of risk management[4] and the "cost of doing business" (as seen in the Ford Pinto case in chapter 2). As long as the costs of unethical and illegal behavior (including fines and the damage to reputation and market capitalization) are less than the profits to be derived from it, then profit-maximizing managers have no reason *not* to behave unethically or break the law, particularly if fines are paid by the corporation and not the individual.

Social Media

Much of what people are exposed to in modern mainstream and social media celebrates manifestations of the seven deadly sins:

> *Being greedy, prideful, gluttonous, wrathful, envious, lazy, and obsessed with lust is no longer frowned upon; it is widely celebrated. Deadly vices are no longer seen as evil outcomes; they are now retained societal norms. In fact, our most successful media (books, TV, movies) and public figures celebrate the human manifestation of the classic seven deadly sins.*

> . . . Our fascination with greed and envy makes reality TV shows celebrating money, lust, arrogance, and excess immensely popular. A gluttonous "Fabulous life" with unaffordable personal assets is the new American, if not global dream. Worse, it is accepted that we should commit whatever acts are necessary, regardless of their ethical consequences, to get there . . .

> *Our CEOs are only citizens, just like you and me, in a global society that has systematically rejected moral fiber and sound governance . . . If we wish for global business and markets to become more ethical and decent, we must look within ourselves. No silver-tongued politician, authentic CEO, or other leader can systematically create change for us. Catchy slogans are fables. Personal accountability is pure necessity.*

> In today's world, we can accept fraud, corruption, and scandal in established norms and outcomes of our societal fabric; in fact, we already have. Or we can expect more. We can expect the opposite, a more virtuous and honorable path.

> Expecting more does not just mean reforming government legislation and implementing tougher rules that rein in our fallen heroes on Wall Street. *Expecting more means knowing that, in many cases, the villain lies within us.*[5]   [Emphases ours]

Behaving ethically and consistently is difficult.

Decision-making

Chapter 2 showed how ethical decision-making depends on the circumstances and context. Five factors complicate matters: 1) ethics often reflect what *"ought to be,"* not *"what is"*; 2) reconciling "duty-based" and "consequential ethics" can be impossible; 3) different religious and cultural axioms lead to different ethical conclusions and answers; 4) individuals and organizations have multiple ethical personas and reference groups, the salience of which depends on circumstances and context; and 5) the impact of rewards and punishments. Choices made vary, depending on the interaction of these five factors.

In the world *as it is,* as opposed to the world *as it ought to be,* people routinely engage in unethical acts.[6] Reflecting ideas of how the world *ought* to be, people try to refrain from behaving in ways that violate their personal morality. When faced with conflict between "ought" and "is" people use one of four ways to reduce the resulting cognitive dissonance. The first is Machiavelli's justification in *The Prince* that "the ends justify the means." There is no point in being ethically or ideologically pure, but powerless. The second is to say that that is how the world is and accept it. The third is to appeal to "alternative facts," conspiracy theories, and untruths to justify unethical outcomes. The fourth is to treat "others" as inferior beings.

Vested Interests

The challenge to ethical *and* successful behavior also comes from vested interests, in government, business, academia, professions, the media – and among stakeholders. Vested interests defend or expand the circumstances with which they are comfortable and seek to protect and enhance the emotional and economic benefits they have acquired (or hope to acquire) at the expense of others.

Machiavelli explained how establishment vested interests operate:

> The innovator makes enemies of all those who prospered under the old order, and only lukewarm support is forthcoming from those who would prosper under the new. Their support is lukewarm partly from fear of their adversaries, who have existing laws on their side, and partly because men are generally incredulous, never really trusting new things unless they have tested them by experience. In consequence, whenever those who oppose changes can do so, they attack vigorously, and the defence made by the others is only lukewarm.[7]

Similar conditions apply within organizations reflecting levels of seniority; departmental differences, priorities and resources; cultural differences resulting from differing ethnic and religious backgrounds; and different "political" and economic interests driven by job function and responsibility.

Long-established elites defend their interests above all else, a mark of what Émile Durkheim called "anomie,"[i] individuals who think and act regardless of what is for the good of society.

Cognitive Dissonance

People shy away from considering complicated ethical dilemmas because they cause the brain to consume too much energy. Humanity is hardwired by System 1

---

i "Durkheim considered anomie to be an abnormal form of the division of labor where there was too little regulation to encourage cooperation between different social functions.

For example, in the antagonism between capitalists and workers, there is little contact between the capitalists themselves and the workers. Thus, these individuals do not realize they are working toward a shared goal and anomie results (Durkheim 1893; Lester & Turpin, 1999)."

Nickerson, C. (2021), "Anomie Theory", *Simply Psychology*, September 28, 2021, https://www.simplypsychology.org/anomie.html#:~:text=Durkheim%20considered%20anomie%20to%20be,capitalists%20themselves%20and%20the%20workers., accessed on May 14, 2022.

thinking to prefer instructions and cognitive processes that make it easy to decide what to do. Consequential ethics – considering the implications of decisions based on things we do not fully know – requires effortful System 2 thinking.

The increase in access to information and connectivity provided by Internet-based social media was seen as positive. Sadly, as people became connected, increasingly aggressive behavior manifested. People retreated into a world of "alternative facts" and conspiracy theories because they could not deal with the cognitive load arising from disagreements on what facts were, endless cries of "fake news," and the systematic peddling of lies by Internet trolls in a "firehose of falsehood."

It is hard for people to admit they were wrong about views in which they have considerable emotional investment. The reason why people remain loyal to religious cults, political beliefs, parties, and candidates after discovering that promises made were empty or misleading is the pain of recognizing they got it wrong. A culture of increasing impunity and declining accountability has resulted.

Inappropriate Regulation

Chapter 3 showed that regulations can be viewed as an opportunity for patronage, bribery, and corruption. Regulations are often written without paying sufficient attention to how the regulated will respond to the rules. Some people will always try to "game the system," aided by lacunae in "black letter law" that allow legal but unethical behavior in line with the letter, but not the spirit, of the law.

Deception

Chapter 3 explained how once an individual and/or group have lied and it remains undetected, increased incentives and rationalization make it likely they will repeat and escalate the deception at individual, interpersonal, and organizational levels. If the deception is detected early, it can be corrected. If the deception is unaddressed, it can infect the entire organization. The spiralling cycle of deception begins when a lie told deliberately is backed up by those who do not correct the record, and go on to cover up the initial and perhaps insignificant misdemeanor.

As long as deception is confined to a few individuals, the "bad apple" defence may be justified but skepticism is warranted. What matters is whether senior levels in the organization are aware of the existence of "bad apples," condoning their misbehavior because of their seniority or impact on the bottom line. As the situation deteriorates, the likely punishments for the perpetrators increase, encouraging them to take ever greater risks to delay the discovery of their malpractice. Failure to adopt a "no broken windows" philosophy regarding adherence to values and codes of conduct makes it easier for such escalating deception to take root and infect the organization.

Inappropriate KPIs and Investor Demands

KPIs are indicators of what matters to superiors. If set inappropriately, they focus the attention of subordinates on the wrong things.

If KPIs only measure results and ignore how they are achieved, they encourage cutting corners, undermining organizational values. Matters are made worse if the only KPIs that matter are financial numbers because 1) financials are easy to manipulate and 2) numbers obscure the fact that real people – and their aspirations, ambitions, and pains – are affected by the decisions made.

Shareholder demands based on short-term speculative attitudes to investments put pressure on managements to ignore long-term ethical issues created by decisions that affect the environment, communities, and future generations because 1) there are no undisputed ways of measuring the external costs of such decisions and 2) neither they nor their shareholders are likely to feel the effects of such externalities, if they materialize outside the time horizons being measured and for which they are held directly responsible.

Handling Ethical Dilemmas

The ethics and culture of organizations reflect the ethics and character of their leaders, whose first task is to set a "virtuous and honorable path" recognizing:

> Our CEOs are only citizens, just like you and me, in a global society that has systematically rejected moral fiber and sound governance . . . If we wish for global business and markets to become more ethical and decent, we must look within ourselves . . . knowing that, in many cases, the villain lies within us.[8]

Dealing with the "villain within" requires leaders establishing their own ethical baselines and accepting that those of the people they depend on to get things done may be different. They need to handle ethical dilemmas successfully, confronting and reconciling them.

Establishing Ethical Baselines

Chapter 4 explained the importance of establishing one's own ethical baselines and the "moral injury" individuals may suffer when these are violated, and understanding that they may be different from those of other people. This requires leaders to first establish their own personal "Moral Capital" and then define their own "kaleidoscopic ethical personas."

1. *Personal "Moral Capital":* the result of what people are taught about ethics; and their experience of the world *as it is* rather than *as it ought to be*. Personal

"Moral Capital" forms three concentric circles. At the centre is the "Universal Core" of values that are the basis of ethics everywhere. Next comes the "Cultural Mantle," representing the histories, cultural beliefs, values, and axioms of different peoples that create tension when they come into contact with one another. Finally, humanity has created a "Regulated Atmosphere" that provides for the different conditions required for law and order in different jurisdictions.

Leaders need to recognize that, apart from the values and beliefs in the "Universal Core" that are shared everywhere, the differences in values and beliefs in the "Cultural Mantle" and "Regulated Atmosphere" create disagreement and friction. Senior management and employees may belong to different cultures and consequently experience dissonance and disengagement when conflicts arise. Friction between goals of ingroups and outgroups are contextually conditional, making it hard for leaders to decide which set of values and beliefs has priority when deciding on codes of conduct.

When people are faced with a situation where they have to choose between fundamental "Universal Core" beliefs and values and doing what they are commanded to do, they are likely to refuse, even if it means losing their lives, freedom, careers, or jobs.

Challenges to values and beliefs in the "Cultural Mantle" may not be existential, but can provoke serious resistance if they relate to identities, to emotional definitions of self. They may be based on, for example, culture, gender, ethnicity, class, religion, education, or language. Violations of "Cultural Mantle" beliefs lead to people becoming willing to die for that which differentiates them.

The "Regulated Atmosphere" presents the least emotionally challenging environment. It is the manifestation of the laws, regulations, taxation, licensing systems, and enforcement. Obeying them or not is a matter of legality. The choices are likely to be determined by weighing the convenience and economic benefits of disobeying against the penalties for being caught and being punished.

Leaders need to recognize that the real problem with ethics and personal integrity lies in the so-called gray areas where people are forced to choose between two rights or two wrongs. How they will make these choices is not always obvious and depends on whether people adopt a "duty-based" or a "consequential" ethical approach to decision-making. How people reconcile the approaches depends on who is affected by the consequences and where people are in the hierarchy. For example, the concept of compliance makes perfect sense to people at the top of the organization because it is about protecting the organization from itself to ensure there are no breaches of the law, or of the organization's code of conduct. Yet for compliance to work, it is critical that breaches lower down in the organization be escalated upward. Escalating breaches of codes of conduct or reporting malpractices in the lower reaches of organizations means making difficult personal choices that affect real people with whom one has to work every day.

2. *"Kaleidoscopic Ethical Personas":* People have more than one ethical self. They have a kaleidoscope of ethical selves, depending on the circumstances in which they find themselves. Each choice can be anticipated by developing scenarios for challenges to "Universal Core," "Cultural Mantle," and "Regulated Atmosphere" beliefs and values.

The decisions people make reflect their response to the ethical challenges and result from a range of different conditions, contexts, needs, relationships; life experiences; and lessons learned. In a sense every ethical choice is unique and depends on the context.

Confronting Ethical Dilemmas Successfully

Chapter 5 discussed ways of confronting ethical dilemmas successfully. It helps people if they 1) determine the potential areas of conflict beforehand, 2) determine the potential costs of any such conflicts, 3) make appropriate decisions as a result, 4) apply a six-step ethical framework to ensure decisions are both ethical and effective, 5) assess the level of "moral injury" suffered as a result of the outcomes of their actions, and 6) re-assess their resulting levels of "Moral Capital" to see if they increased or diminished and how they feel as a result.

1. *Areas of conflict:* Conflicts may relate to personal purpose, mission, and vision and how those align with organizational goals; they may represent the different priorities they place on shareholder value maximization versus other stakeholder priorities; they may reflect the culture of the organization and the demands made by the organization on work–life balance; or they may reflect the organization's philosophy and treatment of employees in practice.

2. *Costs of conflict and "moral injury":* If the only reason employees have for staying is the money, remaining in such an environment may ultimately lead to serious employee "moral injury" with resulting stress, unhappiness, ill-health, and depression.

3. *Making ethical and effective decisions:* This requires leaders to consider six steps: a) establishing their "Moral Capital" based on their own beliefs, values, and purpose; b) determining whether what they intend to do will be *effective* – that is, do the ends justify the means; c) ensuring that such actions are acceptably *mutual/reciprocal* in that they affect everybody equitably; d) checking that they lead to *predictable* outcomes and when; e) checking whether consequences create the "greatest good for the greatest number" – that is, their *utility*; and f) whether the leaders themselves are comfortable with what they are proposing and how it will affect their *self-image* and their personal "Moral Capital."

4. *Applying the six-step framework:* Chapter 4 explained how leaders apply the six-step framework for ethical decision-making to the "Five P" performance framework to check whether any ethical complications might have been overlooked. The "Five P" framework comprises "Purpose," "Principles," "Power," "People," and "Processes"; and they each have an important ethical element.

    a. "Purpose" defines the mission and vision for any organization and is both an ethical and commercial decision. Ethics are involved in deciding what kind of business the organization should do and in deciding what products or services are going to be offered, to whom, and how.

    b. "Principles" are the values that define what business the organization is willing to do, with whom, and how; and have to be translated into policies that are to be observed when doing business (discussed in detail in Chapter 5).

    c. "Power" is a function of organizational design. It includes structural relationships between business units, divisions, departments and teams; and reporting relationships within them.

    d. "People" make organizations. Organizations must have the right number of people to meet organizational design needs, with the right skills, and character, who are comfortable with the mission, vision, and values, and committed to its goals. It is the role of leadership to recruit, retain, train, and develop people with the right mix of skills and values to ensure long-term success.

    e. "Processes" ensure operational alignment with mission and vision. They include all feedback mechanisms, formal and informal, and provide full, relevant, timely, accurate, and actionable information.

When considering whether their strategic directions could lead to unmanageable ethical dilemmas, leaders must evaluate how their intended decisions are likely to affect each of the "Five Ps" with respect to effectiveness (will the ends justify the means), mutuality/reciprocity, predictability, utility (achieving the greatest good for the greatest number), and to their self-image and that of their employees (how they will feel when asked to defend the decisions).

Ethical *and* Successful Strategies

Chapter 5 showed how ethical and successful strategies begin with defining an organization's mission and vision. That is what founders and/or senior management and boards of directors do.

Ethical *and* successful strategies depend on the personal ethics of the top decision-makers in the organization. They must be comfortable with what they are doing or going to do, if they are to maintain the enthusiasm, engagement, and commitment to making the enterprise a success. Equally, if society regards an organization's mission as being unethical, the enterprise will be unable to attract top calibre people needed for long-term success. It may find its strategic room to maneuver limited or eliminated if it loses its "social license to operate." This issue of social acceptability in turn affects the commercial potential by reducing demand and the supply of needed resources and competencies.

The "Five P" performance framework consisting of "Purpose," "Principles," "Power," "People," and "Processes" provides a helpful checklist for leadership to ensure that they will create ethical and successful organizations.

Purpose

Founders and top management need to define and agree who are the organization's beneficiaries, the difference to be made in their lives, and the value they will derive from its products and services, and relate that to the costs of providing them, so as to establish expected rates of return. The appropriate rates of return depend on the type of organization and their different organizational purposes (for details, refer to Table 5.1 "Differences in organizational purpose" in Chapter 5).

There are profound arguments about an organization's "purpose" affected by its type of ownership and whether it is "for profit" or not. Since Milton Friedman's 1970 article, "for profit" organizations have tended to ignore the importance of the customer and have focused on maximizing shareholder value, often interpreting this as maximizing short-term profits. (The debate is discussed in some detail in Chapter 5.)

We do not agree with this interpretation. It ignores the concept of stewardship. Short-term ways of increasing profits or the share price (a key part of the reward system of senior management) may not create sustainable value. Cutting or delaying investment expenditure needed may increase immediate profits, but at the expense of the future. Buying and selling companies to boost the balance sheet is easier than achieving organic growth (even though the evidence is that most mergers and acquisitions destroy value). We prefer the co-founder of Hewlett Packard, Dave Packard's, statement regarding the purpose of business quoted by Charles Handy in 2002 in the *Harvard Business Review*:

> Dave Packard once said, "*I think many people assume, wrongly, that a company exists simply to make money.* While this is an important result of a company's existence, we have to go deeper and find the real reasons for our being. As we investigate this, we inevitably come to the conclusion that *a group of people get together and exist as an institution that we call a company so that they are able to accomplish something collectively that they could not accomplish separately – they make a contribution to society*, a phrase which sounds trite but is fundamental."[9]
>
> [Emphases ours]

Charles Handy defined the purpose of business as being to act as an agent of progress:

> By creating new products, spreading technology and raising productivity, enhancing quality and improving service, business has always been the active agent of progress. It helps make the good things of life available and affordable to ever more people. This process is driven by competition and spurred on by the need to provide adequate returns to those who risk their money and their careers, but it is, in itself, a noble cause. We should make more of it. *We should, as charitable organizations do, measure success in terms of outcomes for others as well as for ourselves.*[10]   [Emphasis ours]

We recognize that the current view that the purpose of business is to maximize stakeholder value is open to the criticism that it is an illusion and that "stakeholderism" is contrary to the interests of stakeholders.[11] We recognize there may be some validity in the criticism levelled, for example, at Unilever by activist shareholders that it is not doing enough to improve its profitability and growth prospects because it has "lost the plot" in its excessive focus on sustainability of purpose.[12] However, in response to these criticisms, Larry Fink of BlackRock argued in his *2022 Letter to CEOs* that stakeholder capitalism is not "woke" whitewash, but the essence of capitalism.[13]

It would help a great deal if governments and regulators tipped the balance away from Friedmanite thinking towards reinforcing stakeholder management by changing "the rules of the game." To quote Tariq Fancy, who used to be in charge of BlackRock's ESG investing:

> Too frequently in corporate life, "purpose" and profit do not overlap sufficiently to drive any meaningful change on the timelines required . . . *Business today is like a competitive sport where players can score points and win by playing dirty. Corporations are playing the game in ways that harm the public interest, driven by a complex web of legal obligations and financial incentives designed to extract profits over purpose at every turn. Existing models of stakeholder capitalism require people who have done business in certain ways their entire careers to embrace "social purpose", even though they remain incentivised to do the opposite.* So, here's an idea: why don't we move to a model based on mandatory compliance? In competitive sports, when a game turns dirty, we ask expert referees to enforce the rules. *By switching to a model of stakeholder capitalism that is based on mandatory compliance and enforced by impartial referees, we increase its chances of success by applying a simple, common-sense aphorism: trust, but verify.* This requires governments to step in and ensure that the game is played fairly . . . Dirty players can pay the referees, undermining their impartiality and protecting loopholes that boost short-term profits but harm the long-term public interest . . . *If stakeholder capitalism fails, the political foundations of the system itself are at risk. I believe in . . . capitalism, but it must better serve the interests of all stakeholders. In pursuit of that goal, those with a voice and a platform should ask corporate America to help ensure the success of stakeholder capitalism by disclosing clearly how much it is paying the referees. Even better, they could start a campaign to stop these payments entirely.*[14]

Leaders can reconcile these different points of view in their "Purpose" by adopting the approach in Johnson & Johnson's *Credo* (for details, see chapter 5, Appendix 5.1:

Two Approaches to Stakeholder Engagement), which puts its customers' interests first (in line with Peter Drucker's definition that "the purpose of business is to create and maintain satisfied customers"), then its employees, then its communities, and its shareholders last, making it clear, in addition, that its shareholders are entitled to expect a fair return and **not** the maximum return.

We would recommend that leaders define their organizations' "Purpose" along the lines of the *Credo* and stop supporting Friedmanite thinking among business schools, the judiciary, and investors that puts shareholders first.

Principles

These represent the values of the organization and need to be translated into policies with regard to *Caveat Emptor*, competition, ethical "fading," equal opportunity, information, marketing, pricing, and technology. Founders, boards, and senior management need to define ethically acceptable and unacceptable behavior, set policy guidelines, and establish codes of conduct for each of these areas.

1. *Caveat Emptor* poses serious ethical issues. Ethical leaders have a responsibility to ensure that their sales forces do not hide behind *Caveat Emptor* to justify unethical behavior resulting from asymmetrical information, exaggerated promises, disclaimers in the fine print that people do not read, or claims made for credence goods that cannot be verified until it is too late for the buyer.

2. *Competition* is at the heart of capitalism. As Chapter 5 explains, it does not always lead to ethical behavior. Part of the reason is the vocabulary used to discuss competition, using metaphors that are violent and devoid of ethical content. Using jungles and evolutionary competition as analogies are inappropriate since business needs rules and fair dealing if it is to be sustained. Cooperating is more appropriate than "every man for himself" for business success. Business is not war. Leaders would do well to remember that customers are not territory to be conquered, occupied, or plundered and competition is not about eliminating the opposition. In the words of Louis Brandeis, US Supreme Court Justice:

    Competition consists in trying to do things better than someone else; that is, making or selling a better article at a lesser cost, or otherwise giving better service. It is not a competition to resort to the methods of the prize ring, and simply "knock the other man out." That is killing a competitor.[15]

    The bitterest battles end up as "lose–lose" and the greatest successes have not been war stories.[16]

3. Ethical "Fading" occurs where people ignore the moral implications of their decisions, creating a culture of "anything goes." Ethical leaders have a responsibility to remind their employees that the financial numbers represent people, their lives, aspirations, and their suffering. "Fading" also occurs when speaking

of employees as costs in the profit and loss (P&L) (where they are recorded in aggregate) instead of as being assets on the balance sheet (where they are not recorded at all) and adversely affects how organizations treat their people.

4. *Equal opportunity* policies can be justified on the following grounds: a) because humans are made in God's image, equal opportunity is every person's divine endowment; b) the "Golden Rule" and its requirement for mutual/reciprocal behavior requires it; c) the Universal Declaration of Human Rights specifies it; and d) organizations do better when their members are given an equal opportunity to be their best.[17] Or e) because diverse workforces offer different experiences relevant where volatility, uncertainty, complexity, and ambiguity (VUCA) is present.

5. *Information* is a form of power and in organizations the flow of information reflects their power structure.[18] The way it flows affects the moral climate of the organization, even more so in countries that have a "High Power Distance" culture,[ii] where the "courage to speak truth to power" is not encouraged. Encouraging "speaking truth to power" is not just an ethical issue; it is sensible because it gives leaders early warning of difficulties that could become too serious to correct if warnings come too late.

   Advocacy and lobbying are legitimate and necessary activities for organizations to get their issues and points of view understood, as long as they are based on truthful information and are not attempts to delay or deny the need for change through the propagation of falsehoods using "alternative facts" or accusing factual information of being "fake news."

6. *Marketing* is an area filled with possibilities for unethical behavior when legitimate processes are pushed too far. Leaders must decide where they draw their organizations' "red lines" and then ensure that the resulting policies are codified and included in their codes of conduct. Ethical companies only sell "fit for purpose" products that satisfy the legal "duty of care" and minimize hiding behind disclaimers.

---

ii "Hofstede's Cultural Dimensions
Power Distance
This is the way people in a society relate to each other on a hierarchical scale. A culture that gives great deference to a person of authority is a High Power Distance culture, and a culture that values the equal treatment of everyone is a Low Power Distance culture. In High Power Distance cultures, "inequality is seen as the basis of societal order". Low Power Distance cultures, on the other hand, see inequality as sometimes necessary (think professor to student), but the more that relationships can be equalized, the better for everyone."

   Hofstede, G., Hofstede, G. J., Minkov, M. (2010), *Cultures and Organizations: Software of the Mind*, 3rd Edition (New York: McGraw-Hill), p. 97, cited by *Center for Global Engagement, James Madison University,* https://www.jmu.edu/global/isss/resources/global-campus-toolkit/files/hofstede-power.pdf, accessed on May 14, 2022.

Great brands have powerful emotional appeal and create a sense of community among users with similar psychographics. Recognizing this can lead marketers to behave unethically, persuading people to buy things they do not need, or cannot afford, or that are bad for their health. Pandering to people's baser instincts such as envy and desire to show off may be good marketing and legal, but it is unethical.

7. *Pricing* immediately raises the ethical question of what is a fair price and can a price be too high? Common law focuses on consent to paying the price that is asked, and so, as long as the buyer consents to the price, under the principle of "willing buyer and willing seller," the law regards the agreed price as being fair and enforceable.

   Deciding how to price is more complicated because price is not just a signal of value; it is also a signal of quality and of status in the case of luxury goods.

   Price gouging, while generally legal, is regarded as being immoral – and the increased profits created by such behavior may not be worth the reputational damage to the organization that raises its price "because it can."

8. *Technology's risks* can be split into risks to the individual and risks to the community. Individual risks are largely chosen voluntarily. What matters is whether individuals were properly informed about the dangers, and whether having been advised, consented to using the products. Risks posed to the community raise serious ethical questions, particularly if the risks are caused by pollution or environmental disasters caused by the actions of companies.

   Technological ethics have a major role to play in environmental issues through climate change, environmental degradation, multi-generational impact, waste, and pollution as the result of the adoption of harmful technologies.

   Leaders must ask themselves what philosophy of risk they adopt when developing and marketing products – the European Union's "precautionary principle" when dealing with environmental, food, health, and safety issues or the US approach that deals with risks and harms once they have materialized.

   In short, leaders must decide "how safe is safe enough" and whether that is "equitable enough," "voluntary enough," and "compensated enough" when evaluating the levels of risk they are prepared to impose on users of their products. Whatever choice they make should be documented and incorporated in codes of conduct so that employees understand what boundaries are acceptable.

Power

This deals with questions regarding organizational design, job descriptions, roles, and responsibilities, and reporting relationships, as well as how people are treated by their superiors, hence the term "Power." The appropriate structures are a function of whether they operate as "Incubators," "Family Firms," "Eiffel Towers," or "Guided Missiles."[19] The differences in operating philosophy of each determine employee relationships, attitudes to authority, ways of thinking and learning, ways of changing, and how to handle criticism and resolve conflicts.

Although the behavioral characteristics of the four organizational archetypes are quite different (refer to Chapter 5, Table 5.2), the ethical issues remain fundamentally the same, and are best discussed under "Purpose," "Principles," "People," and Processes." There are, however, two behavioral areas that are a direct result of power relationships, namely bullying[iii] and sexual harassment; and ethical leadership requires a zero tolerance of both.

People

There are three questions for leaders to answer. Does the organization below them have the right number of people to do the jobs needed, based on the existing and anticipated future organizational design? Do they have the right skills and competencies to do those jobs properly? Do they have the right character and values to work according to the organization's "Principles"?

Leaders should do more than hire or promote subordinates only on the basis of their past track record and catalogue of competencies. They must also consider whether they have the right character to fit with the "principles" espoused by the organization. Too often, organizations excuse people whose behavior does not fit

---

iii Bullying: Bullying is an ongoing and deliberate misuse of power in relationships through repeated verbal, physical and/or social behaviour that intends to cause physical, social, and/or psychological harm. It can involve an individual or a group misusing their power, or perceived power, over one or more persons who feel unable to stop it from happening.

Bullying can happen in person or online, via various digital platforms and devices and it can be obvious (overt) or hidden (covert). Bullying behaviour is repeated, or has the potential to be repeated, over time (for example, through sharing of digital records).

Bullying of any form or for any reason can have immediate, medium and long-term effects on those involved, including bystanders.

Single incidents and conflict or fights between equals, whether in person or online, are not defined as bullying.

What bullying is not
– single episodes of social rejection or dislike
– single episode acts of nastiness or spite
– random acts of aggression or intimidation
– mutual arguments, disagreements or fights.

These actions can cause great distress. However, they do not fit the definition of bullying and they're not examples of bullying unless someone is deliberately and repeatedly doing them.

National Centre Against Bullying, "Definition of Bullying," https://www.ncab.org.au/bullying-advice/bullying-for-parents/definition-of-bullying/ accessed March 7, 2022.

with their values either on the grounds of their seniority or on their ability to make a positive impact on the short-term bottom line. When they do this, they undermine the values they seek to encourage.

Processes

The glue that binds the organization. "Processes" include strategic planning, budgeting, and financial reporting as well as board-approved policies and procedures that reflect agreed "principles", regularly inspected by audits reported to the audit committee or the board on lapses and loopholes and the corrective action being taken.

"Processes" include all internal formal and informal feedback mechanisms, covering reward, remuneration, and appraisal systems; the setting and review of key performance indicators (KPIs) and scorecards; as well as training and personal development schemes; career development and talent management; and appropriate documentation of standard operating procedures and service level agreements.

It is essential the measurement and remuneration processes align with the mission and vision. Performance appraisals are key measurement processes. They often focus on financial numbers. Evaluations should also measure the ability of individuals to reconcile the needs of the current year against those of the next, and the speed and effectiveness with which leaders adapt and redeploy the resources for which they are responsible in the light of changing circumstances. If appraisals are to help leaders ensure that people are aligned with the agreed mission, vision, and values (MVV) they need to incorporate the "Principles" in a way that makes them actionable, observable, measurable, and suitable for setting standards for everybody as well as specific targets for individuals as part of their personal development plans.

Appraisals should assess the capability of superiors in their development of subordinates, and provide effective measurements of investment in training and career development. They should track the types of training undertaken and the return on investment (ROI) achieved by such training and they should include assessments of the attention that managers pay to developing their subordinates and to the effectiveness of succession planning and talent development.

Codes of conduct should be based on translating agreed "Principles" into observable and measurable behaviors and outcomes that are acceptable, clearly identifying which behaviors are unacceptable and consequences and be supported by a robust confidential whistle-blowing policy and procedure.

Personal "Moral Capital"

Responsible moral judgment cannot be transferred to decision-makers ready-made. Developing an ethical approach is partly an administrative process involving recognition of a decision's ethical implications; discussion to expose different points of view; and testing the decision's adequacy in balancing self-interest and consideration of others, its impact on future policy, and its consonance with the organization's traditional values.

The state of an individual's "Moral Capital" account is best determined by using virtue ethics tests as the yardstick on a regular basis to assess whether the decisions they have made have increased or diminished the level of "Moral Capital" in their personal "Moral Capital" account:

> Virtue ethics places a strong emphasis on the pursuit of excellence in business . . .This *"ethical obligation of excellence"*[20] applies to business as well as other spheres of human endeavor . . .
>
> According to virtue ethicists, no humanly successful life is possible without good character. *Having a good character means having virtues such as honesty, integrity, courage, generosity, caring, compassion, and self-discipline.* Among the most important virtues in business are traits such as *justice, fairness, honesty, trustworthiness, cooperativeness, helpfulness, loyalty, integrity, reasonableness, resourcefulness, toughness, diligence, persistence, sensitivity, dependability, civility, congeniality, cheerfulness and decency.*[21] [Emphases ours]

If, as a result of their regular reassessment of their personal "Moral Capital" account, leaders find that they have fulfilled their *"ethical obligation of excellence,"* and they have exhibited the virtues and traits described above in their daily business dealings, then they should continue to do what they are doing. However, should they find that their choices and decisions have violated their values, and led them to failing to have the virtues and traits described above, then they must recognize they have not satisfied their *"ethical obligation of excellence"* and have diminished their "Moral Capital" account as a result.

The reduction in their "Moral Capital" reflects the "moral injury" that they have suffered. They can reflect on their choices and recognize how they have violated their values and take corrective action so that they do not violate their values again. Alternatively, they can choose to live with increased levels of cognitive dissonance by using "motivated forgetting" to deny what they have done to themselves, to become morally disengaged, and change their values to reflect what they have done. If they make this choice, they have consciously or unconsciously committed themselves to entering a downward moral spiral that will ultimately reduce their "Moral Capital" to zero.

Summary

Long-term sustainability depends on firm ethical foundations consisting of the organization's MVV that satisfies stakeholders' needs and meets regulatory requirements. The law, profit maximization, social media, difficult decisions, vested interests, cognitive dissonance, inappropriate regulation and KPIs, and investor expectations may all be obstacles.

The law can only prove minimum ethical guidance and "black letter" law is riddled with loopholes. Profit maximization may lead to amoral decisions that only consider the "cost of doing business." Too much on social media celebrates the seven deadly sins. Making ethical decisions is difficult because of the need to reconcile "duty-based" and "consequential" ethics, differences in culture and religious axioms, individuals' multiple ethical personas, and the distorting effects of rewards and punishments.

The world *as it is* as opposed to how *it ought to be* encourages people to behave unethically, supported by the *anomie* of vested interests. People find it hard to admit error when they are emotionally invested in their decisions because the pain is too great. If KPIs only measure results and ignore how they are achieved, they encourage cutting corners, undermining organizational values.

The ethics and culture of organizations reflect the ethics and character of their leaders, whose first task is to set a "virtuous and honorable path." This requires leaders to establish ethical baselines covering their own personal "Moral Capital" (an amalgam of "Universal Core," "Regulated Mantle," and "Regulated Atmosphere" beliefs and values) and then define their own "kaleidoscopic ethical personas." This allows them to confront ethical dilemmas by establishing potential areas of conflict and their costs to make informed choices as a result, and to apply a six-step ethical framework to ensure ethical and effective outcomes. In so doing, the "Five P" performance framework, consisting of "Purpose," "Principles," "Power," "People," and "Processes," provides a helpful checklist for leadership to ensure that they will lead ethical and successful organizations.

Leaders can assess the levels of "moral injury" created by their actions and whether they have increased their personal "Moral Capital" or not. The state of an individual's "Moral Capital" account is best determined by using virtue ethics tests as the yardstick on a regular basis. If, as a result of their regular reassessment of their personal "Moral Capital" account, leaders find that they have fulfilled their *"ethical obligation of excellence,"* and they have exhibited the virtues and traits described above in their daily business dealings, then they should continue to do what they are doing.

References

1 Atkin, J. (1932), "Donoghue v Stevenson [1932] Doctrine of negligence," *Donoghue v. Stevenson* [1932] A.C. 562, [1932] UKHL 100, 1932 S.C. (H.L.) 31, 1932 S.L.T. 317, [1932] W.N. 139, *LawTeacher*, October 22, 2021, https://www.lawteacher.net/cases/donoghue-v-stevenson.php, accessed December 23, 2021.
2 Thurlow E., *Oxford Essential Quotations*, https://www.oxfordreference.com/view/10.1093/acref/ 9780191826719.001.0001/q-oro-ed4-00010943, accessed January 2, 2021.
3 Thurlow, E. (1978), *The Oxford Dictionary of Quotations, Second Edition* (Oxford: Oxford University Press), p. 547.

4 Sison, A. J. G. (2000), "Integrated risk management and global business ethics," *Business Ethics: A European Review,* Volume 9, Issue 4, October, 2000, https://onlinelibrary.wiley.com/doi/abs/10.1111/1467-8608.00203, accessed January 2, 2021.

5 Malloch, T. R. and Mamorsky, J. D. (2013), *The End of Ethics and a Way Back: How to Fix a Fundamentally Broken Global Financial System* (Singapore: John Wiley & Sons), pp. 238–239.

6 Shu, L. L., Gino, F., and Bazerman, M. (2010), "Dishonest deed, clear conscience: When cheating leads to moral disengagement and motivated forgetting," *Personality and Social Psychology Bulletin,* Volume 37, Issue 3, p. 331, October 2010, DOI: 10.1177/0146167211398138, http://pspb.sagepub.com,, accessed June 21, 2021.

7 Machiavelli, N. (1513), *The Prince* (Harmondsworth: Penguin Books, 1999), Chapter VI, p. 19.

8 Malloch and Mamorsky (2013), p. 239.

9 Packard, D., quoted in Handy, C. (2002), "What's a business for?" *Harvard Business Review,* December, p. 50, https://hbr.org/2002/12/whats-a-business-for, accessed January 17, 2022.

10 Handy (2002), p. 54.

11 Bebchuk, L. A. and Tallarita, R. (2020), "The illusory promise of stakeholder governance," *Harvard Law School Forum on Corporate Governance,* March 2, 2020, https://corpgov.law.harvard.edu/2020/03/02/the-illusory-promise-of-stakeholder-governance/, accessed December 2020.

12 Agnew, H. (2022), "Unilever has 'lost the plot' by fixating on sustainability, says Terry Smith," *The Financial Times,* January 12, 2022, https://www.ft.com/content/7aa44a9a-7fec-4850-8edb-63feee1b837b, accessed February 8, 2022.

13 Fink, L. (2022), "Larry Fink's 2022 letter to CEO's: The power of capitalism," BlackRock, https://www.blackrock.com/corporate/investor-relations/larry-fink-ceo-letter, accessed January 18, 2022.

14 Fancy, T. (2022), "Stakeholder capitalism depends on full corporate disclosure from corporate America," *Financial Times,* February 10, 2022, https://www.ft.com/content/fe148362-595f-42ce-a967-c3cc333c82f1 accessed February 10, 2022.

15 Chief Justice Louis Brandeis (1913), "Competition," *American Legal News,* Volume 44 (January 1913), cited in Solomon, R. C. (1999), *A Better Way to Think about Business: How Personal Integrity Leads to Corporate Success* (New York: Oxford University Press), p. 15.

16 Solomon, (1999).

17 De Vries, P. (1998), "Equal opportunity," in Werhane, P. and Freeman, R. (eds), *Encyclopedic Dictionary of Business Ethics* (Oxford: Blackwell Business), p. 215.

18 Snapper, J. W. (1998), "Ethical issues in information," in Werhane and Freeman, *Encyclopedic Dictionary of Business Ethics,* pp. 235–236.

19 Trompenaars, F. and Hampden-Turner, C. (2006), *Riding the Waves of Culture: Understanding Cultural Diversity in Business,* 2nd Edition (London: Nicholas Brealey Publishing), p. 178.

20 Morris, T. (1997), *If Aristotle Ran General Motors: The New Soul of Business* (New York: Henry Holt & Company), p. 225, cited in ibid.

21 Morris, *If Aristotle Ran General Motors,* quoted in Marchese, Bassham and Ryan (2002), "Work-family conflict: A virtue ethics analysis," *Journal of Business Ethics,* Volume 40, Issue 2, Special Issue on Work Ethics, October.

List of Figures

Figure 4.1   Moral Capital and circles of beliefs and values —— **77**
Figure 4.2   Six-step decision-making cycle —— **89**
Figure 5.1   Four questions to be answered when determining Mission, Vision, and Values —— **100**
Figure 5.2   "'Five P' performance framework": aligning the organization —— **101**
Figure 6.1   Ethical foundations: the basis of long-term sustainability —— **124**

https://doi.org/10.1515/9783110780871-007

List of Tables

Table 1.1   Law and morality compared —— 11
Table 1.2   Rules-based and principles-based regulations compared —— 11
Table 1.3   Rules-based versus relationship-based morality —— 12
Table 1.4   Witnessing a car accident —— 12
Table 2.1   Duty-based and consequential ethics compared —— 27
Table 2.2   Dilemma caused by trust (*xin*) —— 32
Table 2.3   Dilemma caused by benevolence (*ren*) —— 32
Table 2.4   Dilemma caused by filial conduct (*xiao*) —— 33
Table 2.5   Loyalty (*zhong*) —— 34
Table 4.1   Duty-based and consequential ethics compared —— 79
Table 4.2   Relative merits of each approach —— 79
Table 5.1   Differences in organizational purpose —— 102
Table 5.2   Characteristics of the four organizational cultures —— 111
Table 5.3   "Rewarding A while hoping for B" —— 113

https://doi.org/10.1515/9783110780871-008

About the Authors

John Zinkin has co-authored *Criminality and Business Strategy: Similarity and Differences* (2022), and *The Principles and Practice of Effective Leadership* (2021) with Chris Bennett, published by De Gruyter. He has written five books on corporate governance (CG): *The Challenge of Sustainability: Corporate Governance in a Complicated World* (2020), *Better Governance Across the Board: Creating Value Through Reputation, People and Processes* (2019), both published by De Gruyter, and *Rebuilding Trust in Banks: The Role of Leadership and Governance* (2014), *Challenges in Implementing Corporate Governance: Whose Business is it Anyway?* (2010), and *Corporate Governance* (2005), published by John Wiley & Sons. He contributed a chapter on "Corporate Governance in Asia Pacific" and another chapter on "Corporate Governance in an Age of Populism" for the *Handbook on Corporate Governance, 2nd edition*, edited by Professor Richard Leblanc, published in 2020 by John Wiley & Sons.

He is a certified training professional. His specialties are "Leading Brand-Based Change," "Reconciling Leadership and Governance" and "Ethics in Business." He has led board effectiveness evaluations in banking, insurance and government entities and has written codes of conduct and board charters for several development banks. Since 2007, he has trained more than 1,700 directors in CG as well as senior managers of public listed companies. He has trained securities regulators from Cambodia, Hong Kong, Laos, Malaysia, Philippines, Singapore, Thailand and Vietnam on behalf of the Australian Government as part of their CG capacity building programs in ASEAN and APEC.

Starting in 1971, John worked in the UK in fast-moving consumer goods (Unilever), insurance broking (Hogg Robinson), management consulting (McKinsey), and office products (Rank Xerox) before moving to Hong Kong in 1985 for Inchcape Pacific. There John ran marketing and distribution companies in a variety of industries across Asia Pacific, before joining Burson-Marsteller in 1997 as the Asia-Pacific Marketing and Change Management Practice Chair. John moved to Malaysia in 2001 and from 2001 to 2006, was Associate Professor of Marketing and Strategy at Nottingham University Business School, Malaysia Campus, responsible for its MBA program. In 2006 he set up the Securities Industry Development Corporation, the training arm of the Securities Commission Malaysia and in 2011 he was appointed Managing Director, Corporate Governance of the Iclif Leadership and Governance Centre under Bank Negara Malaysia, responsible for training directors of banks and insurance companies in CG. Since 2013, he works independently as the Managing Director of Zinkin Ettinger Sendirian Berhad, a boutique consultancy specializing in CG, brand-based change and ethical leadership.

John graduated from Oxford University with a BA in Politics, Philosophy and Economics (1968) and the London Business School with an MSc in Business Administration (1971).

Chris Bennett has had a wide ranging career as a director, senior executive, researcher, consultant, and teacher/facilitator. His significant international exposure and working experience includes having lived and worked in six countries and held directorships for major British and American companies in 13. Additionally, he has held senior managerial responsibilities in more than 20 countries across Asia, the Middle East, Europe, Australia, NZ, and the Americas. His employers include Bechtel, Honeywell, Burmah Castrol, BP, Towers Perrin, and Watson Wyatt. He has significant experience of directorship, general management, and Senior HR roles across the engineering construction,

https://doi.org/10.1515/9783110780871-009

electronics, oil and gas, and consulting sectors. Much of his board consulting work was in the banking and finance sectors.

His functional career has three main episodes: first as a human resources executive and director, second as a chief executive and director, third as consultant at board level. His observations and experiences led him to a deep interest in the ways in which individual and group behavior manifest in decision making and approaches to corporate governance of individual directors and boards of directors in different cultures, situations, and in complex company groups.

He was a faculty member of ICLIF (the International Centre for Leadership in Finance – an arm of Bank Negara Malaysia – now part of the Asia School of Business) and is currently an adjunct member of the faculty. He also serves on the faculty of Australian Institute of Company Directors and has facilitated programs for directors in Australia, Shanghai, Hong Kong, Singapore, Jakarta, and Dubai.

He is a doctoral researcher at Aston University where he explores the cultural and behavioral aspects of board and top management team decision making in multicultural, multinational, and complex company groups.

Chris lives in Kuala Lumpur. He has co-authored *The Principles and Practice of Effective Leadership* and *Criminality and Business Strategy: Similarities and Differences* with John Zinkin. His publications (with Professor Mak Yuen Teen, National University of Singapore) also include *Guardians of the Capital Markets* (BPA 2016), *Insuring the Future* (The Iclif Leadership and Governance Centre 2015); *The Governance of Company Groups* (CPA Australia & Iclif 2014), *Directors Daze* (BPA 2014), *Corporate Governance of 50 Largest Asian Banks* (BPA 2013), and numerous articles and newsletters (http://www.bpa-australasia.com).

Index

abacus 13
ability 24, 30, 38, 49, 51, 58, 65, 87, 92, 107, 112, 114, 139
academia 58, 127
Acemoglu 6, 21
accomplishment(s) 53
accountability X, 2, 43, 54, 55, 56, 57, 60, 71, 103, 126, 128
accountancy IX, 3, 17, 38, 76
accurate 18, 33, 42, 74, 93, 119, 132
acquiescing 83
acquisition 102, 133
adequacy 94, 140
adherence 2, 17, 124, 128
administrative 54, 94, 139
adulthood 77, 95
advertising 19, 50, 104, 108
advocating 93
advocacy 57, 107, 116, 136
affiliation 38, 44
Afghans 82, 87
agent VII, XIV, 9, 16, 17, 28, 68, 99, 118, 134
aggressive 58, 128
agitate 57
agreement(s) 35, 65, 67, 93, 113, 119, 139
alarmist 105
alcohol 90, 97, 105, 108
alignment 26, 37, 43, 66, 93, 101, 132
allegiance 24
allocation 70, 71, 92, 102
amalgam XIV, 141
ambassadors 92
ambiguity X, XIII, 38, 51, 94, 103, 118, 136
amendment, first 57, 74
amoral 33, 34, 41, 44, 45, 104, 125, 141
amplifying 62, 63
Analects 5, 21, 29, 30, 46
anger 4, 76, 95
anomie 141
antisocial 43
Apartheid 9, 16
Apollo 82
appraisals 92, 114, 139
approbation 23, 24
approval 23, 52
arbiter 8, 61
archetypes 110, 138

Aristotle 28, 29, 44, 46, 98, 115, 122, 142,
– Arête 28, 44
– Eudaimonia 28, 29, 44
– "magnanimous man" 29, 31
– Phronesis 28
Arthur Andersen 62
aspirations 129, 135
assessing XI, 94, 112, 117
associate 20, 38, 44, 84, 147
assumption(s) V, VII, XIII, XV, 27, 39, 49, 71, 88, 104, 115
asymmetrical 104, 108, 135
atmosphere XIV, XV, 77, 78, 82, 83, 84, 85, 87, 88, 95, 130, 131, 141
attitude 8, 18, 43, 55, 62, 65, 72, 92, 107, 110, 111, 114, 129, 138
attrition 93
audits 113, 118, 139
authoritarian 106
authority 5, 6, 8, 11, 21, 24, 26, 50, 51, 52, 73, 110, 111, 136, 138
axioms IX, XV, 10, 23, 28, 29, 31, 33, 35, 43, 67, 77, 126, 130, 141

bad apples 39, 45, 63, 64, 65, 72, 128
balancing 18, 83, 94, 140
bankruptcy 64
baseline X, XI, XV, 4, 76, 95, 129, 141
basins of attraction 58, 59
battles 105, 135
Belfort, Jordan 61, 74
beneficiaries XIV, 118, 133
benevolence 29, 32, 44, 83, 145
benevolent 5, 31
bias(es) 6, 14, 42, 48, 79
black letter law 13, 61, 128
BlackRock 103, 121, 134, 142
Blair, Tony 84
bodies 13, 14, 16, 68, 125
Boeing IX, 42, 43, 45, 47, 106
Bogle, Jack 69, 75
"Boots' Theory" 109, 122
bottom line 64, 72, 90, 91, 112, 128, 139
bottom-up 106
boundaries 3, 26, 48, 77, 95, 99, 107, 137
brain XIII, XV, 22, 48, 71, 115, 127
brand 3, 69, 90, 105, 108, 137, 147

https://doi.org/10.1515/9783110780871-010

Brandeis, Louis, US Supreme Court
  Justice 105, 121, 135, 142
Brazil 10, 22
Brexit 18, 56
British 10, 21, 55, 80, 147
Buffett, Warren 69
Bugs Bunny 49
bullying 84, 107, 138
burden of proof 68
buybacks 70, 114

calculation(s) 39, 45, 63, 83, 85
calibre 133
callous 41
Cameron, David 55, 73
cancer 90
Capital, Moral X, XI, XIV, XV, 4, 76, 77, 84, 87,
  88, 90, 94, 95, 96, 129, 130, 131, 139, 140,
  141, 143
capitalization 14, 125
car accident 10, 12, 145
career 32, 55, 70, 80, 81, 82, 86, 92, 93, 113,
  114, 117, 119, 130, 134, 139, 147, 148
case
– "Heart Transplant" 80
– "Trolley" 80, 96
cash 55, 69, 70, 109
cause and effect 24, 25
caveat emptor XIV, 104, 108, 118, 135
century 21, 33, 58, 73, 84, 109
certainty X, XIII, 2, 14, 16, 27, 51, 53, 136
checklist VII, XVI, 101, 133, 141
childhood 77
China 5, 31, 54, 84, 97
Chinese 29, 30, 83, 84, 97
circle(s) of beliefs 77, 143
civil war 10, 24, 58, 107, 115, 116
clarity 19, 27, 35, 44, 90, 102
class 10, 38, 44, 54, 59, 67, 70, 82, 130
climate 40, 59, 74, 107, 116, 136, 137
code(s)
– conduct IX, XIV, XV, 2, 3, 15, 16, 17, 19,
  21, 26, 27, 38, 44, 51, 67, 81, 83, 84,
  90, 91, 104, 118, 128, 130, 135, 136, 137,
  139, 147
– moral 6, 61, 72, 125
cognitive XI, XV, 4, 26, 42, 43, 48, 49, 51, 58, 61,
  71, 72, 73, 76, 79, 124, 126, 127, 128, 140

collective 28, 31, 38, 44, 45, 52, 53, 58, 63,
  103, 133
collegiality 3
Commonwealth 13, 16
community 5, 10, 20, 52, 99, 108, 109, 110, 116,
  117, 120, 137
communitarian 31
compensation 41, 65, 120
competency(ies) 17, 20, 52, 99, 112, 113, 118,
  133, 139
competition XIV, 53, 57, 60, 65, 74, 104, 105,
  118, 121, 134, 135, 142
complexity X, XIII, XV, 27, 51, 62, 63, 136
compliance 66, 67, 81, 82, 115, 124, 130, 134
confectionery 90
confronting ethical dilemmas X, XI, 85, 87, 131
Confucian 29, 31, 33, 35, 44, 83
Confucius 5, 21, 28, 29, 30, 35, 44, 46
confusion VII, VIII, 4, 53, 76, 88, 95
conscience 11, 13, 46, 74, 87, 97, 99, 112,
  125, 142
consonance 94, 140
conspiracy 26, 57, 127, 128
consumption 53, 65
context XV, 11, 18, 23, 28, 37, 38, 43, 67, 76,
  79, 84, 85, 92, 96, 126, 131
contiguity 24, 25
contract 6, 12, 31, 32, 35, 44, 51, 55, 56, 90
convenience 82, 130
core, universal XV, 77, 78, 82, 83, 85, 87, 88,
  95, 130, 131, 141
corporation(s) VII, XIV, 13, 14, 97, 99, 116, 118,
  125, 134, 147
corruption 8, 30, 31, 53, 56, 57, 60, 65, 90,
  103, 126
Countrywide Financial 64
court(s) chancery, Delaware 42, 47
covid-19 35, 46, 52, 53, 83
credence 104, 135
Credo 102, 103, 116, 118, 119, 120, 134, 136
crime, organized (OC) XIII, 48, 83
criminality VIII, XIII, 4, 23, 48, 76, 101, 147
CRM 105
Cuba XIV 10, 22
cultural, mantle XIV, XV, 77, 78, 82, 83, 84, 85,
  86, 88, 95, 130, 131
culture 10, 13, 25, 27, 31, 33, 38, 42, 53, 54, 57,
  58, 71, 78, 81, 82, 84, 86, 87, 95, 97 111,

122, 124, 129, 130, 131, 135, 136, 141, 142, 146,148
customer(s) 3, 4, 15, 18, 41, 67, 89, 90, 91, 103, 105, 108, 114, 116, 117, 118, 119, 120, 135
"cut and paste" 67
cyber-bullying 107

damage, moral XV, 23, 43
Daraprim 109
dealings 4, 15, 19, 29, 30, 90, 95, 140, 141
deaths 41, 97
deception, systemic 63
decision(s), making 148
decree 8
defendant 13, 14
degradation 137
degree 6, 25, 48, 78, 110
delivery 93
depression 82, 86, 131
derivatives 63
deviant 63
diabetes 90
dictatorial 8, 16
diffuse 6, 111
director(s) 14, 33, 42, 68, 99, 101, 112, 132, 147, 148
disagreements 86, 128, 138
disapprobation 23
disapproval 23
disclaimers 108, 135, 136
discomfort 18, 84
discourse 107
disengagement 26, 43, 46, 61, 66, 74, 78, 91, 130, 142
Disneyland 49
dissonance Xl, 26, 43, 48, 61, 71, 78, 79, 125, 126, 127, 150
dividends 69, 70, 114
divines 91
Dodd-Frank 13
Donoghue v Stevenson 6, 21, 141
Douglas-Home, Sir Alec 54
Drucker, Peter 100, 121, 135
Durkheim, Émile 127
duty of care 107, 108, 130
dynamics 38, 58, 59, 60, 71

education 5, 10, 20, 30, 38, 44, 73, 82, 120, 130
emails 107

ends 1, 26, 44, 88, 89, 127, 131, 132
energy 49, 51, 54, 119, 122, 127
elites VIII, 15, 127,
 – political 8, 16
 – ruling 5, 6, 9
Elizabeth the First, Queen 41
emotion(s) 23, 25, 50
empathy 3, 15, 24, 29, 106
empire 10, 37
engagement XI, 26, 43, 46, 57, 61, 66, 74, 78, 91, 103, 114, 117, 118, 119, 120, 122, 130, 132, 135, 136, 142
engineering IX, 1, 3, 17, 42, 69, 147
enforce(ment) X, 5, 6, 7, 8, 9, 10, 11, 16, 26, 38, 65, 66, 67, 68, 69, 72, 82, 108, 109, 130, 134, 137
Enron 33, 62, 64, 75
environment VIII, 1, 3, 20, 25, 26, 48, 58, 61, 68, 72, 86, 90, 102, 108, 110, 117, 119, 120, 122, 129, 131, 137
errors 11
equity 3, 17, 69, 70, 71, 102, 110
ESG 3, 117, 134
establishment 9, 127
ethical
 – baselines X, 4, 76, 95
 – blindness 41
 – business X, 3
 – challenge(s) 85, 96
 – conflict XVI
 – decision-making XIII, XV, 43, 126, 132
 – dilemmas VII, X, XI, XVI, 1, 4, 25, 51, 76, 81, 8587, 127, 129, 131, 132, 141
 – fading 41, 106
 – framework X, XVI, 85, 89, 91, 93, 96, 131, 141
 – obligation of excellence 94, 95, 140, 141
 – obstacles XI, XVI, 124, 125, 127
 – personas VIII, IX, X, XIII, XV, 4, 23, 37, 43, 76, 82, 83, 84, 85, 95, 126, 129, 131, 141
 – resolutions XV
 – selves 82, 131
ethics
 – applied 2, 20
 – business IX, XV, 1, 3, 4, 15, 21, 22, 29, 32, 33, 34, 89, 97, 99, 118, 121, 122, 142
 – consequential IX, XIII, XIV, 23, 25, 26, 27, 28, 43, 51, 78, 79, 80, 95, 126, 128, 145
 – duty-based 27, 43, 78, 80, 81, 95, 96
 – personalistic 36, 44

– professional IX, 2, 15,21
– virtue 28, 29, 31, 44, 46, 90, 94, 95, 97, 140,
    141, 142
ethnic(ity) 25, 37, 38, 44, 59, 82, 127, 130
Eudaimonia 28, 29, 44
eugenics 81
Europeans 84
European Union 110, 137
evolution X, XIII, 48, 49
exaggeration 104
excellence 28, 44, 52, 94, 95, 97, 140, 141
executive(s) VIII, 9, 14, 32, 42, 55, 68, 70, 75,
    102, 115
expenses 87

fabric 128
Facebook 107
fact(s), alternative 26, 107, 127, 128, 136
fairness XIII, 1, 9, 15, 17, 19, 30, 35, 95, 106,
    109, 122, 140
"fake news" 107, 128, 136
Fancy, Tariq 134
feedback XIV, XV, 62, 63, 93, 113, 118, 132, 139
fight or flee 48
filial piety 29, 30, 44, 84
finance IX, 3, 18, 64, 75, 80, 99, 106, 123, 148
fine(s) 34, 68, 121, 135
Fink, Larry 103, 121, 134, 142
"firehose of falsehood" 128
fit for purpose 107, 136
"Five Ps" XIV, XVI, 132
Foot, Philippa 80
foolish consistency 91, 97
Ford IX, 41, 42, 105, 106, 123
– Pinto IX
forgetting, motivated 26, 43, 46, 74, 140, 142
founder VIII, XIV, 69, 118, 133
fraternities 84
free riding 39
freedom, economic 7
Friedman(ite) 13, 16, 69, 133, 134, 135
frontiers 77

game the system 61, 71, 128
garbage 63
gender 23, 24, 25, 38, 44, 82, 93, 106, 130
genocide 81
Global Financial Crisis (GFC) 64, 65, 115
"go the extra mile" 125

Goldman Sachs 13, 22
"Golden Rule" 34, 35, 44, 46, 78, 90, 92, 96,
    106, 136
God 1, 80, 81, 86, 106, 115, 136
goodwill 78, 118, 119
gorilla(s) 49
Gove, Michael 56
governance 3, 11, 15, 22, 56, 61, 69, 70, 75, 97,
    102, 113, 117, 121, 122, 124, 126, 129, 142,
    147, 148
government XV, 7, 8, 9, 10, 16, 19, 24, 31, 54,
    55, 56, 57, 58, 60, 61, 65, 71, 76, 116, 126,
    127, 134, 147
"gray areas" 3, 78, 95, 130
greed 41, 60, 64, 75, 126
Greeks 82
GSK 117
guarantor 10, 54
guidance XIII, XV, 14, 16, 35, 44, 113, 125, 141
guidelines VII, XV, 2, 10, 104, 118, 121, 135
guilt(y)

Handy, Charles 102, 121, 133, 134, 142
happiness 1, 28, 29, 36, 44, 82, 86, 131
harmony 36, 93
hazing 84, 97
Hewlett Packard 133
hegemon 53
heuristics 48, 51, 71
"High Power Distance" 136
history 2, 4, 5, 9, 15, 46, 67, 73, 74, 76
Hitler 112
Hobbes 7, 16, 21, 51
hobgoblin of little minds 91, 97
honesty 1, 2, 17, 24, 28, 52, 56, 61, 63, 87,
    95, 140
honor 12, 17, 20, 26, 30, 61, 106, 126, 129, 141
horizons 27, 104, 106, 129
hospital 55, 80, 81, 84
humanity XIV, 1, 7, 15, 36, 44, 77, 95, 107,
    127, 130
Hume, David 23, 24, 25, 36, 45, 46
hygiene factor 114
hypocrisy 53

Iacocca, Lee 41, 42
Ibadah 115
Ibn Zafar al Siqilli 23, 33, 45
ideal 5, 10, 15b, 26, 29

illiberal 8, 16
impartiality 17, 106, 134
impulse 49, 50
impunity 53, 54, 55, 57, 128
independence 8, 22
indifference 61, 72, 86
individualistic 31
inequality 53, 71, 136
inferior 26, 29, 127
infrastructure 6
ingroup 37, 38, 39, 44, 45, 76, 130
injunction 6, 25
injury, moral XI, XV, 4, 76, 83, 84, 85, 86, 87,
    94, 95, 96, 129, 131, 140, 141
innocent 14, 68
innovation 21, 104, 105, 119
Instagram 107
institution(s) 1, 2, 4, 6, 8, 9, 10, 15, 52, 57, 60,
    63, 64, 65, 68, 116, 133
integrity 7, 8, 17, 18, 19, 30, 52, 54, 56, 7, 94,
    95, 97, 99, 112, 118, 120, 140
intentions 1, 11, 40, 41, 45, 48, 61
interest(s), vested 59
intergenerational 110
interpretation 8, 14, 105, 107, 133
investors, activist 69, 117, 134
irresponsible XIII

Jamestown 9
Japan 84, 97
Jenkin, Bernard 55, 73
Johnson & Johnson 102, 116, 118, 119, 120, 134
Johnson, Boris 55, 56, 74, 112
Johnson, Robert Wood, General 102
journalism IX, 3, 18, 56
judge(s) VII, 5, 9, 14, 16, 25, 35, 50, 74, 91, 104,
    109, 110, 125
judgment(s) 50
judiciary 6, 68, 73, 138
junk food 90
jurisdiction(s) XIV, 13, 15, 16, 67, 68, 90, 130
jurists 5, 8
justice XIII, 5, 7, 8, 9, 13, 16, 18, 19, 21, 35,
    43, 51, 52, 53, 74, 95, 99, 105, 121, 135,
    140, 142,
– social 7
justification 2, 18, 25, 26, 84, 103, 126

Kabul 82
"Kaleidoscopic ethical personas" X, XV, 4, 76,
    82, 83, 84, 85, 95, 131, 141
Kant, Immanuel 35, 36, 46
Kellerman, Barbara 66, 75
kings 24
"Know thyself" 82
Koch, Charles 56, 74
Korea 6, 84
Kouzes, Jim 115, 122
KPIs X, XI, XIV, XV, 41, 45, 67, 69, 72, 92, 113,
    119, 124, 129, 139, 140, 141

Labaton Sucharow 64, 65, 75
lacunae 61, 128
language 24, 82, 105, 106, 108, 115, 130
law(s)
– application of 7, 15
– "black letter" 13, 61, 128
– commercial XIII, 13
– common 108, 109, 125, 137
– moral 45, 96
– natural 5, 7, 15, 21
– rule by XV, 7
– rule of IX, XV, 7, 9, 11, 19, 21
– "spirit" of 11
lawsuits 41
leader(s), toxic 52, 53, 54, 73
legislation 13, 39, 45, 78, 126
Leviathan 7, 16, 21
Levin, Senator Carl 13
Lewis, C. S. 25, 45, 78, 96
liberty 1, 8, 57, 74
life support 81
"line of sight" 93, 115
litigation 14, 16, 47
living will 81
lobbying 41, 55, 59, 103, 107, 116, 136
logic 1, 49, 50, 71
long-term 69, 102, 103, 113, 116, 117, 120, 124,
    129, 132, 133, 134, 138, 140, 143
loyalty 1, 2, 29, 30, 34, 44, 83, 95, 105, 112,
    140, 145
lying 22, 41, 42, 51, 62, 63, 64, 72, 74, 92, 104

Macmillan, Harold 21, 54
Major, John 54

malefactors 39, 68, 69

malfeasance 6, 64, 68

malpractice(s) VII, 6, 15, 38, 44, 62, 63, 64, 66,
68 69, 72, 81, 128, 130

manipulate 58

mantle, cultural XIV, XV, 77, 78, 82, 83, 84, 85,
86, 88, 95, 130, 131

margin 52, 59, 93

marketing XIV, 90, 104, 107, 108, 109, 117, 118,
122, 135, 136, 137, 147

Maslow X, 51, 73

measurement 72, 113, 114, 139

media X, XI, XIII, XV, 1, 18, 34, 38, 42, 48, 54,
56, 57, 58, 71, 73, 87, 102, 110, 114, 115,
116, 124, 126, 127, 128, 133, 137, 138,
140, 141

medicine 3

memory 48, 49, 61, 72

Mencius 5, 28, 29, 44

merger 102

metaphors 105, 135

military 3, 84, 105, 121

misalignment 87

misdemeanor 62, 81, 128

misdirection 48, 71

misinformation 50, 73

model X, XIII, XV, 21, 22, 46, 53, 60, 71, 134

modesty 24

monolithic 37, 38

monopolies 60

morality 1, 4, 5, 6, 7, 9, 10, 11, 12, 15, 16,20,
21,25, 27, 29, 32, 34, 61, 72, 82, 105, 125,
126, 145

moral
– Capital X, XI, XIV, XV, 4, 76, 77, 84, 85, 87,
88, 90, 94, 95, 96, 129, 130, 131, 139, 140
141, 143,
– conflict XV, 15
– disengagement 26, 43, 46, 61, 66, 74, 142
– injury XI, XV, 4, 76, 83, 84, 85, 86, 87, 94,
95, 129, 131, 140, 141
– relativists 78

mores 76

"motivated cognition" 62, 72

motivator(s)
– extrinsic XIV, 39, 41, 42, 45, 114, 115, 119
– intrinsic XIV, 39, 45, 48, 73, 111, 114, 115, 119

Mozilo, Angelo 64

mutuality IX, 34, 35, 44, 90, 91, 92, 93, 132

MVV 124, 139, 140

Myanmar 54

nation 25, 37, 39, 53, 56

need-to-know 92

"Negative Manifestos" 25

Netanyahu, Benjamin 56, 73

Neuberger, Lord 14, 22

New Testament 40

newspaper test 94

neurons, mirror 24

Nolan Report 55, 56, 73

Notre Dame 65, 121

nudging 26

nurture 37, 52, 64

obedience 73, 112

objective(s) 3, 4, 14, 16, 17, 26, 34, 42, 48,
58, 71, 92, 93, 94, 105, 109, 111,
113, 116

obstacles VII, XI, XVI, 124, 125, 127, 140

oligopolies 60, 71

Olmert, Ehud 56

on-time 93

opportunity, equal XIV, 104, 108, 118, 120, 121,
135, 136, 142

opposition 27

optimize 15

"ought to be" VII, XV, 5, 7, 15, 23, 25, 43, 126,
129, 141

outgroup 37, 78, 130

overpromising 104

ownership, concentration 58

pack(aging) 108

Packard, Dave 133, 142

pain 23, 25, 26, 29, 36, 39, 41, 44, 82, 84, 128,
129, 141

pandemic 35, 46, 52, 53, 83

Parliament 54, 55, 74

particularist 10, 12, 13, 16, 29, 31, 68

patronage 60, 128

peace 7

peer X, 63, 81, 84, 96

Peltz, Nelson 117, 123

permissiveness 26, 61, 72

pesticides 109

philosophers 5, 91

Phronesis 28

Pink, Daniel 115, 122
Plato 5, 21, 24, 27, 28, 29, 44, 45, 46, 73
plaintiff 14
plan 87, 93, 117
policy(ies) VIII, XV, 8, 28, 32, 35, 36, 50, 60,
   74, 94, 104, 108, 117, 118, 122, 135,
   139, 140
polities 76, 95
positivists 7, 15
Posner, Barry 115, 122
powerless(ness) 4, 52, 76, 95, 127
predatory value extraction 69, 70, 75
predictability IX, XIII, 13, 16, 27, 28, 35, 444,
   88, 90, 91, 92 93, 132
press VIII, XIII, 3,4, 6,9, 10, 15, 21, 22, 25, 35,
   38, 41, 44, 46, 48, 52, 53, 54, 56, 57, 61,
   63, 65, 70, 73, 74, 75, 78, 82, 84, 86,
   87, 102, 108, 116, 120, 121, 129, 131,
   141, 142
prestige 53, 109
price-earnings 114
pride 25, 93, 126
primacy 100
prince(s) 23, 24, 26, 34, 44, 45, 74,
   128, 142
principle(s), precautionary 110, 122
privacy 2, 18, 20, 107
privileges 59, 106
procedures 3, 8, 19, 35, 36, 44, 88, 93, 101,
   111, 113, 118, 119, 139
processes VII, XI, XIV, 11, 16, 39, 48, 50, 51, 52,
   61, 63, 71, 92, 93, 96, 99, 101, 102, 107,
   111, 113, 118, 124, 128, 132, 133, 136, 138,
   139, 141, 147
productivity 70, 92, 102, 113, 134
profession IX, XV, 1, 2, 3, 4, 1517, 18, 19, 20,
   21, 22, 38, 58, 59, 65, 83, 107, 111, 117,
   127, 147
profit(s) XI, 5, 14, 40, 60, 66, 68, 70, 93, 102,
   103, 104, 105, 108, 109, 110, 115, 116, 119,
   120, 123, 124, 125, 133, 134, 136, 137,
   140, 141
Profumo, John 54, 73
prospect theory 62, 72, 74
psychographics 108, 137
punishment IX, XIII, XV, 10, 11, 23, 39, 41,
   43, 45, 47, 62, 67, 72, 83, 126,
   128, 141
Putin, Vladimir 54, 112

Quaker 115
quality 3, 14, 17, 19, 30, 31, 32, 53, 71, 90, 102,
   105, 109, 113, 119, 134, 136, 137
Queen Elizabeth the First 41

ranking XIV, 103
rationalization 1, 62, 72, 87, 128
Reagan, Ronald 82
reality, boundaries of 48
reciprocity 6, 34, 44, 106, 125, 132
reconcile XIV, 28, 67, 80, 114, 116, 117, 130,
   134, 139
recruit 84, 112, 132
red flag 88
redemption VIII, 41
reference, group(s) 23, 43, 126
refusal 83, 86
regime(s) 8, 9, 13, 16, 54, 70, 95
regulation(s) VIII, X, XI, XIII, XIV, XV, 6, 10, 11,
   13, 16, 35, 38, 39, 44, 45, 55, 60, 61, 65,
   66, 67, 68, 69, 71, 72, 78, 82, 90, 91, 116,
   121, 124, 127, 128, 130, 140, 145
regulators XVI, 18, 67, 68, 91, 107, 116, 124,
   134, 147
religion 4, 35, 37, 50, 76, 78, 80, 82, 93, 130
remuneration 64, 65, 92, 93, 113, 119, 139
rents 60, 69, 70, 71
rent-seeking 60, 71
repeat offenders 68
Republic 5, 9, 34, 54, 57
reputation 11, 14, 17, 36, 41, 45, 61, 81, 102,
   109, 124, 147
resignation 56, 73, 83, 84
respect XV, 8, 15, 18, 20, 23, 24, 29, 30, 31, 53,
   87, 90, 92, 99, 110, 115, 119, 120, 132
responsibility 1, 13, 17, 19, 20, 30, 59, 67, 91,
   99, 107, 119, 120, 127, 135
retribution 41
revelation 5
rhetoric X, XV, 50, 71
righteousness 5, 29, 30, 31, 44
right(s) human 7, 10, 25, 52, 121, 136
risk management 14, 22, 142
Robinson role 6, 21, 147
Roe v Wade 8, 21, 64, 126
ROI 114, 139
Rousseau, Jean-Jacques 35, 46
ruler(s) 5, 24, 29, 30, 33, 34, 53
Ruskin, John 86, 97

safety X, 17, 41, 42, 43, 51, 63, 68, 71, 90, 110, 122, 137

salience XV, 23, 24, 25, 43, 48, 126

sanctions 39, 45, 48, 54, 69, 76

sanctity 80

scandals 45, 87

scenarios 82, 85

Scent of a Woman 81, 96

scorecards 113, 119, 139

self-categorize 37, 38

self-image IX, 28, 36, 44, 87, 88, 89, 90, 91, 92, 93, 131, 132

self-interest 2, 54, 140

self-respect XV, 90

selling 43, 102, 104, 105, 108, 133, 135

sensitivity 18, 95, 140

sentiments 23, 24, 25

shades of gray VII, XIII, 96

shareholder(s) VII, XIV, XV, 4, 14, 15, 16, 43, 45, 64, 69,70, 86, 87, 102, 103, 104, 114, 116, 117, 118, 120, 131, 133, 135

Shell, Richard 87, 97

Shkreli, Martin 109, 122

short-term 69, 102, 110, 112, 115, 117, 125, 129, 133, 134, 139

signal, quality 3

simplicity 27, 53, 71, 78

sins 58, 59, 122, 126, 141

Singapore(an) 14, 22, 31, 48, 78, 97, 122, 142, 147, 148

situational X, 34, 44, 61, 78, 79, 81, 95

six-step decision-making X, XVI, 85, 89, 91, 93, 96, 131, 132, 141, 143

skepticism 64, 72, 128

slippery slope 28, 43, 81

Smith, Adam 60, 74, 104

Smith, Terry 177, 142

snitching 38, 81

Solomon, Robert 116, 121

sororities 84

souls 13, 14, 16, 41, 125

South Africa(n) 9, 16

sovereign 5, 7

speak truth to power 41, 92, 106, 136

speculative 129

stakeholder(s) Xl, XlV, XVl, 4, 58, 86, 90, 99, 102, 103, 116, 117, 118, 119, 120, 122, 123, 124, 134, 135, 140,142

standards, minimum 2

state, reasons of 34, 44

statesmen 91

status quo 58

statute 8, 16

stewards 30, 102, 113, 114, 133

strategy XIII, 4, 23, 48, 51, 76, 87, 101, 103, 112, 123, 147

strain(s) 78, 95

stress(es) 4, 76, 82, 86, 95, 131

structures XIV, XV, 52, 63, 65, 110, 118, 137

subjective(s) 36, 44, 72, 78, 111

subordinates 30, 39, 45, 86, 92, 114, 129, 138, 139

suicide 82, 86

superiors 29, 30, 32, 39, 45, 81, 85, 86, 110, 114, 118, 129, 137, 139

superordinate 39, 58, 78, 83, 93

supremacists 26

surprises 83

sympathy 24

Syracuse 5

Syria 54

system 1; X, 38, 48, 49, 50, 71, 127

system 2; X, 49, 50, 51, 66, 71, 128

talent 3, 20, 94, 114, 119, 139

Taliban 82, 97

targets 39, 93, 114, 117, 139

taxes 90, 103, 120

team 25, 38, 44, 92, 108, 113, 132, 148

technology XIV, 85, 104, 109, 110, 118, 122, 134, 135, 137

Thatcher, Margaret 54

Thucydides 53

Thurlow, Lord 13, 16, 22, 125, 141

"tick in the box" 13, 16

Timberwolf 13

tone 21, 81, 114, 115

toxic 52, 53, 54, 64, 73, 87, 97

track record 112, 138

tracking 93, 107

traits 29, 95, 140, 141

transparency 2, 8, 55, 120

treaties 54

tribe 30, 37, 78

Trump, Donald 84, 112

trust 2, 3, 4, 17, 22, 31, 32, 35, 46, 55, 75, 76, 79, 82, 83, 84, 90, 97, 104, 115, 118, 123, 134, 145, 147

trustworthiness 2, 29, 30, 44, 140
Turing Pharmaceutical 109
TV, reality X, 56, 57
Twitter 107

UK ministerial code 56
uncertainty X, 27, 51, 53, 136
unethical VII, 13, 14, 19, 25, 26, 27, 39, 40, 41,
    43, 45, 53, 57, 61, 62, 63, 64, 65, 66, 74,
    88, 105, 107, 108, 109, 125, 126, 127, 128,
    133, 136, 137, 141
Unilever 117, 123, 134, 142, 147
United States 10, 16, 22, 41, 69, 70, 78, 105
unfairness 106, 122
universalist 10, 12, 16, 31
US Business Roundtable Declaration 103,
    119, 120
untruth 52, 62, 127
utilitarian(ism) 36, 106
utility IX, 28, 36, 44, 88, 90, 91, 92, 93,
    131, 132

value
– creation 70, 71
– extraction 69, 70, 75
values VII, XIII, XIV, 2, 4, 13, 15, 16, 18, 21, 36,
    37, 38, 39, 44, 45, 55, 58, 59, 65, 66, 71,
    76, 77, 78, 82, 83, 84, 85, 86, 87, 88, 90,
    91, 92, 93, 94, 95, 99, 100, 101, 103, 104,
    112, 114, 118, 124, 128, 129, 130, 131, 132,
    135, 138, 139, 140, 141, 143
Vanguard 75
veracity 40, 50
verify 82, 97, 134
viability 33, 69, 90, 99, 113, 116
"villain within" 126, 129

virtue(s) VII, IX, 1, 21, 24, 28, 29, 31, 44, 46,
    78, 88, 89, 90, 91, 92, 93, 94, 95, 97, 99,
    106, 140, 141, 142
vision VII, XI, XIV, XV, XVI, 3, 20, 25, 32, 38, 44,
    49, 52, 54, 66, 68, 83, 86, 89, 92, 93, 99,
    100, 101, 103, 105, 107, 109, 111, 113,
    114, 115, 116, 117, 118, 124, 127, 131, 132,
    139, 143
violation 10, 24, 32, 54, 74, 79, 80, 82, 83, 84,
    105, 130
vocabulary 135
volatility X, XIII, 51, 136
Volkswagen 41
Voltaire 10, 22
voluntary 49, 110, 137
VUCA X, XIII, XV, 51, 71, 138

waivers 12, 91
Wall Street 61, 64, 75, 122, 126
war 10, 105, 135
watchdogs 57
Wharton 87, 97
whistleblowing 39, 45
whitewash 103, 134
Wilson, Harold 54
withholding 62, 104
woke 103, 134
Wolf, Martin 103, 121
WorldCom 82
World Justice Project 8, 9, 21

Xunzi 5

yardstick 94, 140, 141
YouTube 45, 96, 107, 122

www.ingramcontent.com/pod-product-compliance
Lightning Source LLC
Chambersburg PA
CBHW081107220326
41598CB00038B/7260